W9-AEY-577

Mavis Gallant

Twayne's World Authors Series
Canadian Literature

Robert Lecker, Editor
McGill University

TWAS 871

MAVIS GALLANT
Alison Harris

Mavis Gallant

Danielle Schaub

Oranim, University of Haifa

Twayne Publishers
An Imprint of Simon & Schuster Macmillan
New York

Prentice Hall International
London • Mexico City • New Delhi • Singapore • Sydney • Toronto

Twayne's World Authors Series No. 871

Mavis Gallant
Danielle Schaub

Twayne Publishers
An Imprint of Simon & Schuster Macmillan
1633 Broadway
New York, NY 10019

Library of Congress Cataloging-in-Publication Data

Schaub, Danielle.
  Mavis Gallant / Danielle Schaub.
    p. cm. — (Twayne's world authors series ; TWAS 871. Canadian literature.)
  Includes bibliographical references and index.
  ISBN 0-8057-4553-X (alk. paper)
  1. Gallant, Mavis—Criticism and interpretation. 2. Women and literature—Canada—History—20th century. I. Title. II. Series: Twayne's world author series ; TWAS 871. III. Series: Twayne's world author series. Canadian literature.
PR9199.3.G26Z88 1998
813'.54—dc21   98-21554
                                                            CIP

10 9 8 7 6 5 4 3 2 1

Printed in the United States of America

To David and Maya,
who have grown up with Mavis Gallant.

Contents

Preface

In her creative sphere, Mavis Gallant takes no notice of academic or feminist issues, and she refuses to address them or even to theorize about her own creative process. But from the ironic and detached perspective from which she has chosen to observe the drabness of our century's mores, she has depicted, among others, the plight of women and has metaphorically evoked how her writing functions, securing the attraction of both women and academics. Over the years, her readers have recognized her prominence while learning to delight in her pungent stories, which require her readers' active participation; slowly but surely, they have become aware that unless they add their own building blocks, the stories will not stand. Fascinated by Gallant's ability to shock her readers, I have decided to discuss her use of techniques and their impact on the thematics of her work. In other words, this study reconciles matter and manner, respectively the inherent tension governing the lives of Gallant's characters and the way she strains language and exploits narrative devices to translate the tension.

I contend that Gallant's irony, the multiple perspectives of her stories, narrative voice/s, stylistic devices, interaction between text and image, atmosphere, and structural frame build up a tension that mirrors the characters' displacement and disconnectedness. Finally, the analysis of the various narrative strategies that Gallant exploits leads me to inscribe my conclusion in a postmodernist manner. My final sub/version of her writing should highlight the pleasure of "interventing" the text.

Acknowledgments

A book is seldom the product of a single hand, and I am indebted to other readers of Mavis Gallant's work, even though our approaches and conclusions may differ. I am indebted to those friends who have encouraged me by repeatedly supplying me with new critical material; my thanks go to Mary Condé, Janice Kulyk Keefer, and Neil Besner for their careful and incisive readings of my writings at earlier stages. My students also deserve my thanks for their congenial and critical response to my ideas about specific texts. I am also grateful to Sam Wajc for his unfailing generosity of time and spirit. Finally, I would like to thank Mavis Gallant for having written such delightful prose, thereby giving me a good excuse to combine pleasure and work; in addition, I would like to express my gratitude to her for having taught me indirectly how to distance myself from those predicaments in life over which I have no control.

I am also grateful to Mavis Gallant for permission to quote from her work.

Chapter 3 in part combines earlier and shorter versions that appeared in *Multiple Voices: Recent Canadian Fiction,* ed. Jeanne Delbaere (Sydney, Mundelstrup, and Coventry: Dangaroo Press, 1990), 234–46, and *Historiographic Metafiction in Modern American and Canadian Literature,* ed. Bernd Engler and Kurt Müller (Paderborn: Schöningh, 1994), 435–45. Parts of chapter 4 appeared in *Canadian Literature* 136 (Spring 1993): 45–57. Part of chapter 6 appeared in modified forms in *Critique* 34, no. 1 (Fall 1992): 33–46 [Heldref Publications], and *Studies in Canadian Literature* 18, no. 2 (Winter 1993): 132–55. Part of chapter 7 appeared in *Image et récit: Littérature(s) et arts visuels du Canada,* ed. Jean-Michel Lacroix, Simone Vauthier, and Héliane Ventura (Paris: Presses de la Sorbonne Nouvelle, 1993), 77–95.

Chronology

1922   Mavis Gallant (née Young) born 11 August in Montreal.

1926   Attends Pensionnat Saint-Louis de Gonzague.

1932–1941   Attends various schools in Canada and the United States.

1932   Father's death.

1940   Graduates from Pine Plains High School in Pine Plains, New York.

1941   Returns to Montreal. Works for the Canadian National Railways.

1943–1944   Works for the National Film Board, Ottawa.

1943   Marries John Gallant.

1944   "Good Morning and Goodbye" and "Three Brick Walls," her first published stories.

1944–1950   Works as a journalist for the Montreal *Standard*.

1948   Divorces John Gallant.

1950   First story accepted by the *New Yorker*. Leaves for Europe.

1952   First reading agreement with the *New Yorker*.

1950–1953   Lives in Paris, Salzburg, Rome, and in Sicily and Spain.

1951   "Madeline's Birthday," first story published in the *New Yorker*.

1953–1961   Lives in Menton-Garavan near the French-Italian border.

1956   *The Other Paris*.

1959   *Green Water, Green Sky*.

1960   Settles in Paris.

1960–1965   Travels to Germany frequently to document *The Pegnitz Junction*.

1964   *My Heart Is Broken*.

1968   Awarded National Magazine Award for fiction, Columbia University Graduate School of Journalism.

1968–1975   Lives in Menton half the year, and the other half in Paris

1970   *A Fairly Good Time.*

1973   *The Pegnitz Junction.*

1974   *The End of the World and Other Stories.*

1979   *From the Fifteenth District.*

1981   *Home Truths.* Receives Governor General's Award for Fiction. Made an Officer of the Order of Canada.

1982   Production of *What Is to Be Done?* in Toronto.

1983   *What Is to Be Done?* Awarded Canada-Australia Prize.

1983–1984   Writer in residence, University of Toronto.

1984   Awarded Honorary Doctorat ès Lettres, Université Sainte Anne, Nova Scotia, and Honorary Doctorate of Letters, York University.

1985   *Overhead in a Balloon.*

1988   *Paris Notebooks. In Transit.*

1989   Made a Fellow of the Royal Society of Literature, England, and an Honorary Foreign Fellow of the American Academy of Arts and Letters.

1990   Awarded Honorary D.Litt., University of Western Ontario.

1991   Awarded Honorary LL.D., Queen's University.

1993   *Across the Bridge.* Made a Companion of the Order of Canada.

1994   Awarded Honorary Doctorate, University of Toronto.

1995   Awarded Honorary Doctorate of Civil Law, Bishop's University, and Honorary Doctorat ès Lettres, Université de Montréal.

1996   *Collected Stories.* Canadian and British title *Selected Stories.*

1997   Awarded Molson Prize for the Arts.

1998   Awarded Honorary Doctorate, University College of Cape Breton.

Abbreviations

AB	Across the Bridge: New Stories
EW	The End of the World
FFD	From the Fifteenth District
FGT	A Fairly Good Time
GWGS	Green Water, Green Sky
HT	Home Truths
IT	In Transit
MHB	My Heart Is Broken
MW	The Moslem Wife
OB	Overhead in a Balloon
OP	The Other Paris
PJ	The Pegnitz Junction
PN	Paris Notebooks
SS	The Selected Stories of Mavis Gallant

Chapter One
Life as Exile

Gallant has always been discreet about her life, claiming that "curiosity about the writer's life kills interest in the work itself."[1] More outspoken in her Linnet Muir sequence than many other Canadian writers ever have been, perhaps with the exception of Mordecai Richler, she strongly reacts against critics who maintain that she has surrounded her life with an aura of secrecy.[2] If her expatriation puzzles critics on the lookout for some bizarre revelation about her life, so be it. Entirely devoted to literature, she spends hours working at home, as deeply absorbed in the search for her truth as academics, whose pattern of life is rarely questioned (cSchaub 93). Responding to Gallant's discretion, Kulyk Keefer aptly remarks that "it's doubtful that intimate knowledge of Gallant's own life would in any authentic way illuminate her work. For one thing her fiction is rich with dreams and images, recurrent motifs and situations which work supremely well within the fictive structures she creates—we have no need to drag in biographical fact to improve their eloquence" (Kulyk Keefer 1988, 197–98). After all, readers gain no insight from the knowledge that Gallant experienced personally what she describes in a story such as "When We Were Nearly Young" nor that Jane's vixen of a mother in "The Wedding Ring" shares Gallant's own mother's nastiness, to give only two examples.[3] Whether the Linnet Muir sequence is autobiographical or fictional does not detract from, or add to, its quality. The stories stand on their own; their themes, style, atmosphere, and irony—those are the pertinent features. Reconstructing Gallant's life amounts to highlighting the experience of incoherence, disjunction, disconnection, displacement—the very subject of her work.

Perhaps one of the most significant elements in her life, one that she has stressed over and over again, is her bilingual upbringing, unusual in view of the period during which she was raised. Born in Montreal in 1922, she was sent, at the age of four, to a Jansenist convent school, unsurprisingly French-speaking, "where by all the rules of the world [she and her parents] lived in [she] did not belong."[4] She spent four formative years there, literally exiled from her own background, an experience resulting in her dual perspective; having had in one instance to certify that a nun's inaccurate translation from English into French was correct, she became aware that "black is white" (*HT,* xvi) in the other community. Similarly, the hostility she met in the schools she attended, because she could speak the "other" language of the country, gave her the feeling of being alien or of being with "alien . . . children" (xvii).[5]

From an early age, she therefore had two measures for all things— the French and the English—which shaped her specific turn of mind: "It left me with two systems of behavior, divided by syntax and tradition; two environments to consider, one becalmed in a long twilight of nine-teenth-century religiosity; two codes of social behavior; much practical experience of the difference between a rule and a moral point."[6] The resulting awareness that whatever she saw, heard, and said could be interpreted in two diametrically opposed manners led her to realize that she herself could not utter, let alone write, anything without having an ironic inner smile, mirroring the "other" position. This tendency was, of course, reinforced by her second uprooting when she decided to leave Canada in 1950 "to get free" and try her luck as a writer in Europe.[7] As she lived in different places and mixed with all sorts of impoverished or downtrodden refugees and exiles because she "didn't want to go into the . . . expatriate Anglo-American thing" (Kulyk Keefer 1988, 206), her perspective multiplied, increasing her ironic twist.[8]

Like many writers, Gallant needed (and still needs) to distance herself from her homeland, to free herself from bonds and social norms that would prevent her from making the most of her vocation.[9] She repeat-edly uses her sense of marginalization in Canada as a theme in her work, especially in the Linnet Muir sequence, in which she expresses most poignantly that "poetry was leaving" her (*HT,* 248), that her writing was starting to resemble "dead butterflies, wings without motion or lift" (249)—an "artistic sclerosis" resulting from the atmosphere. Her choice of France, and of Paris in particular, she ascribes to freedom; in her inter-view with Barbara Gabriel, Gallant explains that she felt freer in France because "there was much more openness to women in general."[10] In addition, Paris offered her anonymity, at least until 1988, when she appeared in "Apostrophes," the most widely watched literary television panel in France.

Besides the dual perspective her early experiences gave her, they have undoubtedly aroused her compassion for children and her need to describe their fate. Raised by parents who had no deep interest in her, she did not enjoy a privileged treatment and was often disposed of over the weekend. An unwelcome guest in her parents' house, she lived as if in exile in a world of her own. She suffered from the inconsistency and unpredictability of her "half-crazy" mother, who could take her somewhere, tell her she would be back in a minute, and not come back. Her mother's strange behavior resulted in Gallant's insecurity and lack of trust in adults. Her father's sudden and unexplained disappearance impressed her sensitive mind with the sense of "mysteries over life and death" (cSchaub, 93), so devastating for a child.[11] As a result of these unsettling childhood experiences, many of Gallant's stories show her concern with children, whose perspective she even adopts at times.[12] The children she portrays live in "the prison of childhood," "trapped in the adult world of muddle," suffering from the whimsical, negligent, egocentric, or tyrannical behavior of the adults on whom they depend.[13] Children without meaningful ties, her young characters can be compared to waifs and strays, maybe a memory of her own "rather sad childhood" (cSchaub, 93).

Having felt as a child "at the mercy of adults" (iGirard-Valette, 90), Gallant aspired "to grow up and have nobody tell {her} what to do. It was a need of autonomy rather than independence" (cSchaub, 93). This need helps to explain why Gallant married so young: she married John Gallant to be emancipated from her unpredictable mother. And her refusal to remarry may well be ascribed to her youth; in any event, she remarks: "I'm not really the marriageable person. . . . And every time the question came up I always found that I was thinking, 'Well whatever happens, I wouldn't abandon children, that's absolutely out. And I wouldn't take children away from their father, as I was taken away from mine. . . . So I'm walking into a trap.' So—I said no, no, no, because I could see myself in an awful dilemma. And unless you go on writing, {marriage} takes up more and more of your life" (Kulyk Keefer 1988, 209–10). Having been hard hit by her parents' separation, she adamantly refuses to be tied down to any man, lest her sense of independence should estrange her from him and make her desert him, to the detriment of their child or children. Perhaps "the experience of betrayal, loss, injustice" (Kulyk Keefer 1989, 97) she suffered in her childhood has maimed her so much that she cannot bear the sheer idea of doing harm to a child of her own.

A likely consequence of her childhood struggles with the adult world, Gallant's censorious outlook on adults blackens their idiosyncrasies. As a keen watcher and listener, she observes people around her, scrutinizing them, ready to record a ridiculous trait, habit, or behavior. Drawing her attention at its first manifestation, the least flaw in an adult is pinned down and mocked. Any scene displaying human folly catches her eye and ear and eventually reemerges in one or another form in her work. Abuse of power, pretentiousness, affectation, ostentation, sententiousness—these she denounces with gleeful derision. During a meal in a Parisian restaurant, she once treated me to hilarious comments on the foolish behavior—the freakishness and whimsicality—of some people living in Montparnasse; her anecdotes, which she shares with her readers, highlight the precision of her observations and convey her ironic standpoint.

In contrast to her vivid discussion of people, Gallant declines to talk about her writing from a critical point of view. She has written minimally about it; the much-quoted essay "What Is Style?" contains about as much as she has agreed to reveal.[14] To critics eager to fathom all the secrets of her art, she usually answers with statements such as "*You're* the critic, *I'm* the writer. The minute I would become seriously interested in the techniques I use, I'd stop writing." Questioned about her reluctance to talk about her own craft, she argues that self-consciousness would work against creativity, a danger she does not sense when she reviews other writers' books.[15] She nevertheless admits the influence of her early career as a journalist on her development as a writer: "Newspaper work was my apprenticeship" (*SS*, xiii), she confides; "digging out facts and putting them together was fascinating. It gave me the grounds for writing. One prepares for the other" (cSchaub 93). In addition, journalism also proved pivotal from a stylistic viewpoint, if only for the ground rules of the newspaper for which she was writing.

Gallant does not attribute her predilection for the short story to her training as a journalist. She simply claims that the genre perfectly suits her temperament; it "satisfies me fully; the more I write stories, the more I develop a taste for them and acquire technical mastery. Why bother about the unnecessary? The novel requires weaving ties between events, and only Stendhal, or, better still, Flaubert, succeed in turning every passage into an interesting one. In contrast, with the short story, the whole connective tissue, that is, what binds the muscles to the bones, is done away with" (iGirard-Valette, 83; translations mine throughout). She sometimes writes sequences, such as the Paul stories, the Linnet Muir cycle, the Carette Sisters, the Edouard, Juliette, Lena stories, or the Henri Grippes stories, which she places one next to the other without "weaving ties between events" as does Alice Munro in *Lives of Girls and Women* or Isabel Huggan in *The Elizabeth Stories*.[16] By presenting these sequences as short stories rather than integrating them into a novel,

Gallant "[keeps] the strong beats, eliminating the rest" (iGirard-Valette, 83). The rest implies descriptions, a superfluous and often tedious addition pertaining to the traditional novel. She prefers to evoke places and landscapes rather than describing them at length; her pictures convey an atmosphere by mere hints. Aiming at perfection, Gallant usually lets her material rest for quite a while in a mental drawer, as it were, extracting it from there only once it has taken shape; then she writes and rewrites until the sounds of the words satisfy her.[17]

A great reader, she acquired her style by reading extensively from a very early age. "I owe it to children's books . . . that I absorbed once and for all the rhythm of the English prose, the order of words in an English sentence and how they are spelled" (*SS,* xvi). "Je lisais comme on boit de l'eau," she says;[18] her life was and still is "built on books: nothing can replace them."[19] When she was a child, she notes, "there were only good books for children; there was no junk then, so all I read was very formative" (cSchaub 94). She thinks that, with their sense of retributive justice, the well-written fairy tales of Hans Christian Andersen and the Grimm Brothers influenced her to some extent. As an adolescent and a young woman, she turned to other types of books, "[reading] more British writers than American writers" and "[reading] what French writers [she] could get" (cSchaub 94), not to mention her enthusiasm for Russian fiction. Numerous writers, she claims, marked her early and later reading, and she acknowledges the influence of Maupassant, Chekhov, Hemingway, Mansfield, Kipling, and Saki, among others. Although Canadian, Gallant does not come out of a Canadian tradition; unavailable in the family home, Canadian literature exerted no influence. An avid reader, her mother encouraged her to read the classics, not Canadian fiction. In addition, Gallant remarks that "there were no Canadian writers when I was a child. I remember some Canadian poetry. People my age are the pillars of Canadian literature. I did read some stories by Callaghan. Other than that I read American and European writers" (cSchaub 94). As a result, Gallant writes out of the European and American tradition.

Nonetheless, as a writer with a strong sense of her Canadian identity, Gallant should be situated in the Canadian context.[20] At the outset, she developed on the margins of the local tradition by keeping aloof from the counterculture and nationalist writing of the sixties and seventies that evolved into the postmodernist revival.[21] She has not shown interest in this kind of writing, and the critics and writers who have chosen the new modes of expression and subvert traditional forms openly (like

George Bowering or Robert Kroetsch, for instance) have reciprocated her lack of interest. To them, she seemed, and still seems, marginal, like a "modernist anachronism"—witness her long-standing contribution to the *New Yorker*.[22] Even Canadian internationalists with a vested interest in defining Canadian literature as intertextually and politically interwoven with world literature, or at least with European and North American literature, did not respond to Gallant's work earlier.[23] Because of her invisibility in Canada until the eighties, critics started to appraise her work rather late, the more so as women critics delayed reclaiming and advertising women writers. Combined with the wane of literary nationalism, their slowness accounts for the lack of enthusiasm among certain critics and writers. The first article by Peter Stevens appeared in 1973; it was followed in 1978 by Grazia Merler's monograph and Geoff Hancock's special issue of the *Canadian Fiction Magazine,* and the odd article in the early eighties.[24] By the mid-eighties, with the notoriety achieved by the 1981 Governor General's Award for *Home Truths,* Gallant started receiving more critical attention.[25] Today critics even allocate her a central position in the history of the Canadian short story.[26]

Her importance can also be assessed by the influence she has exercised on the next generation. It can be traced in Janice Kulyk Keefer, one of the prominent Gallant scholars who has savored every word she wrote. Prolonging an admired pattern, Kulyk Keefer somehow carries on Gallant's tradition: direct and sharp focus, incisive style, detachment—all these she seems to have assimilated, but in an original manner. Wasting no word, spoiling no image, she creates a sharp fictional world on a level with the model in many ways. Even her topics in some short stories are reminiscent of Gallant's: in *Traveling Ladies,* for instance, Kulyk Keefer examines the attitudes of female characters—at all stages in life—as they are traveling to Europe and attempting to bring about a change to their lives.[27] Of course, these are not exiles à la Gallant, but they are, nevertheless, divorced from their familiar backgrounds and also strive for self-knowledge. Interestingly enough, Kulyk Keefer too has a predilection for third-person narratives, which allows her to distance herself from her characters; out of her collected stories, only three are first-person narratives, and a few experiment with direct address. An expert word spinner, Kulyk Keefer spontaneously uses patterns typical of Gallant, displaying an uncommon mastery of style, exploiting all the resources of language to bring out her themes. And like all good disciples, she transmutes the inheritance from her master, giving her voice a tone, emotionality, and sensuality of its own.

If Gallant's work did not attract fame in her homeland for years, it has definitely received the honors it deserves in the last two decades. It has earned her exceptional honors, such as her Honorary Foreign Fellowship of the American Academy of Arts and Letters, prestigious prizes such as the Governor General's Award and most recently the Molson Prize, as well as several honorary doctorates from distinguished universities. Gallant's work has known renewed interest, one marked by new collections of previously collected short stories. The 1994 New Canadian Library selection of stories, *The Moslem Wife and Other Stories,* with its fine selection, was followed in 1996 by the colossal McClelland and Stewart volume *The Selected Stories of Mavis Gallant.* With its chronological organization, not by date of original publication but by decades referred to in the narratives (to the exclusion of the cycles, which are set apart at the end), this collection offers the advantage of delineating the evolution of the world as seen through the sharp eyes of the master ironist. Reviving the interest in her works, these two collections mark the importance of Gallant in the literary world, and most particularly in her own country, a happy denouement for a writer whose fiction was regarded with suspicion because of its un-Canadianness.

Chapter Two

Distance and Disharmony:
The Other Paris and
My Heart Is Broken

Written in the fifties, *The Other Paris* and *My Heart Is Broken* "begin to suggest many of Gallant's . . . major themes" and approaches to the fictional world.[1] Disclosing her sharp eye for detail and unquenchable curiosity in the realms of postwar politics, family institutions, and cultural and social trends, these early collections expose how Gallant embeds her vision of the world in her cunningly crafted fiction. Although they deal with episodes in the lives of one or more characters, the stories are set in a wider social and political context, which Gallant powerfully turns to profit in the political and sociological narratives of *The Pegnitz Junction* and *Overhead in a Balloon*. While heralding the thematic concerns of the later collections, *The Other Paris* and *My Heart Is Broken* also prefigure Gallant's clever exploitation of narrative strategies, more subtly postmodern than those of George Bowering, Audrey Thomas, and Rudy Wiebe, for instance. In particular, with their clashing visions of life, the narratives generate and sustain tension through oppositions of varied forms: between romance and realism ("The Other Paris," "Autumn Day," "The Deceptions of Marie-Blanche," "My Heart Is Broken," "The Ice Wagon Going down the Street," "Its Image on the Mirror"), liberalism and traditionalism ("Bernadette"), the private and the public face ("Señor Pinedo," "The Other Paris"), pretended and real concern ("A Day like Any Other," "Bernadette"), selfishness and generosity ("Poor Franzi"), children and parents ("Going Ashore," "About Geneva," "An Unmarried Man's Summer," "The Legacy," "A Day like Any Other"), inner life and external behavior ("Acceptance of Their Ways," "Its Image on the Mirror," "The Cost of Living," "Bernadette"), the past and its questionable recollections ("The Moabitess," "Its Image on the Mirror," "The Cost of Living," "Wing's Chips"), and inner life and ideologies ("Sunday Afternoon"). In addition, with the contrast afforded by the oppositions, the stories give prospect of the split levels of discourse, multivoiced narrations, and ironic disruptions so characteristic of Gallant's later fiction.[2]

At first puzzled by Gallant's disturbing approach, critics and reviewers criticized her "refus[al] to make . . . connections," "the sophisticated foreign tour in which one is taken to see only the digressions and parentheses of each culture," "the elements [that] never quite coalesce, never seem more than preliminary notes for a novel which was never written," and that "too much is left out of the world of [her] stories."[3] Such a lukewarm response may be ascribed to "the reader's fear that she may mistake the author's intent, or fail to discover some stable meaning in a text, may lead her to behave defensively, to shut the compelling complexities out."[4] Yet the refused connections, digressions, parentheses, and blanks contribute to the greatness of Gallant's fiction, for they create "numerous corridors we might take in our journey through the text" (Rooke, 25). Drawn into action, the readers somehow have to invent their own personal versions of each story.

In her introduction to *Home Truths,* Gallant mentions that "fiction, like painting, consists of entirely more than meets the eye; otherwise it is not worth a second's consideration" (xii). Her comment echoes Wolfgang Iser's assumption that "no author worth his salt will ever attempt to set the *whole* picture before his reader's eyes. If he does, he will very quickly lose his reader, for it is only by activating the reader's imagination that the author can hope to involve him and so realize the intentions of his text."[5] Gallant's earliest collections, *The Other Paris* and *My Heart Is Broken,* prove just that; her stories' blanks—the aspects of scenes left unwritten and the parts of dialogues left unspoken—allow the readers' creative participation, encouraging them to realize the text (Iser 1974, 125).[6] In Gallant's writing, "the very precision of the written details . . . increases the proportion of indeterminacy" (136), and the constant changes in perspective add further angles from which to look at the text. Part of the difficulty of her writing results from the dual, if not multiple, lenses with which she looks at the world, contributing to a detached perspective, verging on aloofness. Although "there is no milieu [she] do[es]n't feel comfortable in, that [she] do[es]n't immediately understand,"[7] thanks to her itinerant life as a child and then as a young woman, she always retains the candid perspective of the outsider too, which contributes to the confusing vision of her writing. She indeed provides the readers "with a bundle of multiple viewpoints, the center of which is continuously shifted" (Iser 1971, 20). As one perspective always contradicts another, the text "simultaneously stimulates and frustrates our desire to 'picture' " it, causing a fair amount of disorientation (Iser 1974, 136).

In this respect, the short story "The Other Paris" informs Gallant's writing most obviously and serves as a model for both collections because of the indeterminacy engendered by suppressed information and ironically conflicting perspectives combined with the narrator's "detachment and disinterestedness vis-à-vis the experiences [of the] characters . . . [and] refusal to take sides and pronounce judgements" (Kulyk Keefer 1989, 41).[8] Through twists and turns, the story discloses how Carol Frazier, a young, educated American woman, "set[s] about the business of falling in love"[9] with her American boss, Howard Mitchell, who has proposed to her "over a tuna-fish salad" (*OP,* 3) to avoid "just [being] a person who fills in at dinner" (5). She has learned "from helpful college lectures on marriage" that "a common interest, such as a liking for Irish setters, [is] the true basis for happiness, and that the illusion of love [is] a blight imposed by the film industry" (4), but in spite of her pragmatism, she is convinced that the Parisian setting will provide the right emotions. Idealized to extremes, her vision of Paris is contrasted with her perception of the drabness around her, a perception she eventually sets out to forget and replaces by her idealized version, a decision guiding her romantic approach to love and marriage, in spite of her college lectures. Contrasting Carol's approach, Odile, the French secretary from aristocratic—but destitute—origins, lives by real emotions supporting her lover, Felix, an unemployed refugee almost 15 years younger than she. Her life drastically contradicts the message of the lectures Carol attended, according to which "similar economic backgrounds, financial security, belonging to the same church—these [are] pillars of the married union" (4). Even this bare plot summary evidences the irony contained in the story and the disharmonious pictures of life, but it illustrates neither the gaps of indeterminacy nor the jumps of perspective nor the narrator's detachment contributing to both the irony and the discontinuous relation.

The opening of the story immediately sets the pattern: "By the time they decided what Carol would wear for her wedding (white with white flowers), it was the end of the afternoon. Madame Germaine removed the sketchbooks, the scraps of net and satin, the stacks of *Vogue;* she had already, a professional look of anxiety, as if it could not possibly come out well. One foresaw seams ripped open, extra fittings, even Carol's tears" (*OP,* 1). Left undefined in the opening sentence, the nature of the personal pronoun *they* is clarified in part in the second sentence but is fully appreciated only in the next paragraph when Odile, Carol's friend, comes into the picture. Yet the parenthetical information in the first sentence reflects Odile's ironic outlook, and no one else's (except perhaps the narrator's), for the seamstress would have described the dress and the material, leaving the color aside as obvious. The parenthetical information, contrasted with the temporal marker indicating the lengthy period of indecision, implies the ironic smile of an outsider, like Odile, who, left out of the picture at this stage, derides the conventional "white dress with white flowers"—and perhaps even the concept of marriage. The next sentence transcribes the scene from the detached perspective of the narrator: the first section of the balanced sentence clinically records the gestures of the seamstress; the second conveys the impression of an emotion difficult to understand, puzzling the readers. What "could not possibly come out well"? The dress? The wedding? Upon a second reading, the second option imposes itself as a plausible, if ironic, interpretation. The last sentence removes the readers to a distance because of the use of the indefinite personal pronoun, yet the topic signifies the perspective of the seamstress. Thus from the very opening the story unfolds different views for which the readers must establish a pattern of plausible connections.

Increasing the distance from which the scene is perceived, the next paragraph introduces Odile's critical attitude: "Odile, Carol's friend, seemed disappointed. 'White isn't *original,*' she said. 'If it were me, I would certainly not be married in all that rubbish of lace, like a First Communion.' She picked threads from her skirt fastidiously, as if to remove herself completely from Carol and her original plans" (*OP,* 1). Although focusing on Odile, the paragraph does not render her standpoint; it merely depicts her attitude and repeats her deprecatory words ("not original," "rubbish," "like a First Communion"—the last one implying childlike choice), whose critical connotation appears through hypothetical markers such as "seemed" and "as if" in the descriptive sentences. At once detached and presuming to decode Odile's feelings, the paragraph calls upon conventional religious habits, and through their criticism also upon nonconformist approaches, widening the scope of the story.

The next paragraph embraces several perspectives, causing a fractured perception and therefore disconcerting the readers, who have no thread to hold on to:

> I wonder if anyone has ever asked Odile to marry him, Carol thought, placidly looking out the window. As her wedding approached, she had

more and more the engaged girl's air of dissociation: nothing mattered until the wedding, and she could not see clearly beyond it. She was sorry for all the single girls of the world, particularly those who were, like Odile, past thirty. Odile looked sallow and pathetic, huddled into a sweater and coat, turning samples of lace with a disapproving air. She seemed all of a piece with the day's weather and the chilly air of the dressmaker's flat. Outside, the street was still damp from a rain earlier that day. There were no trees in sight, no flowers, no comforting glimpse of park. No one in this part of Paris would have known it was spring. (*OP*, 1–2)

This paragraph contains such a multiplicity of viewpoints that the readers are tossed about like a boat at sea, never having a firm anchor. While the first sentence reflects Carol's viewpoint, the next one implies the standpoint of the detached narrator or possibly Odile. The third sentence reverts to Carol's viewpoint, whereas the fourth sentence could be from either her perspective or the detached narrator's. The fifth sentence, with its impressionistic comparison, corresponds to the narrator's wider perspective, alien to Carol's materialistic approach. The sixth remains unclear, for it evokes the weather as experienced outside, and yet the characters do not seem to have left the flat of the seamstress. Only retrospectively, when reading the next paragraph still set indoors, do the readers realize that omniscience is at hand. The seventh and eighth sentences could be from either the narrator's or Carol's perspective. The oscillation between one standpoint and another dizzies the readers, who have no control over the whirling mechanism of the machine into which they have stepped. Propelled centrifugally, the readers never reach the central platform where the characters move about. Kept at bay, the readers also experience detachment.

This "distanciation" results from the detached tone of the narrator, who even in passages from a character's perspective neutralizes the emotional impact. The narrative reads as if the narrator had filtered emotions and transmitted them analytically, adding qualifiers that increase the distance between the characters and the readers. Witness the following passage recording Carol's reaction to Odile's irony: "People had assured Carol so often that her engagement was romantic, and she had become so accustomed to the word, that Odile's slight irony was perplexing. If anyone had asked Carol at what precise moment she fell in love, or where Howard Mitchell proposed to her, she would have imagined, quite sincerely, a scene that involved all at once the Seine, moonlight, barrows of violets, acacias in flower, and a confused, misty background of the Eiffel Tower and little crooked streets. This was what everyone expected, and she had nearly come to believe it herself" (*OP,* 3). While echoing Carol's feeling, the first sentence manifests a clinical detachment by qualifying Odile's irony as if Carol were examined under the magnifying glass of a psychologist or sociologist, for no innocent subject of verbal irony would stand back and ponder over the quality of the irony. Similarly, the next sentences lay bare a hypothetical situation, which Carol would not even think of. So although the passage discloses Carol's attitude toward her engagement and toward Odile's ironic perception of it, the narrator does not, strictly speaking, transmit Carol's thoughts and emotions from within. Halfway between neutral and editorial omniscience, the narrator adds a tinge of irony to the discourse by modifying the perception of emotions from a detached, even cynical, standpoint. In the same manner, the sentence informing Carol's eventual realization that Odile's comments are ironical combines the narrator's and Odile's ironic perspective: "It penetrated at last that Odile was making fun of her" (*OP,* 3). The ironic phrase "at last" contributes to upsetting the perspective, balancing it between Carol's, Odile's, and the narrator's, as in a cubist painting, which instead of showing different angles of the same person would show apposed parts of different subject matters.

When turning to Howard, the narrative discourse effects similar shifts of perspective. At first the narrator apparently transmits a voice closer to his: "He was touched by her shy good manners, her earnest college French. His friends liked her, and, more important, so did the wives of his friends. He had been seriously in love on earlier occasions, and did not consider it a reliable emotion. He and Carol got on well, which seemed to him a satisfactory beginning" (*OP,* 5–6). Although less critical, the narrator emphasizes the lack of genuine feelings by juxtaposing statements that do not connect smoothly. Jumping from Howard's superficial feelings through his friends' appreciation and then his past passions to his tolerant acceptance of the situation, the discourse sounds like an ironic counterpoint to Carol's college lectures. Allusions to the normal course of romantic development contribute further irony: "His friends, however, told him that she was obviously in love with him and that it was pretty to see. This he expected, not because he was vain but because one took it for granted that love, like a harmless familiar, always attended young women in friendships of this nature. Certainly he was fond of Carol and concerned for her comfort. Had she complained of a toothache, he would have seen to it that she got to a dentist" (*OP,* 6). Knowing how Carol feels, how she sets about to love Howard, the readers smile while reading the first two sentences, for they reveal how romantic ideals color the perception people have of Carol, whether such ideals are implicated or not in the relationship; generated by the readers' active reading process, the ironic smile highlights the connections drawn. The abrupt transition to Howard's feelings and concerns jumps back to the last sentence of the previous passage, emphasizing contentment with the situation; but the next sentence hilariously reduces the romantic appeal, translating it onto a different, more pragmatic plane. An awareness of the change in registers effected in this passage allows the readers to surmise that passion does not characterize the new couple's relations.

The narrative then evidences a far more complicated course of relationship than at first assumed. To discern a plausible thread, the readers have to decode a jumble of incidents, thoughts, and allusions. Their understanding of Carol's dissatisfaction with her life goes back to allusions attributing her lack of love to the unromantic weather, to the as yet undiscovered true Paris, to the nonexistent connections with French society. Originating in her awareness that she does not share anything with anyone, Carol's disappointment is disclosed every day when "thinking that a special kind of evening [is] forming all over the city, and that she ha[s] no part in it" (*OP*, 8). It is further silently voiced through questions and hypotheses interspersed in the text: "Where was the Paris she read about? Where were the elegant and expensive-looking women? Where, above all, were the men, those men with their gay good looks and snatches of merry song, the delight of English lady novelists?" (6); "There must be more to it than this" (8). Thus here and there the fractured narrative implicitly insists on the absence of real emotional involvement from the start and a refusal to examine its implications as evidenced in the following revelatory passage: "Temporarily, she put the question of falling in love to one side. Paris was not the place, she thought; perhaps it had been, fifty years ago, or whenever it was that people wrote all the songs. It did not occur to her to break her engagement" (13). The readers have to make out from the previous jumble of statements—taking them in all directions—that Carol's allusions to the picture of Paris in the famous love songs suggest her refusal to address its romantic, thus unreal, nature as well as inform the unsound grounds for her engagement. The latter is evoked from an omniscient perspective that awakens the readers to the necessity to direct their attention to another track, to forget the official engagement and look for another plausible plot.

As the readers look for other tracks, they eventually realize that Carol does not want to see where the emotions lie for fear of their unconventional character. She may well think that "if she spoke to the right person, or opened the right door, or turned down an unexpected street, the city would reveal itself and she would fall in love" (*OP,* 9), but the minute she faces the right person or place, she rejects the emotions inspired because they do not correspond to the image of love and Paris imprinted in her mind. The readers have to put this picture together from different passages. The first corresponds to the abrupt introduction of Odile's friend, Felix, in the analeptic narrative in the first section. Brought in apparently for no explicit purpose, Felix puzzles Carol. The oxymoronic look on his face, "at once bold and withdrawn" (9), engenders equally contradictory feelings in her—attraction and repulsion. The meandering narrative then takes the readers through confusing developments recording Carol's confusion. Her voiced question as to Felix's origins is followed by a curiously bizarre reported speech: "Howard didn't know. Felix was Austrian, he thought, or Czech. There was something odd about him, for although he obviously hadn't enough to eat, he always had plenty of American cigarettes. That was a bad sign. 'Why are you so interested?' he said. But Carol was not interested" (10). Often mentioning unreproduced dialogues that the readers must reconstruct in order to bridge the gaps left by the unwritten, Gallant offers here an interesting combination of direct and reported discourse. Whereas the first two statements undoubtedly correspond to the report of Howard's words, the third and fourth statements leave the identity of the speaker uncertain; they could represent anybody's words, though the context would direct the readers' assumptions toward Howard, who appears to understand obscure aspects in the life of Felix—further referred to in elusive terms as "other things" he does (10). At first reported as if reproduction would add nothing, the conversation is then represented in direct discourse for no obvious reason. Standing in striking contrast to the rest of the paragraph, the question reproduced in direct discourse should encourage the readers to turn to discourse analysis and examine the switch. If it is justified by the importance of the question, then the reported answer amounts to brushing off the topic as irrelevant.

No matter how justified the interpretation of the switches might appear, they might be decoded differently and signal just the opposite, for the next sentence in the following paragraph implies a link, however superficial, that ties Carol and Felix: "After that, Carol [sees] Felix every evening" (*OP,* 10), keeps registering his appearance, and discusses him with Odile—all signs of interest rather than indifference. Soon after Carol gleans information about Felix, the link appears stronger, even if contrived: "That night, before going to sleep, she thought about Felix, and about how he was only twenty-one. She and Felix, then, were closer in age than he was to Odile or she herself was to Howard. When I was in school, he was in school, she thought. When the war stopped, we were fourteen and fifteen . . . But here she lost track, for where Carol had had a holiday, Felix's parents had been killed. Their closeness in age gave her unexpected comfort, as if someone in this disappointing city had some tie with her" (10–11). This passage exposes the lie of Carol's previous claim to disinterest. Subsequent confrontations, nonetheless, disclose that Carol keeps denying Felix a real part in her life. Ignoring him or objecting to one or another aspect of his personality (11, 16, 19, 22, 24), she minimizes the impact of her encounters with him.

Complicating the readers' decoding task, Carol's conscious decision to ignore Felix and her attempts to enforce it expose another reality: "In the morning she was ashamed of her disloyal thoughts—her closest tie in Paris was, after all, with Howard—and decided to ignore Felix when she saw him again. That night, when she passed his chair, he said 'Good evening,' and she was suddenly acutely conscious of every bit of her clothing: the press of the belt at her waist, the pinch of her earrings, the weight of her dress, even her gloves, which felt as scratchy as sacking. It was a disturbing feeling; she was not sure that she liked it" (OP, 11). Carol obviously cultivates an illusion: once again, though one sentence expresses her claims to love Howard and to will Felix out of her sight, the next sentence turns to Felix and gives ample details of the physical stirrings his presence elicits in her. The concluding statements of the passage signify Carol's blindness to the emotions that would lead her to experience love. The to-ing and fro-ing between the assumed pose and the real feelings nonetheless keep unsettling the readers, who cannot advance any interpretation with certainty, for at any time the narrative shifts back to a previous set of data, negating the most recent ones.

Further instances of intense closeness and emotional excitement prove that Carol will ignore "the right person," "the right door," the turning into "an unexpected street." To discover her self-imposed exclusion, the readers have to follow Carol in her meanderings through Paris and in the text's complicated intersections of past and present. Carol's reaction when she sees Felix at a concert given by Martine, Odile's sister, informs the awkward wavering that pulls the readers along: "She felt a spasm of annoyance, and at the same time her heart began to beat so quickly that she felt its movement must surely be visible" (*OP,* 16). But she refuses to understand the emotions, or at least misinterprets them. For immediately after recording her heartbeats, she weighs their occurrence in a most confused manner: "What ever is the matter with me, she thought. If one could believe all the arch stories on the subject, this was traditional for brides-to-be. Perhaps at this unpromising moment, she had begun to fall in love. She turned in her seat and stared at Howard; he looked much as always. She settled back and began furnishing in her mind the apartment they would have in Chicago" (16). Ironically Carol decodes her emotions correctly; she *has* begun to fall in love, but not with the man who fits her idealized picture of marriage. The contrast between her emotional reaction to Felix and her indifference to Howard becomes clearer as she sets out to forget the feelings by letting her pragmatic sense take over. After several oscillations between one and the other, the readers eventually attribute her attitude to a fight between conventionalism and nonconformism.

Such an interpretation may have been facilitated by a typographical device singling out a scene. Halfway through the story, the concert attracts the readers' attention by virtue of its highlighted position between blank lines before and after. On the one hand, the initial blank line might correspond to the break necessitated by the readers' pondering over the three sentences Carol writes in a letter to her parents to mention the concert. Whereas the upcoming event kindles her imagination and stirs up her excitement, Carol's correspondence tones down emotions to the point of suppressing them altogether. Since she privileges surface smoothness over deep feelings, she makes sure that her letters "sound properly casual" (*OP,* 15). Unreproduced, the letters set the readers' minds at work; the degree of indeterminacy caused by the unwritten forces the readers to picture the content of the letters. As the latter "ha[ve] not contained much of interest" (15), the readers visualize a jumble of irrelevancies interspersed with hints at another world, a reflection of her life in Paris.[10] On the other hand, the blank line announcing the scene might signify the crucial value of the experience. Carol is convinced that the concert will introduce her into French society; yet the event itself is dismal, set in "an ordinary, shabby theatre" on "an obscure street," and the audience turns out "odd and shabby" (15, 17). The scene would then serve to contrast her ideals, setting the glamorous picture of French society against its drab reality, and by extension the passionate love stories associated with Paris against the emotionless landscape she has visited.

The concert certainly causes a drastic change in Carol's approach: "For Carol, the concert was the end, the final *clou*. She stopped caring about Paris, or Odile, or her feelings for Howard" (*OP*, 20). Having witnessed the disdain of Odile's family for outsiders, Carol articulates her discontent and consciously erases any previous concern of hers. Her dissatisfaction also stems from Felix's catchphrase describing the attitude of Odile's family, "No admission for us foreigners" (19), for the suggested lack of discrimination between Felix and herself vexes Carol: "[I]t was even less kind to include [her] in a single category of foreigners. Surely Odile could see the difference between Carol and this pale young man who 'did other things.' She felt that she and Felix had been linked together in a disagreeable way, and that she was floating away from everything familiar and safe" (19). Carol's frustration curiously echoes the readers' feeling when confronted with the indeterminate gaps of a narrative that puts together so many apparently disparate elements.

As if the indeterminacies did not suffice to fragment the readers' perception of both characters and events, halfway through the story, the narrative unexpectedly resumes the first scene. Aggravating the fracture, the disruption of chronology severs the tenuous thread from which the readers were suspended. Odile's reference to her nastiness at Madame Germaine's indeed directs the readers back to a long-forgotten scene interrupted by the description of Carol's life after her engagement. Only then do the readers realize that Gallant has led them astray; the comparison between the illusory scene Carol would picture and the actual proposal has led to retrospective narration. Astutely concealing the anachronic nature of the information through successive speedy developments, Gallant distorts the readers' sense of chronology. Her cutting technique calls to mind the conceptually similar cinematic technique of montage: film directors often cut a story into several parts, change their natural order, and splice everything together again to highlight an important scene. With this technique, Gallant forces the readers to reconstruct the scene at the dressmaker's in the light of the anachronies (chronological deviations).

The drastic break in the narration allows the readers to weigh Carol's approach to Odile's irony and to Felix's marginality in different terms. Indeed, in the aftermath of the highlighted scene, Carol disconnects herself from her previous concerns. The change presumably helps the readers to understand why "Odile's slight irony was perplexing" in the first section of the story, the more so as the account reiterates people's assumptions concerning Carol's engagement: "Everyone seemed to think it normal that now her only preoccupation should be the cut of her wedding dress. People began giving parties for her. The wash of attention soothed her fears. She was good-tempered, and did not ask Howard to take her to tiresome places. Once again he felt he had made the right decision, and put her temporary waywardness down to nerves. After a while, Carol began lunching with Odile again, but she did not mention the concert" (*OP,* 20). Justifying Carol's lack of insight, the passage alternates points of view, thrusting the readers in all sorts of directions because of their allusive character. While the first sentence reflects Carol's innocent outlook on the decisions made at the dressmaker's, thus precluding any irony and begging the readers, as it were, to share her perspective, the second and third jump by mere narratorial allusions to completely different aspects of the period, left to the readers to connect and visualize. Furthermore, the reference to Carol's fears evokes her lack of love for Howard and her suppressed emotions for Felix while calling to mind her desperate attempts to enter French society so as to fall in love. The fourth sentence curiously combines the narrator's, Carol's, and Howard's approach: the use of the adjectives "good-tempered" and "tiresome" have different values depending on the angle of vision the readers decide to share. These words definitely evoke Carol's decision to be satisfied with her present lot, to refuse passion; on the other hand, they recall Howard's previous allusion to his sisters' composure and contentment. The fifth sentence, from Howard's perspective, alludes to previous scenes and thoughts when Carol did not deserve his assent. Faced with these multiple allusions, the readers need both intense concentration and associative minds to fathom the connections and grasp Carol's defeated ideals.

Further perplexing allusions await the readers. The last section of the story, resuming the action of the first one, begins with an apparently unnecessary allusion to the weather. As Gallant professes that "only the essentials remain" in her stories (iGirard-Valette, 82), the allusion cannot be brushed off as irrelevant. Indeed, it refers back to Carol's conviction that once the weather turns better, she will fall in love. However, it must also connect with future events, particularly because Odile's comment—"This was the longest winter I remember, although I think one says this every year" (*OP,* 21)—alludes to patterns, forgotten and resumed time and again, an allusion that will connect with Carol's approach to marriage: just as seasons come back, her disappointment over her lack of passion will return and will always be followed by her refusal to break the frail bond of her marriage. Of course, this realization

comes only on rereading the story; at first, the general implications of
the reference to the weather will be lost for want of a wider frame of reference achieved only by retroactive reading.

The analepsis taking the readers back to the first scene of the story
allows Odile to mention how she worries about her sister and Felix, and
to take Carol along to visit Felix. The walk in a part of town with
"crooked, narrow streets," "a section of Paris Carol ha[s] not seen" (*OP,*
22), recalls Carol's conviction that some side street would inspire her
love. She does discover love in two ways. First, she witnesses Odile and
Felix's love (25). Second, she senses her intimacy with Felix (25) and presents an interesting case of transferal of emotions when Felix lets her
know that "Odile loves [her]": "Her heart leaped as if he, Felix, had said
he loved her. But no, she corrected herself. Not Felix but some other
man, some wonderful person who did not exist" (28). Evidenced by the
simile in the first statement, the transferal leaps to another transferal
conveying that Carol reverts to an ideal, not to a reality, repeating a pattern started before. Her dream comes true, but its materialization contrasts her vision of a romantic setting, far from the one she finds herself
in: "For a moment, standing under the noisy trains on the dark, dusty
boulevard, she felt that she had at last opened the right door, turned
down the right street, glimpsed the vision toward which she had strug-
gled on winter evenings when, standing on the staircase, she had
wanted to be enchanted with Paris and to be in love with Howard" (29).
Although the sentence repeats the very words of Carol's original conviction that certain conditions are needed to fall in love (9), the scene ironically contradicts her vision by presenting a setting alien to her dreams.

At this point, the readers wonder what track Carol will choose—love
or its appearance? A mental somersault pulls her away from her dream
as she weighs her emotions and the conditions under which they would
flourish and rejects the whole picture because of its material sordidness.
She refuses a vision "com[ing] from Felix and Odile" (*OP,* 29) no matter
how much she has longed for it: "She remembered in time what Felix
was—a hopeless parasite. And Odile was silly and immoral and old
enough to know better. And they were not married and never would be,
and they spent heaven knew how many hours in that terrible room in a
slummy quarter of Paris" (29). Echoing the discourse of a child, this passage, characterized by its abundant coordination, reflects how Carol
needs to punctuate the negative aspects of Odile and Felix to convince
herself to reject the vision. In a similar manner, when she reverts to her
relation with Howard, coordinators stress their assets as if she needed to

count them: "What she and Howard had was better. No one could point to them, or criticize them, or humiliate them by offering to help" (29). Carol's outlook pushes her away from her ideal into a conventional reality that she will nevertheless romanticize. The conditional used throughout signals a likely condition, though by no means assured:

> Soon, she sensed, the comforting vision of Paris as she had once imagined it would overlap with reality. To have met and married Howard there would sound so romantic and interesting, more and more as time passed. She would forget the rain and her unshared confusion and loneliness, and remember instead the Paris films, the street lamps with their tinsel icicles, the funny concert hall where the ceiling collapsed, and there would be, at last, a coherent picture, accurate but untrue. The memory of Felix and Odile and their distasteful strangeness would slip away; for "love" she would think, once more, "Paris," and, after a while, happily married, mercifully removed in time, she would remember it and describe it and finally believe it as it never had been at all. (*OP,* 30)

The final paragraph recalls a sordid scene made fun of and told with much flourish that causes Carol's awareness about the truthfulness of accounts: "She realized for the first time that something could be perfectly accurate but untruthful—they had not found any part of that evening funny—and that this might cover more areas of experience than the occasional amusing story" (*OP,* 13). Putting the last paragraph in parallel with this sentence, the readers eventually visualize the intricate patterns that the story has drawn for them by contrasts and blanks to fill in. Thus the pattern of excitements and the rejection of their source eventually leads to the erasure of any trace of past brief encounters with a disturbing reality.

The story thus exhibits how Gallant makes the most of contrasts and gaps of indeterminacy, involving her readers in the conception of a creative design encompassing all the patterns of her story. Combining detachment and involvement, the presentation of perspectives unsettles the readers because it constantly moves in utterly opposed directions. Now coming closer, now pulling away, it prevents the readers from even attempting to empathize; any such attempt is indeed frustrated because of the irony or conflicting revelation disclosed every so often. Such revelations highlight Gallant's understanding of culture from within and without; she conveys their differences by exposing the rather romanticized North American perception of France together with an insider's version revealing the nonglamorous aspects of French society after the war. With the protagonist's idealized version of Paris contrasting its real picture, the narrative hints at the human tendency toward delusion that manifests itself through a need to stick to an invented vision of life and the concomitant refusal to acknowledge even the existence of another reality.

Like the title story, all the stories in *The Other Paris* emphasize a disharmony of views and behavior. So do the stories in *My Heart Is Broken*. Owing to their discontinuous narrative perspectives, the stories present gaps of indeterminacy that draw the readers into the action.[11] In addition, except for in "Autumn Day" and "Wing's Chips," the readers cannot identify with the characters because of their despicable or ludicrous approaches or the distance the narrator puts between the readers and the characters. "Poor Franzi," for instance, contrasts the title character's total lack of emotional involvement with his fiancée's selfless concern for others as well as opposes Americans and Austrians. The thoughts of the attendants at the funeral of Franzi's grandmother do not encourage the readers to empathize with any of them. The same applies to the absent Franzi, who "often commit[s] . . . absurdities in conversation, following only the rhythm of the sentences and thinking all the while of something else" (*OP,* 63), a tendency reminiscent of the disrupted thread of the narrative. Likewise, in "The Deceptions of Marie-Blanche," the detached observer offers a comic account of the multiple engagements and amorous deceptions of the title character and her family's reactions to them but regularly delays or omits pieces information, so that the readers have to piece the facts together. The distance and detachment characteristic of the first-person narrator provoke the readers' lack of concern for the victim of the narrator's irony.

In the stories portraying the conflicts between parents and children, the oscillation between the various standpoints and the detachment of the narrator also keep the readers at bay. At the same time, the readers are made to feel for the children because of their dependence on the tyrannical or negligent behavior of the adults, who take notice of their children only when it suits their own needs. Thus in "Going Ashore" the fragmented narration with its distortions of reality reveals how Emma, a 12-year-old girl, has to adjust to her divorced mother's forever picking up men to live with. The contrast between the real Tangier and "the imagined city, full of hazard and adventure" (*OP,* 95) Emma experiences reflects the unreal nature of the life she leads with her mother. "About Geneva" explores the tension in a broken family between the children's memories of a stay with their father and their mother's and grandmother's vision of the visit. The mother asks questions about their stay only because she is trying to figure out why her marriage collapsed.[12] "A Day like Any Other" shows that Jane and Ernestine Kennedy are a burden to their parents, who refuse any involvement in the children's upbringing. Their mother rarely has "time to enjoy or contemplate something not directly dependent on herself or fated by one of her husband's decisions" (239). Their hypochondriac father takes even less interest in them: "Mr. Kennedy seldom saw his daughters. The rules of the private clinics he frequented were all in his favor. In any case, he seldom asked to see the girls, for he felt that they were not at an interesting age" (223). In "An Unmarried Man's Summer," Mary and Johnny Osborne are mostly referred to as "the children," a sign of their uncle's and parents' disconnection from them. If it were not for Angelo, the uncle's young Italian servant, the Osbornes' holiday would turn out a disaster, for the story's various jumps into the minds of the adults bring to the fore their self-centered intention not to bother over Mary and Johnny.

Other stories disclose the characters' memories in such a way as to alert the readers to the characters' questionable authority and force the readers to work out a more accurate picture. "Its Image on the Mirror," for instance, focuses on Jean Price's seemingly detached, but unfaithful, recollections of the past, particularly of her relationship to her younger, bohemian sister, Isobel.[13] Like Jean's dreams, the narrative of her life consists of "love remembered, a house recovered and lost, a climate imagined, a journey never made," in short a confused account of dreamed-for love and recognition.[14] With all the breaks in continuity offered by Jean's reconstruction of the past, the readers have to disentangle the various narrative threads to discover a pattern in her life. The alternation between objective account and subjective representation of the past, between mean calculation and distress, reveals how the narrator suffers from her own delusions, forever aspiring to replace her sister, yet incapable of doing so. Almost reversing that pattern, "The Cost of Living" offers another first-person account of two Australian women's life in Paris from the perspective of Puss, the younger, bohemian sister. The story also calls attention to the questionable reliability of memories, for Puss misconstrues the past and presents it in a haphazard fashion. Confronted with this seemingly artless and spontaneous jumble of memories and omissions, the readers have to decipher the pattern of Puss's life, her self-denial. Lily Littel in "Acceptance of Their Ways" also manifests a meanness of approach that she conceals for the sake of company. No longer a paid lady in attendance, Lily engages in mental fights with Mrs. Freeport, whom Lily repeatedly abandons to pay visits to an imaginary sister; instead she succumbs to the pleasure of wine drinking on her own. The two women's fear of loneliness emerges from their conversations, their thoughts, and the information the detached narrator chooses to impart.

The contrast between external manifestation and inner life also creates a pattern in several stories. The readers discover the tensions of human relations through the omissions, sidetracks, and multiple standpoints of the narrative. "My Heart Is Broken" exemplifies how talkative Mrs. Thompson fails to understand the distress of Jeannie, a young married woman who has just been raped by one of her husband's colleagues. Mrs. Thompson's recollection of her past and its romanticized tragedy—the death of Jean Harrow—smothers Jeannie, who never expresses her distress. The readers must decode the narrative's indirection and digressions to learn that Jeannie's silences and apparent detachment conceal her heartbreak.[15] In a similar fashion, "Sunday Afternoon" unfolds the inner life of unpoliticized Veronica Baines while Jim, her American lover, and Ahmed, his Algerian friend, discuss politics. The men's invested interest in ideologies prevents them from acknowledging her presence, afflicting her greatly. But unlike Jeannie, Veronica does manage to voice her frustration and her need for recognition, albeit indirectly: "Jim never spends anything. He needs a reason, and I'm not a reason. . . . It's not my fault if you don't like me. Both of you. I can't help it if you wish I was something else. Why don't you take better care of me?" (*MHB*, 217). Veronica's distress recalls Cissy's in "Autumn Day." The story focuses on Cissy, a young American woman who, after joining her husband posted with the Army of Occupation in Salzburg, experiences utter solitude. With its different threads, her account of her experiences evidences disconnection from her husband—"this stranger, mute, helpless, fumbling, enclosed" (*OP*, 53). But eventually she consciously suppresses her disillusion about married life by sticking to a wishful conviction that "we'll be all right" (53).

Further stories illustrate how Gallant's multiple perspectives, deliberate omissions and digressions, and indirection enhance the conflicts opposing her characters. "The Picnic," for instance, is concerned with the preparations for a picnic meant to gather the French population with the Americans from the army base. Yet the twists and turns of the narration throw light on the gap that separates the main representatives of the two groups, so that toward the end, the Major "rallie[s] his forces for the coming battle" (*OP*, 121), not for a social function. An ironic "symbol of unity" (119), the picnic itself never acquires narrative attention in the picture of disharmonious concerns, a foreboding sign of its failure. By not depicting the event for which all prepare themselves, Gallant provokes the readers to anticipate its outcome, allowing them to prolong the text, so that it becomes a "living event" with lifelike pictures (Iser 1974, 142).

With its different viewpoints and its "narrator at once detached enough to observe and engaged enough to comment on social rituals in their settings" (Besner 1988, 17), Gallant's fiction highlights the discontinuity and disharmony attendant on human life. She borrows from her personal experience as an insider-outsider by combining multiple perspectives without warning as if to merge one perspective into the other, contributing to the confusing vision of her fiction. "The intensity and ruthlessness of her vision that makes Gallant such a disturbing and demanding writer" (Kulyk Keefer 1989, 37) originates, among others, in her ability to blend the various perspectives. The narrators indeed direct the reading of the stories by alluding implicitly or explicitly to their views and interpretations of the events depicted, but the shifts in standpoint offer other lines of thought that disrupt the readers' sense of continuity and harmony. Detached, if not ironically critical, while also presenting the views of the characters, the narrators regulate the distance between the readers and the characters or events, thereby contributing to the aesthetic effect of the story (Iser 1971, 18). Full comprehension results from understanding the aesthetic principle that governs the presentation of views. With the multiple interconnecting perspectives, the alternation between involvement and observation, between closeness and distance, and the deliberate omissions and indeterminacy, Gallant encourages the readers to connect several phases of the text to fill in the blanks and discover a pattern. Thus with Gallant "the act of reading" involves the readers in "a process of seeking to pin down the oscillating structure of the text to some specific meaning" (Iser 1971, 10) that emerges only from an active interaction with the text.

Chapter Three

Multivoiced Narration and Historiographic Discourse: *The Pegnitz Junction*

At the age of 22, Gallant was among the first Canadians to see photographs of the concentration camps and was supposed to write the captions and a 750-word article on them. Stunned by the sight, she started questioning the foundations of civilization, for "there was hardly a culture or civilization [she] would have placed as high as the German" (iHancock, 40).[1] She kept wondering for years why "neither culture nor civilization nor art nor Christianity had been a retaining wall" (40), as well as why and how German fascism was born. *The Pegnitz Junction* answers her question; while letting different voices be heard, the collection gives a picture of postwar Germany that secures an enlightening dialogue between past and present, between history and fiction. Gallant felt "that in every day [*sic*] living [she] would find the origin of the worm—the worm that destroyed the structure" (iHancock, 40), contrary to Ricoeur's opinion that "either one counts the cadavers or one tells the story of the victims" (Ricoeur, 188). Gallant was convinced "that the victims, the survivors that is, would probably not be able to tell us anything, except for the description of life at point zero. If we wanted to find out how and why this happened it was the Germans we had to question" (iHancock, 39–40). The collection thus "depict[s]" by "making visible" (Ricoeur, 188) the potential destructiveness in people, not by re-presenting the victims and the conditions in which they were kept.[2]

The stories thus expose "where Fascism came from. . . . [n]ot the historical causes of Fascism—just its small possibilities in people" (iHancock, 40–41). Whether they inflicted or suffered from the hardships of the Fascist regime, postwar Germans are entitled to add their voices to the Gallantian chorus. But the stories are so closely related to history and politics that each individual character is on trial; indeed the specific scenes depicted stress "the instability of the self" not only "in relation to itself" but also in relation to others.[3] Furthermore, the multiple voices evoke social, economic, political, religious, and gender-based issues, diversifying the perspectives from which German society and history are considered. Since these voices suggest sociocultural and political contexts of exchange, the stories become the perfect media for historiographic discourse.

The most popular piece of writing among her critics,[4] the title story of *The Pegnitz Junction* offers the richest example of Mavis Gallant's polyphony and historiographic discourse.[5] Evoking numerous sets of voices, the story opens up so many possible routes into the text that the readers wonder with whom to side.[6] To this should be added that the "layering of points of view, and the potential (if not inevitable) gaps between what is, what is perceived, and what is said, can create a virtually endless set of relations between 'reality' and 'words.' "[7] To make the reading even more complex, the novella's suggestive information becomes all the richer as it reverberates beyond the text by reflecting a more general state of affairs beyond the mere relation of events. Indeed, with the help of the protagonist-narrator, who tunes in to the experiences of other characters, the grim contextual reality emerges from the specific instances of emotional insulation.[8]

Centered on Christine, an awkward and unpromising young German woman, the third-person narrative relates her brief stay in Paris and the interminable train journey back to Germany with her lover (Herbert) and his son (Bert). Although she is engaged to a theology student, the issue at stake is not her amorous dilemma. Instead the train journey provides the focal point: "Only one thing matters now—this train running all over the map."[9] Since the train covers Germany and gathers people from all walks of life, the journey allows Gallant to survey numerous attitudes to life evoked through different voices—German mainly, but also French and American, and others. These in turn transmit yet another combination of discourses—cultural, historical, political, racist, or social—that awaken the implied reader's response to the information imparted.[10] These multiple voices are filtered through Christine, who, like a medium, picks up messages and interior monologues from the people around her: as she shares in the experiences of people to whom she has no relation except for spatial closeness, the initial, fairly "traditional" narration takes a paranormal turn.[11]

Through Christine, the story mingles different experiences and gives the readers so many glimpses of unrelated microcosms. Here she witnesses scenes that evoke divergent sets of values; there she records various personal memories that contribute to the picture of postwar Germany. At other times, an omniscient narrator reports facts in an apparently detached tone. The fast alternation of broken narratives creates such a distance that the readers never feel like identifying with any of the characters. This is actually not very surprising, as Mavis Gallant's challenging use of narrative techniques intimates that the grounds for the atrocities prevalent during World War II result from the universal human potential for fascism (iHancock, 40).[12] To put it differently, through a series of horrible, unrelated, and multifaceted experiences perceived from uncountable perspectives and disclosed through similes, symbols, and allusions mostly inserted in free indirect discourse, one conviction emerges: people entrapped in their own egocentric world are liable to lapse into fascism.[13]

At the outset, in accordance with the general message conveyed, the neutral omniscient narrator establishes a cold, distant, and critical mode that prevents the readers from sympathizing with the main characters.[14] Voicing the implied—and undoubtedly the real—author's contempt for absurd views and positions, the omniscient narrator's bias marks the story's style: originally depreciative descriptive statements are further amplified by cascades of subclauses or subsequent clauses that color them negatively.[15] Thus the first picture of the protagonist and her background is not devoid of criticism. Christine immediately strikes the readers as not very attractive:

> She was a *bony slow-moving* girl from a *small bombed baroque German city,* where all that was worthwhile keeping had been rebuilt and which now looked as pink and golden as a pretty child and as new as morning. By the standards of a few years ago *she would have been thought plain;* she was *so tall* that she bumped her head getting in and out of airplanes, and in her childhood she had often been told that her feet were like canal boats. *Her hair would have been brown,* about the color of brown sugar, if she had not rinsed it in camomile and whenever possible dried it in sunlight; she could not use a commercial bleach because of some vague promise she had given her late grandmother when she was fourteen. . . . She had heard a man say of her that you could leave her in a café for two hours and come back to find she was still smoking the same cigarette. She had done some modeling . . . but now she was trying to be less conscious of her body. She was at one of those turnings in a young life where no one can lead, no one can help, but where someone for the sake of love might follow. (*PJ,* 3–4; emphasis added)

Since Christine is implicitly presented in a critical mode enhanced by the distance the modal verbs create—a favorite device of Gallant's—the readers may safely assume that the entire narrative is critical, too. The criticism even extends to the general attitude to life: the comment about the town where Christine comes from reveals the human ability to patch things up and produce beautiful, impersonal, and ageless substitutes. Detached comments thus manifest disapproval of clumsy repairs, and the disparaging expositional report defines Christine as a passive and superficial being, circumventing promises, though altogether determined to refuse compromises.

The portrait of Christine's lover, Herbert, a 30-year-old engineer, is not more favorable. He is first defined by contrast to the theology student, as if he could not stand on his own. Indeed, his sole concern for his child turns him into a shallow being where others are concerned:

> Unlike the student of theology, he had not put up barriers such as too much talk, self-analysis, or second thoughts. In fact, he tended to limit the number of subjects he would discuss. He had no hold on her mind, nor any interest in gaining one. The mind that he constantly took stock of was his child's; apparently he could not be captivated in the same way by two people at once. He often said he thought he could not live without her, but a few minutes later he seemed unable to remember what he had just said, or to imagine how his voice must have sounded to her. (*PJ*, 4)

Christine and Herbert do not strike the readers as exceptional people. The narrator's disparaging pen spares none of the characters; they all come out in a rather dismal light. The disconcerting presentation of the main characters clarifies at once the nature of the text: the novella will allude to objectionable self-centeredness and refusal to assume responsibility for personal or national past mistakes, further confirmed through the polyvocal narration and its multiple standpoints.

This critical approach holds for the first two sections of the story. More traditional than the last two, the initial sections, namely the background description, the stay in Paris and the outset of the train journey (*PJ*, 3–14) followed by the stopover at Strasbourg (14–16), nevertheless combine a variety of narrative techniques announcing the subsequent experiments. Owing to the constant shifts from neutral to selective omniscience—a frequent device in Gallant's third-person narratives—the readers often wonder whose voice they hear, whether a negative comment is objective or reflects Christine's frustration with her present situation.[16] Similarly, conversations can be confusing. Direct speech is often not marked except for an inquit form at first, so toward the end of a long passage, the readers never know whether they are dealing with direct speech or reported thought unless a declarative verb concludes the passage.[17] The following extract illustrates this point clearly:

> Little Bert would have breakfast on the French train, said Herbert, to distract him. He had never done that before.
>   "I have never been on a train," was the reply.
>   "It will be an exciting experience," said Herbert; like most parents, he was firm about pleasure. He promised to show little Bert a two-star restaurant at the Gare de l'Est. That would be fun. The entire journey, counting a stopover in Strasbourg and a change of trains, would take no more than twelve hours; this was fast, as trains go, but it might seem like a long day to a child. He was counting on little Bert's cooperation, Herbert concluded somberly. (*PJ*, 9)

Unmarked by inverted commas, the very beginning of the speech act seems to be internal, not really spoken out, as if it all happened in Herbert's mind. But the declarative verb marks it as indirect discourse, mimetic to some degree, that is, the transcription of a speech act whose original style has been preserved.[18] After the two explicit retorts in direct discourse, a statement ("like most parents . . . pleasure") voices Christine's or the omniscient narrator's detached consideration—definitely not Herbert's, as he is in no position to distance himself—of the father's educational system. The rest of the conversation is transmitted in indirect discourse, mimetic to some degree, which, out of context, could be considered in part—namely in those sentences without a declarative verb—as free indirect discourse. Internalized and externalized discourses merge, offering hazy clues.

Such intermingling of discourses abounds. The passage just after the night porter has locked the threesome out of their bathroom offers another example of such a combination: " 'We shall never come to this hotel again,' he remarked. Was that all? No, more: 'And I intend to write to the Guide Michelin and the Tourist Office' " (*PJ*, 8). Between the two sentences in direct discourse, two comments in free indirect discourse express most presumably Christine's thoughts, although they could also mark Herbert's hesitations, as rendered by the narrator, concerning the completion of his speech act.

Dashes have a clearer function: they often mark the beginning and end of passages in free indirect discourse.[19] Nevertheless, if the latter tend to modulate Christine's thoughts, they sometimes present another voice; occasionally, within Christine's inner monologue, the readers can hear Herbert's voice, as if they were hearing a voice within a voice. Take, for instance, the description of the rooms the characters have in the hotel: "They had two dusty, velvety rooms with a bathroom between. The bathroom was as large as the bedrooms together and had three doors, one of which gave on the passage. Leaving the passage door unlocked soon turned out to be a trick of little Bert's—an innocent trick; the locks were unlike those he was used to at home and he could not stop fiddling with them" (*PJ,* 5). The dashes preceding the reference to "an innocent trick" presumably announce Christine's thought about the child's behavior. But, over and above her voice, the readers can hear Herbert's trying to excuse his son and minimize the child's provocation. The explanation about the locks on the doors echoes Herbert's justification, but Christine's voice is also heard finishing the sentence.

At times, abrupt transitions between sentences—a characteristic of Gallant's vigorous and pungent style—force the readers to infer the missing links between them and to supply mentally a word or a clause that is left unmentioned; bits and pieces must be tied together for the readers to have a more coherent picture of the characters or situations. The readers then inevitably add another voice to the story; by supplementing the links, they draw on their own experiences and color the text differently, contributing to the multiplicity of voices: "Little Bert had been settled in one of the corner seats; the other was reserved for someone who had not yet appeared. Christine and Herbert sat facing each other. They were both so tall that for the rest of the afternoon someone or other would be tripping over their legs and feet. At last the freight sheds began to glide past the windows" (*PJ,* 16). The transition between the last sentence and the preceding one could easily be "they were relieved when," "luckily," "but no one would for," or any other type of transitional phrase to that effect. Since more than one connector could fill in the narrative gap left by each abrupt transition, the readers are invited to contribute to the polyphony.

The last two sections present the same combination of techniques. Moreover, during the journey through the Rhine valley into Germany, with a scene at a castle (*PJ,* 16–34) followed by the rerouted train journey, a stopover in the country, and the final stopover at Pegnitz Junction (34–88), the text offers an unexpected presentation of psychic experiences. As mentioned before, Christine actually serves as a medium disclosing the inner and outer lives of the people who happen to be in her vicinity.[20] This paranormal turn of the narrative would be surprising if former details had not given away Christine's exceptional ability. Before, she indeed showed sudden—almost supernatural—awareness of the Parisian night porter's ill health: "[T]he knowledge came to her—she did not know how, but never questioned it either—that he suffered from a form of epilepsy" (*PJ*, 7). Distressed by the porter's outburst, she looks out of the window and she sees a scene of her past, as if it belonged to the narrative present. Similarly, at times, "her face [looks] totally empty-minded, when in fact her thoughts and feelings [are] pushing her in some *wild direction*" (4, emphasis added). Obviously, these three instances of rare intuition already announce her unusual insight into people's lives and her exceptional mind reading skill as well as stress her dissatisfaction with the state of the world, while highlighting her creative imagination.

Episodes of people's lives—past, present, and future—are thus recorded as if by a neutral omniscient narrator, whereas it is Christine who decodes such information. Her perception of other people's lives allows her to know what is going on in each person's consciousness. Here, she picks up their inner monologue transmitted in free indirect discourse, as with the old diabetic woman, the would-be American young woman, and Herbert, to mention only a few. There, her clairvoyance allows her to see in people totally unrelated to her so that the passage has the earmarks of an omniscient narration. The first such passage (*PJ*, 27–34), "an episode . . . of surrealist kitsch" (Kulyk Keefer 1989, 175), might have inspired Luis Buñuel. A nouveau riche, referred to as Uncle Ludwig as if he had been introduced before, is seen on an excursion. He goes with his provincial and obtuse family to a castle where he wants to buy Christmas trees for the winter market. The assumed omniscient narrator relates their further intrusive behavior in the castle, which they suppose to be a museum, reports their conversation, and even goes as far as to foretell their imminent deaths from cancer or murder. The preparatory scenes to the murder and the murder itself are even described in detail. Without further transition, the relation shifts back to the train from which Christine looks at this odd party of people. "The train [trembles] and [slides] round a curve, out of sight of the dappled lawn and the people climbing slowly up to the castle, on their last excursion together" (34). This information leaves the readers with Christine witnessing the party's entering the castle grounds, that is, at the beginning of their visit. Who is to thank for the report of supposedly posterior events would remain an unanswered question if it were not for Mavis Gallant's determination to experiment with narrative techniques.

Further passages in the narrative offer a similar treatment of information. The photographer's private life could easily be revealed by an omniscient narrator if Mavis Gallant did not obviously want to stress Christine's unusual turn of mind. For by now, the readers may assume that such private matters are transmitted through—and thus colored by—Christine's mind regardless of their omniscient rendering. Likewise, when the train slows down at a level crossing, the narrative focuses on several figures. One of them, a pregnant woman, seems to attract the attention of three male travelers, among others Herbert. This leads to the confusing comment that *"we* are going to learn something more about Herbert" (*PJ,* 41; emphasis added). The nature of the addresser and/or addressee (Lanser, 71) remains vague.

As a result, the readers regularly hang in doubt about the nature of the narration; they constantly question whether they hear the voice of the omniscient narrator or whether the narrator transmits Christine's voice, itself transmitting other characters' voices. The following passage gives a clear example of the readers' difficult task:

> She remembered the elaborate lies and stories she had needed for the week in Paris and wondered if they were part of the pattern he had mentioned. Suddenly Herbert begged her to marry him—*tomorrow, today. He would put little Bert in boarding school; he could not live without her; there would never again be interference.* Herbert did not hear what he was saying and his words did not come back to him, not even as an echo. He did not forget the promise; he had not heard it. Seconds later it was as if nothing had been said. (*PJ,* 46; emphasis added)

The initial memory of past discourse is an example of what Cohn calls psycho-narration, in which the narrator offers a discourse about a character's consciousness or, to put it in other words, in which mental verbs (in the present case: "remembered," "wondered") taint the discourse with internal analysis provided by the narrator.[21] The narrator's voice thus joins that of the character involved. The italicized sentence presents an interesting bivocal quality, for it voices Herbert's indirect discourse, mimetic to some degree, but also Christine's free indirect discourse as she conveys what she "hears" from Herbert.[22] Similarly, the last sentences are bivocal too, but of a different nature: Christine is heard, as well as the omniscient narrator, who relates Herbert's mental activity. Indeed, "free indirect speech is never purely and simply the evocation of a character's thought and perception, but always bears, in its vocabulary, its intonation, its syntactical composition and other stylistic features, in its content or its context, or in some combination of these, the mark of the narrator."[23] In this case, the distance necessary to assess Herbert's insouciance cannot just be Christine's. Knowing how forgetful he tends to be, she can only assume that the words were spoken without being taken in. Clearly, the certainty conferred to the sentence is the narrator's. Embedding is thus typical of the narrative mode chosen.[24]

Through Christine, the internal focalizer who sees the focalized from within and from without in turns,[25] the readers can also perceive the voice of tradition, both literary and musical.[26] The passage with Uncle Ludwig and his party definitely brings to mind Kafka's *The Castle*.[27] As to the four conscripts waiting at the level crossing (*PJ*, 42), they offer another interesting reference to the literary sphere. Seen in the narrative present and future, the conscripts recall Wilhelm Busch's satirical strips. Equally evocative, the episode with the little girls going home from camp and invading Christine and Herbert's compartment (20–22) suggests similar pictures. The girls' physique, their alternate bullying and charming behavior, their submissive attitude in their family's presence, and their mean relatives—all evoke the satirized figures so popular in Germany. Further on, the leader of a group of middle-class concertgoers tries to "[wipe] out of their memories every vexation and discomfort they [have] been feeling" (69). To lull them, he mechanically enumerates a long list of writers, philosophers, composers, and musicians—further vibrating voices of the German-speaking cultural tradition.[28]

As if such cultural suggestions did not suffice, a historical voice further enriches the polyphonic narration. History is ever present, for "images of the past, specifically of the war, intrude everywhere into the present" (Besner 1988, 151), which gives a sense of "historical *déjà vu*" (Kulyk Keefer 1989, 173).[29] The past weighs on Christine and influences her imagination, or rather colors her present perception of things. When she hears orders compelling the passengers to keep windows shut because of fires along the railway, Christine immediately "[imagines] the holocaust they might become" (*PJ*, 36). Throughout the novella, the past war is obliterated or pooh-poohed as a far-off situation, for the simple reason that it unsettles the characters. At the *Gare de l'Est,* a "plaque [commemorates] a time of *ancient* misery, so ancient that two of the travellers [were] not born then, and Herbert, the eldest, [was] about the age of little Bert" (11; emphasis added). Herbert feels so embarrassed about the war that he speaks French in public so as to pass himself off as French. He also constantly erases allusions to World War II, supposedly to protect his son but also for sheer fear of its memory.

But reminders abound.[30] The simple-witted porter at the hotel calls them "Dirty Boches" (*PJ*, 8). One of their fellow travelers, a Norwegian bass baritone, mentions the German reparations, forcing Herbert to consider the matter. Then, at their first stopover, they cannot overlook the barbed wires separating the West from the East. Refugee-like travelers, too, curiously conjure up past atrocities, as does the conductor's repeated authoritarian behavior. That Christine reads Dietrich Bonhoeffer's essays further refers to the political past, as the minister who had planned to overthrow Hitler was hanged in a concentration camp.

Further allusions to World War II create vivid images echoing the readers' personal or historical experiences.[31] The warning in the neighborhood of the barbed wire frontier with its reference to "hostile police guards, guns, soldiers, dogs, landmines" (*PJ*, 54) specifies the fictional setting but also alludes to the real setting of postwar Germany as well as to the past decor of World War II. Hitler's ideal race is brought to mind twice. When Christine notices a detachment of German conscripts, "she [sees] them as she [imagines] Herbert must be seeing them: small, round-shouldered, rather dark. Blond, blue-eyed genes were on the wane in Europe" (50). The abrupt transition between the actual description and the genetic statement makes it unclear whether the latter marks disappointment or is merely an objective statement. But when the museum curator "with the funny name" (64) is later harangued for "contributing to the artistic decline of a race" (64), little doubt is left about the implication.

In this context, the train in which Christine and her fellow passengers are endlessly rerouted, without knowing where to, is a mild version of other trains, as clearly conveyed by Christine's allusion to the Holocaust. The distressed travelers, the endless journey, the unwelcoming landscape, all re-present the nightmarish journey home, back from the camps, in Primo Levi's *The Truce*.[32] Gallant's novella prolongs Levi's account, the latter present in the former as a subtext of resistance whose transformed traces result from the changed perspective. The behavior of the little girls going back home from camp and invading Christine and Herbert's compartment curiously brings to mind that of the Hitler Jugend, ready to bully and threaten nonconformist citizens. The conductor of the train too is seen frightening a number of refugee-like travelers—inscribed in the text as possible survivors from concentration camps. Bullying and threatening them, he terrorizes them with authoritarian attitudes reminiscent of SS officers'; although these attitudes are fake—remember Hitler's theatrical behavior—and little Bert sees through them, the victims decode them as threats. The conductor's worry about being denounced for ill behavior evokes the postwar search for Nazi officials to be brought to justice:

> The conductor leaned over them, his face so near that she could see specks of gold in his brown eyes. He said, "You won't say bad things about me, will you?"
> "To the stationmaster? I'm not sure."
> "No, to anyone. If anyone asks."
> "You were rude a moment ago," she reminded him.
> "But I was kind on the train. I let you keep the windows open when we went through the fire zone." True enough, but had he really been kind? "You'll testify for me, then?" he said. "If you are asked?"
> "What about these passengers?" she said, meaning the other women. "You were making faces—scaring them. They're still frightened." Indeed some of them looked positively ill with terror. (*PJ*, 81)

Because of the text's constant interaction with the past, the frightened passengers also remind the readers of the concentration camp inmates, whose fate depended on the officer keeping a close watch over them. In this respect, Herbert's imaginary letter of protest to the mass media not only expresses his complaints about their own travel conditions but also echoes and amplifies the horrors of World War II: all his complaints reflect a still more appalling historical past. "Blind obedience to obsolete orders, pig-headed officials, buck-passing, locked toilets, shortage of drinking water, absence of someone responsible, danger to health, indifference to others" (*PJ*, 55)—all suggest the inhuman conditions in which the inmates of concentration camps were kept as a result of barbaric policies.

The characters' unawareness of their attitudes' implications with regard to the past should be inscribed in a large sociological context, revealing human tendencies. In such a context, Herbert's discourse sounds ironic; not only does he not perceive the connection between his complaints and their inscription in a past that he consciously obliterates, but his attitude implies that the conditions in which the victims of the Holocaust lived seem less important to him than the lack of comfort *he* experiences. He manifests the same indifference to others as all the characters. The GI's letter to the German country girl's former lover—another instance of Christine's mind reading—bears the same indifference, selfishness, and lack of concern for others, which enlarges the scope of the text to the world at large. By generating an alternative reading of postwar Germany, the text establishes that the inherent potential for fascism is not just a German characteristic; it is human.

Many similes call up past situations as well as a whole set of attitudes to life and the war. Some concern the characters' conditions, compared at times implicitly, at times explicitly, to the predicament of the inmates of concentration camps. While Christine is refreshing herself at the station in Strasbourg, after her interrupted attempt at having a bath in the hotel, she reviews the sordid facilities with several similes whose allusive impact cannot be overlooked:[33] "The cubicle was *as cold as a cellar;* no sun, no natural light had ever touched the high walls. She stepped from the towel to her sandals—she did not dare set a foot on the cement floor, which *looked* damp and gritty. . . . She said to herself, If this is something you pay for, what are their jails *like?*" (*PJ,* 15; emphasis added). Christine's description leads the readers to visualize cells, but also to read her perception as ironically closed to a widening of her vision—or rather to putting things in the right perspective—probably for sheer lack of experience or because of a reluctance to remember the past. Nevertheless, as the description comes straight after other similes concerning the noises heard in there, other realities, contextual as well, are brought to mind: "Noise from the platform *seemed* to seep between the cracked tiling and to swirl and echo along the ceiling. Even the trains *sounded* sad, *as though* they were used to ferry poor and weary passengers—refugees perhaps" (15; emphasis added). The similes no doubt evoke World War II—trains packed with prisoners bound for camps whose cells were incomparably worse than the washroom cubicle.

Similarly, as Christine describes Herbert's reaction while the porter throws them out of the room, war images of another kind emerge: "He really *seemed* extraordinarily calm, picking up toothbrushes and jars and tubes without standing his ground for a second. It was *as if* he were under arrest, or *as though* the porter's old pajama top masked his badge of office, his secret credentials. The look on Herbert's face was abstract and soft, *as if* he had already lived this, or always thought that he might" (*PJ,* 7; emphasis added). As well as reinforcing his guilt, the description calls to mind the helplessness of people under arrest, calling to mind works such as Kafka's *The Trial.*[34] With the "lights flashing and signal stations like sentry boxes" (74), the readers have to call on outside information, on their knowledge of history, to be fully aware of the author's intentions. For the comparison takes the readers back to the years when sentries guarded concentration camps, and to the not so distant time when soldiers watched the Berlin Wall. In the same way, Uncle Ludwig, "who always [sounds] like a piece of metal machinery" (29), recalls SS officers, their yelling and threatening guns.

So by having recourse to their historical awareness, the readers get another picture: they sense in the background the presence of prisoners in constant fear, or rather panic, at seeing an SS officer approach. This also brings back the recollection of questionings under threat, which are clearly evoked when Herbert catches a glimpse of untidy German soldiers: "Herbert's expression gradually changed to one of brooding. He *seemed* to be dwelling on a deep inner hurt. His eyes narrowed *as if* he had been cornered by beams of electric light. Christine knew that he felt intense disgust for men-at-arms in general but for untidy soldiers in particular" (*PJ*, 50–51; emphasis added). While suggesting questionings, the passage conjures up an attitude that popular wisdom attributes to Germans, namely an obsession with order, neatness, and cleanliness— the very qualities that made it possible for Hitler to promote his fancies about racial purity.

Such concerns disclose yet another voice, racist this time.[35] Xenophobic as he is, Herbert does not want his son to get anywhere near the frontier coffeehouse patronized by guest workers: these foreigners have brought new diseases into the country, he says. Incidentally, this racial consideration echoes the prejudice of Herbert's mother when she returned, an embittered woman, from the camps. Nevertheless, Herbert is intelligent enough to know that his son should not "breathe the slightest whiff of racial animosity" (*PJ*, 61). Bert would definitely do so if he shared Christine's intuition. Indeed, the fat old woman in their compartment verbalizes her anti-Semitism in her telegraphic inner monologue. She does not seem to question the past; as she reviews her reasons—and her closest relatives'—for disapproving of the American decision to side with the Allies, she gives vent to her anti-Semitic obtuseness. To her, a Jew is a stereotype, and America joined the wrong side. She even produces "historical fantasies" (Kulyk Keefer 1989, 174) justifying her prejudice. Her nonrealistic explanation of the reasons why "during forty years [in America, her closest relatives and herself] would only have voted four times" (39) marks her bias while creating an ironic subtext of opposition: "*In 1940—against wild utterances and attempts to drag the USA into the conflict on the wrong side. The President of the USA at the time was a Dutch Jew, his father a diamond cutter from Rotterdam, stole the Russian Imperial jewels after the Bolshevik revolution, had to emigrate to avoid capture and prison sentence. Within ten years they were running the whole country. . . . Their real name was Roszenfeldt"* (*PJ,* 39). This obvious misconception exposes not only her views but also the anti-Semitic discourse prevailing in some American circles at the time. She then repeats that *"apart from those four times {they} would never have voted"* (*PJ,* 40) or wanted to vote, a sign of their lack of social conscience. Undoubtedly, while listening to the voices Christine perceives, the readers have to bring back to memory this web of emotional, historical, and political facts.

Evoking political distinctions, the choice of Pegnitz Junction as the station from which the rerouted travelers can go back home is not haphazard either: the last junction in West Germany, the obvious way into East Germany, Pegnitz Junction confronts Christine and her fellow travelers with two options—the capitalist West and the Marxist East.[36] They eventually hear only the voice of the system they belong to, that is, that favoring free enterprise. In accordance with this, while silently haranguing a man who seems to long to be in his native village across the barbed wire, Christine advocates the voice of the West: "What are you doing here? . . . Why spend a vacation in a dead landscape? . . . Marie [his childhood girlfriend] wouldn't look even if she remembered you. Wouldn't, couldn't—she has forgotten how. Her face turns the other way now. Decide what the rest of your life is to be. Whatever you are now you might be forever, give or take a few conversations and lapses from faith" (*PJ,* 60).

If Christine emits a political voice in the previous quote, she can also transmit another voice, social this time.[37] A representative of the upper middle class, Christine is used to comfort and expostulates about the poor conditions in which she has to travel. Her complaint to Herbert— "I believe this train has a steam engine. How can they, when we have first-class tickets?" (*PJ,* 17)—indicates her allegiance to her social class. Yet in France, she was "outraged by the undemocratic Paris *métro* with its first- and second-class tickets" (17). But, then, she was most probably voicing her fiancé's left-wing beliefs, not her own. Equally class conscious, Herbert labels the furniture of their compartment as "middle class" (18), a reminder of the social discourse characteristic of the Western world.

In a similar context, language, attire, and manners separate Uncle Ludwig's vulgar, but wealthy, party from the decorous, but impoverished, castle owners. The landed gentry "[speak] with such a correct and beautiful accent" (*PJ*, 28) that the parvenus are baffled. They, in turn, astound the aristocrats, whose privacy they violate without even realizing that they might be upsetting their established ways. While evoking the world of fashion, their dress further increases the gap: the aristocrats wear elegant and stylish country outfits, whereas the nouveau riche clique exhibit the showy "Sunday urban best" (30) and hairstyle fashionable in the 1950s. Funnily enough, the parvenus are quite sure that the castle owner is English rather than German "because of all the aristocratic scoundrels they [have] seen in films" (28). Nevertheless, the narrator notes, "he is as removed from them as any foreigner [might be]" (28). As for Uncle Ludwig himself, "now that he [is] rich he [is] not thought ignorant any more, but simply eccentric" (29). Even Jürgen, Uncle Ludwig's right hand, gives vent to social prejudice in the episode prior to his foretold death. When he surveys the belongings of a debtor, he notices that apart from a small rug, "everything else [is] trash, probably bought second-hand to begin with" (33). At all levels of the social strata, prejudice flourishes.

In addition, the readers have to reframe their mind to accommodate yet another dimension; they also hear, as it were, a universal voice speaking in a neutral tone. When Christine, angered by the lack of comfort, surveys their first-class compartment, her criticism is counterbalanced by a statement that tones it down. Indeed, the universal "one" does not reject the compartment as unfit because, the voice says, "the most one could say [is] that it would do for first class" (*PJ*, 17), but the statement does not reject Christine's criticism either. This points to the all too human subjective perception of things. When one is at peace with oneself, the situation is acceptable, but if, like Christine, one is at odds with oneself, it becomes intolerable. Later, as she tries to reflect on their situation, she manages to encompass three different levels of perception by using the pronoun "one": "But some times on those days one feels more. More than just one's irritation, I mean. Everything opens, like a pomegranate. More things have gone wrong than one imagined" (26). This observation reveals her impatience at the lack of comfort, her awareness of their failed relationship, as well as her realization that civilization has taken the wrong turn.[38] What with the extended vision and the numerous superimposed voices, an even more arduous task faces the readers.

That they are constantly perplexed need not surprise, the more so as few clues indicate whether one episode or another reflects Christine's paranormal gift. Even Christine's definition of information is vague: "Christine thought that she knew what 'information' truly was, and had known for some time. She could see it plainly in fact; it consisted of fine silver crystals forming a pattern, dancing, separating, dissolving in a glittering trail along the window. The crystals flowed swiftly, faster than smoke, more beautiful and less durable than snowflakes" (*PJ,* 23). True, here and there she announces "creaking thoughts," "crystals," or "interferences."[39] But most clues are muddling, for they often come after the transference of thought, leaving room for doubt. To make matters worse, it could be argued that the alleged clue does not give evidence of Christine's prior clairvoyance. A case in point concerns her comment following the local curator's silent diatribe against narrow-minded artistic perception. As he thinks out ways of putting his counterarguments, Christine reveals "that Herbert could [help] him because he [is] good at that kind of letter" (65), that is, a letter denouncing libel. The novella displays the same ambiguity in the episode with a stranger whom they meet in the country at one of their stopovers. The narrator recounts the distressful experience of a child during the war as he and his parents fled from their village. Now, years later, the child grown a man returns to the village and meets Christine. "She [sees] that he [knows] she [knows] everything" (60), and she has a conversation with him "as they silently [pass] each other" (60). So the readers must be on the lookout for the odd significant word.

Typographical clues can also be confusing. At times, italics reveal thought transference. But this technique emphasizes more than one character's inner monologue. Thus the readers have to keep in mind the different threads and styles of, for example, the old diabetic woman, Herbert, and the pregnant German woman passing herself off as American. Otherwise the readers cannot grasp what these people actually mean.

As already mentioned, the readers' task is rather intricate; not only do they have to recognize the originator of emitted discourse, but they also have to decode the essentially petty information that Christine absorbs and imparts as stories within the story. Eventually, the readers are bound to realize that every single message reveals a fictional character's inability to accept others as they are, and that, beyond fiction, the novella also points to real attitudes and beliefs further accepted or rejected by the readers. The diversified views of the writer, the implied author, the narrator, a fictional character or several characters, the nonfictional world, and the readers with their possibly conflicting intellectual and emotional responses may and must be superimposed on the text.

No matter what attitude is evoked, the war is a parameter that haunts Europeans, whether they try to obliterate it as in Germany, or intend to emphasize it elsewhere. Take, for instance, Christine's early perception of the altercation during which the Parisian hotel night porter voices his aversion to the Germans in a most antagonistic discourse: "Dirty Boches, you spoiled my holiday in Bulgaria. Everywhere I looked I saw Germans. The year before in Majorca. The same thing. Germans. Germans" (*PJ,* 8). Through the French porter's insults and reproaches, the views prevalent in certain circles all over Europe stream forth. A German, no matter how young or innocent, is still verbally or mentally attacked for belonging to the country of the hated invader who lost the war and became the richer for it. The readers may recognize their own views in this approach or, on the contrary, object to it on the grounds of unfair generalization. As to Christine, she is obviously upset: her tears reflect the powerlessness of the Germans faced with their own reputation, resulting from their elders' behavior. But Herbert, although he probably objects, pretends nothing has happened, for he does not "want any unpleasantness in France" (7). He merely considers not going to that hotel again and eventually mentions his intention—genuine or pretended—to complain in writing. At this stage, the readers are reminded of the implied author's contempt—shared by the author herself—for the general refusal "to talk or ask questions about [the country's] immediate past" (Kulyk Keefer 1989, 175), indeed for the compulsion to obliterate the unpleasant signs of the past war, to which Herbert's attitude might be ascribed. Depending on their political convictions, the readers accept or reject this view, thereby adding other layers of nontextual information based on their personal experience. The different layers intertextually obtained therefore highlight the different aspects and views of the period.

Further direct allusions to Germany's recent past make it clear that the novella centers on the attempt or refusal—real and fictional—to be reconciled with the past. Thus the scarred man at one stop looks for his own self across the barbed wire. His past, as seen by Christine, takes the readers across the barbed wire separating East Germany from West Germany in the early times after the separation, when no close watch was kept to prevent people from sneaking out of the East. The story of the lens factory has numerous counterparts in recent German history. Schott Iena, for instance, the Iena glass factory, was rebuilt in Mainz across the now-discarded border by the workers who had fled to freedom and economic success. For the scarred man, however, freedom does not mean happiness: his scar signals a deeper inner wound left by the separation of East and West Germany.

The text offers other instances of refused commitment. Herbert's reaction to the man's comment on the rough time the partisans gave his father in Yugoslavia marks another attempt at refusing any responsibility for the conflict:

> "I hope they gave him a bad time," said Herbert, who always said such things with a smile. People who did not know him had to think again, wondering what they had heard. No one knew how to deal with Herbert's ambiguities. "I hope they gave him a very bad time."
>
> Could I have heard this? the scarred man seemed to appeal to Christine.
>
> Suit yourself, she seemed to answer. I wasn't born either.
>
> "Now the children of the partisans come here as guest workers," said Herbert, still smiling. "And we all drink coffee together. What could be better?" (*PJ,* 62)

Christine's silent repartee not only answers the man's silent question but also reflects the very aim of the novella, that is, to force the readers to clarify their own vision of history and their own moral criteria, thereby adding further contextual layers. Out of context, Herbert's discourse might sound positive. But because it comes just after his xenophobic discourse on the *Gastarbeiter,* his comment can only be another attempt at evading the subject, or at least at closing the question. Indeed, earlier on, he is heard reacting in the same fashion when the Norwegian "[begins] to do what Herbert [calls] opening up the dossier" and touches on "the subject of German reparations" (*PJ,* 49). Similarly, Christine expresses her refusal to make her stance on political issues clear by getting into her book, her shield against unpleasant realities.

Through the disclosure of those people's thoughts and preoccupations, the readers get a pretty grim sample of the German population after World War II. The old woman sitting in the same compartment vents her viperish resentment against a past situation she never explicitly opposed. She is clearly only absorbed in getting her share of the inheritance her husband left to his niece. Her meanness—both in the fictional past and narrative present—is reflected in her obsession with food. While the old woman rots in her repressed resentment, the smell of rot (*PJ,* 26) that she has caused in the compartment offends others' nostrils but does not seem to affect her. She is so engrossed in the resentful survey of her marriage and 47 years of life as an immigrant in America that she does not suffer from the lack of comfort affecting the passengers: she is impervious to it because her self-centeredness makes her incapable of questioning her own views, so that she cannot be part of those searching their identity. Hers is forever fixed in the petty consideration of her meanness.

Besides the old, obese woman, the readers have to put up with a number of symbolic repulsive traits in the other characters. Bert is obviously too young for metaphysical doubts, but all the others feel utterly ill ease with the identities with which they are constantly confronted. Over and over again, they literally or figuratively go "past a landscape baked and blind" (*PJ*, 21), symbolizing their blind refusal of their past behavior. Thus the elegant concertgoers would not admit that the Hitler time "was a sad time for art in the country" (70). The mere reference to Hitler unsettles them, and they readily forget the harmful, not to say fatal, effects of his views. Herbert, who cannot get over his wife's breaking up with him, is indifferent to others, except his son. He dismisses any allusion to the life and death of his ungenerous and embittered mother. His own educational theories reject remembrance of things past, that is, when reminiscent of the war. Abroad, he even pretends not to be German and does not speak his mother tongue for fear of insults. The young country girl, whose pregnancy has resulted from the presence of foreign army bases in the country, also pretends to hold another citizenship. Her one and only concern—showing her determination to have her way—is to obtain compensation from her lover for having got her pregnant.

Further unpleasant characteristics complete the picture that the readers have to put up with. An echo to Hitler's racial discrimination, the Kafkaesque episode staging impoverished but dignified aristocrats and showy nouveaux riches uncovers the segregating gap between social classes. As for the conscripts glimpsed from the train window, their announced future, while pointing to "the decline of the next generation" (*PJ*, 42), also echoes their own decline, for a merged voice—the neutral omniscient narrator's and Christine's—is heard saying that "there [is] no limit to mediocrity even today" (42). Just like Christine, who "*might* [feel] pity for [Bert's] fragile neck and tired shadows around his eyes" (38; emphasis added) but is repelled by "the dirty knuckles, the bread-and-butter breath, the high insistent voice" (38), the readers can neither sympathize with the characters nor endorse their views and lines of conduct. Literally put off by the characters' mean, self-centered, and inauthentic existences, the readers leave them, without the slightest compassion, trapped in their train, each shut up in a self-created hell.

Nevertheless, in spite of the most negative picture emerging from the multiple voices of postwar German society, the prospects brighten toward the end. Christine, the one who is shown, again and again, "as reluctant as ever to make up her mind" (*PJ,* 87) about anything, whether a detail or a major issue, manages to reach a decision concerning her life. She becomes "other" (LaCapra 1985, 140). At Pegnitz Junction, she experiences an epiphany leading her to meet her lot; the maddening stopover forces her to pause for reflection before making a new and decisive choice. With the new perspective gained through meeting others—both inwardly and outwardly—she is brought to decide what turn her life should take. She resolves to stop pretending—a characteristic of all the characters. She no longer thinks of putting up a show for propriety's sake; she starts acting as a true mother would, feeling sincerely sorry for the child's discomfort and herself comforted by his presence, by "his breath on her arm" (*PJ,* 80). She gently explains her decision to Bert: "You must stop calling me 'the lady' when you speak to your father. Try to learn to say 'Christine' " (80), she says to the little boy, who cannot grasp the full meaning of this statement. She resumes the story that she had interrupted before owing to the "interferences" from the other passengers, suggestively announcing the change.

At this stage, Christine—along with the readers who have decoded all the intertexts—has gathered enough material to have a clearer picture of her own country and a better idea about her identity. When, eventually, she shuts her book to tell Bert a story, she has discovered a new awareness and acceptance of their past. Tardy though it may be, her acceptance is a sign that nothing is ever fixed in society. The readers may—for the time being—look forward to a new age cleansed of the petty-mindedness of postwar Germany, to a new age where no one need be ashamed of the human condition—a positive prospect resulting from her having digested, so to speak, the information accumulated through mind reading during the journey.

The constant references to information reveal that the novella focuses on its own creation[40] as well as on its vision.[41] Just as fiction conveys a message and thus relies on how the readers receive the writer's own organization of facts and details, the train journey—the pretext for creation—reveals from within the real nature of Germany and its reception abroad. The novella undoubtedly marks how negative a symbol Germany has become for most outsiders: after disclosing the Norwegian's and most Europeans' past and present fear of German soldiers, a passage in free indirect discourse reveals that "the important part of the journey had ended as far as he [the Norwegian] was concerned because he had finally said what he thought" (*PJ,* 75). Like the journey, artistic creation is the sum of "infinite tracks meeting, merging, and sliding away" (74).

The novella's factual information, like Herbert's, bears on the actual journey with its frustrating stops and appalling conditions. But like Herbert's information, "raising pictures in the imagination" (*PJ,* 23), the text's goes beyond the mere relation of the action. For the action constantly refers to the characters' obsession with the past and their refusal to admit responsibility. Besides, Christine's fluid information, based on a cosmopolitan set of voices, clarifies the picture of Germany and its reception abroad. The quality of her information varies from crystal clear to ashen and muddy as Christine accumulates it and becomes aware of her people's sordid identity and aimless culture.

Surprisingly enough, this information does not estrange her from her country. On the contrary, she comes to terms with its reality just as a writer endorses the finished creation, perhaps encouraging the readers to do so, too. In the end, Christine picks up unpleasant data about Herbert but discards the information as irrelevant, a decision that also signifies her acceptance of his past. She thus transcends the historical acceptance to reach a personal acceptance that should henceforth allow her to change the course of her life. Just as a writer delights in giving birth to an artefact, so does Christine open up to a new start that will allow her to discard any traces of narrow-minded egotism and to be proud of herself. She finally follows Bonhoeffer's "exhortations . . . to assume responsibility for [her] actions" (Besner 1988, 90). At one with her self, she "[relaxes] her grip on the child [Bert] as if he were someone she loved but was not afraid of losing" (*PJ,* 87)—thus showing what turn her life is going to take.

The chain of allusions and voices whirling around the characters takes them back to their home base—or almost—with little change in their outlook, except for Christine. The text indeed confirms her initial comment about not feeling "as if [she] were going home" (*PJ,* 17), for it eventually shows that she has changed: her perception is "other" (LaCapra 1985, 140). As she has absorbed the life stories of others, she has grown away from her originally petty-minded approach to things and people. Taken on its own, the almost circular plot would be meager. Without the allusions to the act of creation, the story would lose its metafictional strength, and without the quest for identity allowing the reenactment of the past, the train journey would be deprived of its most essential message. The novella would lose its impact if it were not for the multiple perspectives, for the interweaving of the fictional characters' personal memories and the wider historical frame they evoke.

The presence of outsiders in this context is also essential. Not only do they express their fear of, and resentment against, Germans, but they also prove capable of the very meanness conducive to the insatiable need to dominate that they fear and resent. Indifference, therefore, is not restricted to Germans; it is characteristic of humanity as a whole. Given the right conditions, any people might have developed into destructive persecutors.

Nevertheless, as mentioned before, the novella ends on a positive note. By telling Bert the story when she should get going, for their train has arrived, Christine implies that she is no longer eager to take the train of social life with its norms, insincere feelings, and failed communication.[42] By choosing to leave her track and relate to others, she eventually emerges as a character capable of understanding and spontaneous generosity in spite of the gloomy world around her. Thus she resumes the story she had started to tell Bert of a family made of "five brothers, all named Georg" (*PJ,* 88), with Georg pronounced differently, a story that "suggests the brotherhood of man" (Hatch 1978, 103). This fictional optimism was recently vindicated when Leonard Bernstein conducted the Berlin Philharmonic Orchestra in Beethoven's Ninth Symphony, letting the "Ode an die Freude" burst on the very ruins of the Wall.[43] Gallant's text is ahead of reality—an unforeseeable reversal in the balance of interactions between the fictional world and the real world. The reading of the world she intimates through her text thus casts a different light on historical readings of World War II, allowing both her characters and the readers to reprocess the past and to arrive at a better understanding of it, "having implications for the present and the future."[44]

"The Pegnitz Junction" is no exception in Gallant's fiction: most of her stories encourage the interplay of intratextual information and extratextual realities.[45] With their inquiry into the origins of fascism, the other German stories definitely set an interesting interdependence of text and history. In "An Alien Flower," for instance, though suppressed, the recent past reemerges through "the streets still smell[ing] of terror and ashes. Every stone [holds] a ghost, or a frozen life, or a dreadful secret" (*PJ,* 168). Erika, the first-person narrator in "An Autobiography," evidences the general suppression of the recent past by noting, "it is no good excavating; the fragments would be without meaning," and adding, "it is easy to put an X over half your life" (103).[46] "O Lasting Peace" stages, among others, Uncle Theo, a former camp guard on the Eastern front whose survival depends on his disciplinarian niece. "Ernst in Civilian Clothes" evokes the attraction of adolescents for the Hitler Youth movement and then the German army, which Ernst erases from his memory thanks to his "life-saving powers of forgetfulness" (143). Other German stories not included in *The Pegnitz Junction,* such as "The Latehomecomer" and "A Report," for instance, take up similar issues. "The Latehomecomer" is concerned with a former member of the Hitler Youth movement who comes back after the war to find his homeland changed. In "A Report," former POW Willy's distorted vision of the past is contrasted with that of M. Monnerot, a French fascist who "despises Germany for having been defeated in the last war,"[47] and that of the Laurents, who blame their half-German servant for all the war atrocities. The various stories do show "the small possibilities [of fascism] in people."

Originally planned for inclusion in *The Pegnitz Junction* but eventually published in *From the Fifteenth District,* "The Latehomecomer" discloses the ultimate annihilation of the character's identity through mingled references to the past, present, and future of a young German man. Returning to Germany after five years spent as a war prisoner in France, the protagonist, Thomas, finds himself homeless.[48] Admittedly, he does have a home, and a better one than before, because while he was away, his mother married a "kind man with a pension" (*FFD,* 117). But spiritually he no longer belongs. At the age of 16, he left the country with the ideals of the Hitler Jugend and returned five years later to a country trying to obliterate the past and the very ideals for which he was sentenced. He thus exchanges his identity as P.G. (*prisonnier de guerre*) for that of D.P. (displaced person).[49]

In her interview with Geoff Hancock, Mavis Gallant explains Thomas's difficulty in becoming integrated and starting a new life: "Try to put yourself in the place of an adolescent who had sworn personal allegiance to Hitler. The German drama, the drama of that generation, was of inner displacement. You can't tear up your personality and begin again, any more than you can tear up the history of your country. . . . To wrench your life and beliefs in a new direction you have to be a saint or a schizophrenic" (iHancock, 51). As the story illustrates the young man's maladjustment, its structure reflects the meanderings of his emotional disorder. Indeed, in his attempt at summing up the situation, the first-person narrator's disrupted narration adopts the pattern of a displaced person's existence with jumps in time and space, and a final inability to relate to both human and physical surroundings.

From the very beginning, the narration establishes Thomas's disrupt-
edness. It indeed starts with his return from France and his immediate
discovery that his mother no longer matches his memories. She literally
belongs to another man, who owns everything Thomas and his mother
are supposed to share. As Thomas later admits in one of the numerous
external anachronies, only the mother of his memories shared their
poverty, not the prosperous wife of a streetcar conductor. He ironically
remembers/imagines their lost poverty as a "paradise," in which he and
his brother incestuously shared their mother: "In captivity I had longed
for her and for the lost paradise of our poverty, where she had belonged
entirely to my brother and me and we had slept with her, one on each
side" (*FFD*, 119–20). Thomas's disconnectedness is made obvious by
the abrupt jumps from thought to thought. However, like the landscape
before the building where his mother lives, the story presents a seemingly smooth succession of recollections that conceals the spikes of unhappiness:

> Cinders and gravel had been raked evenly over the crushed masonry
> now; the broad concourse between the surviving house—ours—and the
> road beyond it that was edged with ruins looked solid and flat.
>   But no, it was all shaky and loose, my mother said. Someone ought to
> cause a cement walk to be laid down; the women were always twisting
> their ankles, and when it rained you walked in black mud, and there was
> a smell of burning. (*FFD*, 123)

Like the buried remnants of the other building, whose ashes and burnt
smell remind the present dwellers of their past existence, the narration
discloses the unforgettable memories that the narrative present and
future try to conceal, showing Gallant's interest in the creative process
of this story.[50] The women forever twisting their ankles are not unlike
Thomas, whose compressed knee and tangled nerves prevent him from
forgetting the past. A residue of past miseries, they cannot be forgotten.
    Since oblivion cannot assuage those sufferings, they remain present in
filigree. Thus, like the flat his stepfather inherited, Thomas is haunted
by "ghosts [who rattle] about, opening and shutting drawers, banging
on pipes, moving chairs and ladders" (*FFD*, 118). The ghosts are nothing but his obsessive thoughts, interrupting the relation of the immediate present: the whole narration is punctuated with persistent leitmo-
tivs. The mother's cupped hand concealing her missing teeth stresses
the difference between Thomas's picture of his mother while young and

carefree and his present realization that age and anxiety estrange her from him. Similarly, the stepfather's mouth hanging open so that he can seize any opportunity to hold the floor emphasizes the new hierarchical order, akin to that prevailing in the army. Likewise, repeated allusions to the adolescent boys and girls protecting older soldiers sitting smugly in bunkers or to older soldiers' disillusioned attitudes to life reveal that Thomas's exaltation is marred by resentment. This is further reflected in the frequent reminders of the stepfather's first wife, her apartments, and her unusual burial place. The silent questions Thomas asks when in front of mirrors also show him in search of an ideal image, forever blurring. These recurrent motifs fill Thomas's mind and unfold regularly, as if to remind him—and the reader—of past atrocities and present opportunism.

Past, present, and future merge in his conscience to form an entity that cannot be done away with. The present and the future must bear the weight of the past; the past is never dead. Only the thoughtless can bear the past: "They just slip through," as Mavis Gallant notes (iHancock, 51). Unlike Willy Wehler, who changes his mind as often as necessary to be on the right side ("All Willy ever had to do was sniff the air" [*FFD*, 133]), Thomas is unable to "forget everything" (134). All he can do is pretend: "I shut the door as if on a dark past, and I said to myself, 'I am free. This is the beginning of life. It is also the start of the good half of a rotten century. Everything corrupt and rotten and vicious is behind us.' . . . I thought, I shall get used to the smell, and the smell of the burning in the stone outside. The view of the ruins will be my view. Every day on my way home from school I shall walk over Elke [his stepfather's first wife]. I shall get used to the wood staircase, the bellpull, the polished nameplate, the white enamel fuses in the hall" (136).

This decision helps explain why he eventually anticipates his marriage to Willy Wehler's young daughter, who is "as whole and as innocent as a drop of water, and . . . without guilt" (*FFD*, 127). Too young to bear the stigma clinging to the older generations, she is the likeliest source of happiness. Characteristically, the passages concerning her are to be found approximately in the middle of the story: she towers as an ideal over a mist of dirt, vice, and guilt. Although Thomas's intentions regarding her are sinister, she stands out as a beacon in a narrative that is otherwise concerned with down-to-earth concerns. A counterpart to the blissful hours Thomas had with the French girl who took to him, Willy's daughter's future comforting role announces a more peaceful age, even if it does not obliterate the past, as is made evident in the subsequent reminiscences. Indeed, the rest of the narration is so bleak that it shows how, deep down, Thomas and his fellow countrymen—at least those endowed with a semblance of conscience—cannot shun the dark times of the war.

Nor can Thomas escape the rule of time: his mother has changed; his country has disowned the ideas he abided by in his youth; his murdered father has become a hero, much to his disapproval. The "shadow that [floats] on the glass panel of the china cabinet" (*FFD,* 137) does not reflect Thomas's own image, for time has altered his father's features. A displaced person, Thomas is rather like his other fellow countrymen: "In their eyes the deepest failure of a certain political authority was that it enticed peace-loving persons with false promises of work, homes, pensions, lives afloat like little boats at anchor; now these innocent provincials saw they had been tricked, and they were going back to where they had started from" (125). Floating aimlessly once his purpose in life has vanished, Thomas has to go back to square one, a difficult task in a world that does not offer any options. In a final attempt at negating time, he wishes to go backward: "I wished that I was a few hours younger, in the corridor of a packed train, clutching the top of the open window, my heart hammering as I strained to find the beloved face" (138). The final hopeless note shows how shattered his beliefs have been by his confrontation with the new image of his mother—the opportunist—and of his father—the hero. Torn between his past goal and his announced future, the narrator/protagonist cannot, in spite of the retrospective presentation of the story, identify with his new image. With its incursions into the past and the future, the narrative thus reflects the crumbling of identity, the devastating reality of the fragmented self.

Also evoking past and present attitudes to historical trends, "The Old Friends" deserves special attention because of its disruptions and multiple perspectives. An old "de-Nazified police commissioner" (Kulyk Keefer 1989, 179) fears the ghost of the recent fascist past so much that Helena, a survivor and renowned actress on whose friendship the commissioner depends, crushes him with mere allusions to the camps or her Jewish origins. Ironically, he feels "orphaned" (*PJ,* 90) when she takes a distance from him; yet *she* lost her mother in the camps. In an attempt to rewrite history, he goes over a mental file, so reminiscent of those Gestapo files that condemned human beings to the camps, if not to death. His mental exercise evidences the fluctuation between committed and contemplated (Rimmon-Kenan, 61) acts, evoking unsettling realities that go beyond the mere fabulation:

To the dossier he adds : (One) She *should never have been* arrested. She was only a child. (Two) She is partly Jewish, but how much and which part— her fingers? Her hair? (Three) She *should never have been* sent out of the country to mingle with Poles, Slovaks, and so on. Anything *might have* happened to her. This was an error so grave that if the functionary who had committed it were ever found and tried, the commissioner **would** testify against him. Yes, he **would** risk everything—his career, his pension, anonymous letters, just to say what he thinks: "A serious mistake was made." Meanwhile, she sits and smokes, thinking she doesn't need him, ready at any second to give him up. (*PJ,* 94; emphasis added)[51]

The old police commissioner—"he" in the extract—desperately tries to safeguard his relationship with Helena—"she." He reveals his attempt to correct the course of the past by creating a mental dossier to which he adds the information contained in the excerpt. A succession of modal expressions, his interior monologue asserts that a series of facts should not have been, or, to quote a specialist of modals, "was 'necessary-not' and would not have happened."[52] The mere use of negated modals implies that the assertion contains in itself the counterproposition, namely that these facts *did* exist. The final assertion, no longer part of the interior monologue, punctuates Helena's detachment, indeed total indifference, and readiness to get rid of her "benefactor." The text even implies that the errors he records were, in fact, perpetrated by people like him, who, in the narrative present, try to redeem themselves by inventing plausible, yet improbable, plots of reparations that would not erase the past. The irony lies in the utterances containing forms of the hypothetical modal "would" (in boldface in the quotation). As pointed out earlier, these statements imply that the speaker is unlikely to suit the action to the word; his past record (presented elsewhere in the story) evidences that when given the chance to do so in the past, he failed to take the opportunity actually to commit what his inner discourse presents as a contemplated act. Since the contemplated acts are never committed, the necessity or possibility is never realized, indirectly securing a pitiless picture of the characters' shortcomings.

Affording further disruptions, Helena challenges the commissioner's prerogative to modify the past by refusing to draw a clear picture of it. When interviewed about her childhood experience in the camps, she refuses to give any information and tells "a story that has long ago ceased to be personal" (*PJ,* 95). Asked whether she was sexually abused, she replies "it was forbidden" (95), rejecting the question as invalid, for the camps did much more than deprive her of her virginity; they obliterated her identity, reduced her to a number. Those spared the experience cannot grasp this reality, indeed would prefer to circumscribe its destructiveness by equating it with rape, minimizing the impact. Having internalized the postwar sense of guilt, Helena refuses to play the interviewer's game; the information she volunteers reveals nothing, let alone hints at the beginning of an answer. Superimposing different perspectives, the scene highlights the fractured perceptions of history,[53] for Helena assesses the others' criteria of evaluation and counterbalances them with her own, pointing also to an ironically informed "we" whose identity can be, at once or separately, the interviewer, the commissioner, or even the readers.

With respect to shifts in perspective, the simile creates analogies that bring together two layers of interpretation. As Besner points out, "[Gallant's] style . . . is marked by . . . reliance on simile rather than metaphor, and by its effectiveness as a vehicle for irony" (1988, 151). The discussion of "The Pegnitz Junction" has shown that Gallant often exploits similes to suggest another way of looking at things, allowing the story to draw upon past circumstances and events. As a result, similes generate ironic readings that reveal the characters' unawareness of their own narrow-mindedness or their own situation, which proves far less alarming when compared with the past. The accumulation of such comparisons creates tension by imposing a connection with some other person, thing, or event as if the original situation could not stand on its own. Thus when Helena laughs and does not reject the commissioner, he thinks that "on crumbs like these . . . he can live forever" (*PJ,* 92), a phrase recalling the nonexistent crumbs the prisoners were supposed to live on, enhancing the futility of his survival. Similarly, in a passage reenacting their first encounter, the commissioner compares Helena to a painting by Holbein, ironically alluding to the Aryan ideal, the very ideal responsible for her internment. Finally, when the narrator expresses that "the knowledge [of Helena's experience in the camps] can produce nothing more than a pain like the suffering of laughter—like pleurisy, like indigestion" (95), the implication is that no description can ever compare with the actual experience, and no insight can ever be gained.

The interaction between text, contexts, and life results precisely from Gallant's constant determination to remain outside the text and to speak with "a true voice" (*PN,* 179), that of detachment. For no matter which point of view she selects to tell a story, distance is what characterizes its reception: the readers cannot empathize with the characters, as the latter dissect themselves and others. Even first-person narratives (with the exception perhaps of the Linnet Muir stories and a few more)[54] tend to have narrators who harbor such despicable attitudes to life and to others or are so estranged from their deeper self that they flatly refuse to commit themselves truly. Dissuaded from feeling sympathy, the readers stay close to the implied author, and no doubt to Gallant herself, whose critical eye and disparaging pen catch, with fascinating acerbity, the follies of the age, in their multifarious variations. The polyphonic quality of the stories, no doubt, adds to the pervading disengagement. Receiving discordant information, the readers do not hear a single voice with whom to identify, which puts them in the position of concertgoers listening to a symphony: they take in all the voices collectively, much as music lovers confronted with the merging tunes from instruments competing for attention. Since the voices in Gallant's texts shower the readers with conflicting messages, the readers stay aloof, not wanting to partake in the general disjunction; never acquiring the status of conductors, they stand apart, closer to the composer of the polyphony than to any of the particular tunes.

Chapter Four

Structural Patterns of Disjunction: *Green Water, Green Sky, A Fairly Good Time,* and *The End of the World*

Gallant's predilection for the genre of the short story has not prevented her from trying out the novel. Significantly, though, her first attempt, *Green Water, Green Sky,* appeared first as three separate short stories— "Green Water, Green Sky," "Travellers Must Be Content," and "August"—like a cycle of stories.[1] Her second, and longer, novel, *A Fairly Good Time,* appeared more than 10 years later and contains one short story published previously—"The Accident."[2] *Green Water, Green Sky* concerns the descent into madness of Flor, whose disconnection from the world goes back to her parents' divorce after the mother's meaningless infidelity and the resulting penitent tribulations in Europe of mother and daughter. *A Fairly Good Time* narrates the events around the dissolution of Shirley Perrigny's marriage to a petty middle-class French reporter who cannot possibly understand his Canadian wife's disorganized life and interest in marginal beings. Her aimless trajectory in a society she does not belong to, let alone understand, reveals the extent of her bafflement and disjunction. Seemingly conventional in plot, the novels nevertheless present organizational principles that turn the texts into an interpretative challenge. Reminiscent in some ways of certain stories, the form of these two novels suits the mental confusion of the characters, indeed structurally reflects their fragmentation.

An example of disrupted chronology, *Green Water, Green Sky* jumps back and forth in time, unsettling the readers' sense of continuity.[3] The first section starts in Venice with Flor Fairlie, aged 14, her mother, Bonnie McCarthy, and her cousin George Fairlie, aged 7, and finishes 10 years later in New York with Flor as the bride of Bob Harris. The second section records the development of Flor's mental disorder while in Paris with her husband, Bob, reaching its peak in her "regression into a perfect childhood reunion with her long-departed father."[4] The third section narrates Flor's starting relationship with Bob in Cannes while Bonnie entertains her friend Wishart. The fourth and previously unpublished section, set in the restaurant of a Parisian hotel two years after Flor and Bob's marriage, no longer stars Flor, who has been interned in an asylum. Instead it gathers Bob, Bonnie, and George, reminiscing about the past and about Flor's madness, sadly unable to help her reconnect with the world.

If the general temporal frame manifests disruption, the reminiscences within the novel's four sections add to it. The very first section seemingly starts with the scenes in Venice, but subsequent anomalies in tenses point to the remembrance of those events, not to their actuality. No marker of reminiscence, such as the use of the past perfect, prepares the readers for George's memory of his parents' abandoning him there with his aunt for the day; the passage refers to the narrative past in the simple past. If it were not for the illogical shifts of tense from the simple past to the past perfect, the readers would not be alerted to the dual levels; the scenes in Venice are so vividly depicted that no one would think of doubting their veracity.

Further anomalies occur. Sometimes, for no apparent reason, Gallant switches from the past perfect (statement [a] in the following extract) to the simple past (statements [b] and [c]) for events happening at the same time in the past, while she narrates episodes belonging to the narrative present or the near narrative present in the simple past (statements [d] and [f]) as if they coincided, causing more confusion: "Oh, they had managed it beautifully [a]. First they were out on the terrace [b], offering him gondoliers, then he was abandoned with Aunt Bonnie and Flor [c]. Even years later, when they talked about that day [d], and his parents wondered how they had found it in them to creep off that way [e] . . . even then, there was an annoying taint of self-congratulation in their manner [f]."[5] Sometimes both the simple past and past perfect correspond to the narrative past, causing a blurred transition with the narrative present: "His Fairlie cousins had called him the Monster [a], while his mother's relatives . . . often said he was being badly prepared for the blows and the thumps of life [b], and wouldn't thank his parents later on [c]. . . . At seventeen he was a triumphant vindication for his parents of years of hell [d]" (GWGS, 3). Both statement [a] and [b], in the past perfect, refer to the time when he was 7 years old and are logically followed by a future of the past in statement [c]. Then the use of the simple past to signal an event belonging presumably to the narrative present, when he is 17, confuses all the issues.

In fact, Gallant masterfully distorts grammatical rules governing the concordance of tenses to convey the sense that none of the characters' memories can be relied on. All the characters reconstruct the past to suit their own vision, or di(s)vision of themselves and from each other. Threatened by George's memory of her breaking and then theatrically flicking her glass bead necklace in the air, as it would alienate her mother, on whose love she depends for survival, Flor mentions that they "don't remember the same things" (*GWGS*, 20). Later, before her final collapse into madness, her final vision (re)constructs a happy scene with her father, the very scene she has been longing for all along, ever since her parents' divorce. In the same vein, Bonnie keeps contradicting herself depending on the momentary confirmation of vision she needs and reinvents Flor's need to be protected so as to absolve herself of her dependence on her daughter, so destructive to Flor that she ends up with a dysfunctional neurosis. Because their reconstructions differ drastically, they cannot possibly "share a life, or a world," the more so as they whirl between different geographical settings, none bearing the notion of home.[6] Juxtaposition of their clashing reconstructions structurally points to their disconnectedness.

As often in Gallant's fiction, images offer a *mise en abyme* (that is, a reduplication, reflection, or mirror) that clarifies the novel's process of creation, structural frame, and style.[7] Here, besides its metafictional imagery, the text reflects the readers' experience through one of George's perceptions. A consciousness that guides, or misguides, the novel, George feels as puzzled as the readers about the other narrative threads, about the images generated by the other characters; like the readers, he "[can] hear their voices, but he [can] not understand any of the things they said" (*GWGS*, 145) for want of a firm anchor. This actually echoes Flor's last vision before she disappears from the scene, which best expresses the organizational frame of the novel: she realizes "she was in a watery world of perceptions, where impulses, doubts, intentions, detached from their roots, rise to the surface and expand" (111). The image conveys the way the characters let their reconstructions of the past—idiosyncratic, changeable, purposeful for their own self-image—surface and guide them. The metafictional value of this quotation resembles that of George's (and the book's) final vision. George visualizes "Aunt Bonnie, and Flor, and the girl [seen earlier] on the Quai Anatole France as one person. She was a changeable person, now menacing, now dear; a minute later behaving like a queen in exile, plaintive and haughty, eccentric by birth, unaware, or not caring, that the others were laughing behind their hands" (154). His vision evokes the contradictions within the narrative threads, the multiple and clashing perspectives, the paradoxical facets of all the characters, the oxymoronic representation of characters, sometimes white, sometimes black, like a picture and its negative—the very representation of disjunction.

If *Green Water, Green Sky* presents a disrupted structural frame, *A Fairly Good Time* diverges even more from the traditionally linear structure.[8] A hotchpotch of unconnected scenes, messages and letters, memories and dreams, phone calls, future steps to take recorded as a list, flyleaf inscriptions, journalistic essays and passages of an autobiographical novel in process, extracts from a terrorist act, erroneously transcribed nursery rhymes, interviews, alluded books, *A Fairly Good Time* derides linearity, resists even a disrupted thread, indeed conveys chaos.[9] Chaos it is, for Shirley refuses to structure her life; the narrative accordingly follows her meandering trajectory with its breaks and jumps, juxtaposing apparently disconnected episodes with bits and pieces of remotely related information.

Reflecting Shirley's life, the opening chapter of the novel—a letter Shirley receives from her mother—is a *mise en abyme* of the novel, also jumping from one idea to another.[10] The letter indeed gives the key to both Shirley's life and the structural organization of the novel. The mother's disorganized letter and its emphasis on peripheral detail reflects the life text of her daughter, who forgets what her priorities are and devotes time and energy to people who will not even be grateful. Thus the mother's letter provides encyclopedic information on European bluebells, with interspersed comments about a myriad other subjects that turn out to be cryptic answers to Shirley's questions about possible ways to cope with the dissolution of her marriage.[11] The uselessness of the botanical information to Shirley and the readers foreshadows the uselessness of Shirley's devotion to peripheral friendship. In the 10 to 11 months that the novel spans, Shirley bestows her thoughtful, though eventually unappreciated, attentions upon Renata (a friend who feigns suicide for attention), James (Shirley's Greek neighbor), and Claudie Maurel (an adolescent sexually abused by her father, whose baby she has borne), following the process that has unconsciously led Shirley to alienation from Philippe, her husband.

The letters also mirror the readers' reception of the novel. If Shirley's mother "[can] not decipher" Shirley's letter,[12] neither can the readers decipher the mother's for its jumps and deliberate silences that convey her avoidance of emotional involvement. The same applies to Shirley's letter; illegible to her mother for its emotionally charged stains and blots, it is equally indecipherable to the perplexed readers for its textual absence, leaving them desirous of more information. They can rely only on the textual reproduction of Shirley's life, with all its diversions and digressions that disclose drop by drop the gist of the letter through the memories of, and allusions to, Shirley's married life. In the same way, Shirley will have to digest for about 10 months the content of her mother's rambling letter to see the light. The beauty of the novel is that at the very end, it buckles its loop as Shirley finds before moving out of her flat her mother's letter and understands its cryptic message. Shirley gives in to Philippe's misunderstandings, ridding herself of the burden of a life not meant for her, ready at last to enjoy "a fairly good time," unattached, free to run her life the way she thinks fit. At last, she has understood the epigraph from Edith Wharton's *The Last Asset,* a clearer message than her mother's: "There are lots of ways of being miserable, but there is only one way of being comfortable, and that is to stop running round after happiness. If you make up your mind not to be happy there's no reason why you shouldn't have a fairly good time." By then, too, the readers rereading the opening of the letter about a "macerated and decomposed specimen . . . sent . . . for identification" (*FGT,* 3) realize its metafictional power. Like the bluebell, the text of Shirley's life has macerated in Gallant's mind before being composed in bits and pieces, indeed de-composed.

Gallant's fictional repertoire offers other structural devices reflecting a character's fragmented perception. Just as she drastically distorts any sense of structure in *A Fairly Good Time,* she manages to fake a sense of order in unchronological narrations. In "The Wedding Ring," one of the stories in *The End of the World,* the first-person narrator/focalizer relates a series of events that seem to be sequential as well as experienced on the spot because of the present tense and its seeming immediacy. But an analysis of the selected events, facts, and thoughts reveals the looseness of the deeper structure that reproduces the protagonist's devious search for identity. The story is presumably concerned with a young girl's memories of a summer spent in Vermont with her mother, a Boston cousin, and a male guest with whom her mother is in love. But the story really deals with the fundamental gaps between the family members: at the core of the group lies an insuperable incapacity to communicate, which the story's structure matches.[13]

To add confusion to chaos, not only is the overall relation of events disconnected, but the internal organization of paragraphs, or even of sentences, also seems to have been chosen haphazardly. Thus the descriptive opening sentence is typical of the story's organization. The weird combination of totally unrelated objects on Jane's windowsill—"a pack of cards, a bell, a dog's brush, a book about a girl named Jewel who is a Christian Scientist and won't let anyone take her temperature, and a white jug holding field flowers"—announces the characters' unrelatedness.[14] It rather rings like Pope's *The Rape of the Lock:* "Here files of pins extend their shining rows, / Puffs, powders, patches, bibles, billets-doux."[15] The long explanatory phrase about the book on the windowsill anticipates the subsequent loose passages on one or another aspect of Jane's life that has deserved the narrator's less sparse commentary. The rest of the opening paragraph is not any more coherent: "The water in the jug has evaporated; the sand-and-amber flowers seem made of paper. The weather bulletin for the day can be one of several: No sun. A high arched yellow sky. Or creamy clouds, stillness. Long motionless grass. The earth soaks up the sun. Or, the sky is higher than it ever will seem again, and the sun far away and small" (*EW,* 126). The terse sentences and telegraphic notes, all presumably dealing with an aspect of the immediate environment in which the events take place, either record the local dryness or give possible weather forecasts that seem to bear no relation to the narrative. But if this mixed bag refers to the actual weather, it also renders the mood of the family and its overall desolation.

The accumulation of unconnected sentences makes the readers actually experience the feeling Jane's mother evokes in one of her favorite lines: "I was divorced from the landscape, as they [her parents] were from each other. I was too taken up wondering what was going to happen next" (*EW,* 128). Jane's situation is like a *mise en abyme* of her mother's experience. She feels as divorced from her parents as they feel from each other. She, too, cannot relate to her surroundings: she simply tells, as if absentmindedly, what she remembers, what she saw and experienced when young. Her alienation is reflected in the loose narration of events, whose exact chronology cannot be determined for want of time markers.[16] Anachronies are actually emphasized in the narration, but they only confuse the readers.[17] Take, for instance, the first paragraph involving a scene, just after the first two descriptive paragraphs:

> The screen door slams and shakes my bed. That was my cousin. The couch with the India print spread in the next room has been made up for him. He is the only boy cousin I have, and the only American relation my

age. We expected him to be homesick for Boston. When he disappeared the first day, we thought we would find him crying with his head in the wild cucumber vine; but all he was doing was making the outhouse tidy, dragging out of it last year's magazines. He discovers a towel abandoned under his bed by another guest, and shows it to each of us. He has unpacked a trumpet, a hatchet, a pistol, and a water bottle. He is ready for anything except my mother, who scares him to death. (*EW,* 126)

The first sentence marks an action followed by a sentence referring to the agent. But then the scene is interrupted by a comment on the couch made up for the agent: the statement in the present perfect points out an external retroversion, but the time reference is left vague.[18] There follows an expository sentence on the nature of the protagonist's connection to the agent in the present tense of permanent truth, not in the narrative present. Another external retroversion in the past simple takes the readers back to the assumption that the protagonist and her mother had presumably just before, or at the beginning of, the cousin's stay with them. But then, as if to confuse the readers, the next sentence, also in the past simple, refers to an action that could hardly take place at the same time. The next sentence reverts to the present simple, so presumably to the original scene, but the nature of the information so unlikely belongs to the scene that it takes the readers back to the recent narrative past: the boy's discovery of "a towel abandoned under his bed by another guest" cannot possibly be a fact worth recalling as a scene, but rather a marker of the rapid turnover of "guests" in the summer cottage. The list of objects the child "has unpacked" seems to suggest that the time reference is the first day of the boy's stay: the present perfect implies an action started in the past that has an impact on the narrative present. The final comment on his reception of his aunt could again belong to at least two points in time: his attitude on arriving or his general fear of his aunt. The constant jumps in time create chaos in the minds of the readers, who constantly waver about the exact chronology of all statements.

What is true for this paragraph holds for the others. The last paragraph of section 2 (and final paragraph of the short story) highlights the overall incoherence:

Uncut grass [1]. I saw [2a] the ring fall into it [2b], but I am told I did not [2c]—I was already in Boston [2d]. The weekend party, her chosen audience, watched her rise, without warning, from the wicker chair on the porch [3]. An admirer of Russian novels, she would love to make an immediate, Russian gesture [4a], but cannot [4b]. The porch is screened [5a], so, to throw her wedding ring away, she must have walked a few steps to the door and *then* made her speech, and flung the ring into the twilight, in a great spinning arc [5b]. The others looked for it next day, discreetly [6a], but it had disappeared [6b]. First it slipped under one of those sharp bluish stones [7a], then a beetle moved it [7b]. It left its print on a cushion of moss after the first winter [8]. No one else could have worn it [9]. My mother's hands were small [10a], like mine [10b]. (*EW,* 128–29)[19]

The natural order in which the events take place *(fabula)* is totally disrupted in the *story* (Bal, 5): Jane's mother must get up first, then walk out so as to throw the ring theatrically before it can fall into the grass that happens to be uncut. The ring lodges itself under a stone, which explains why the mother's friends cannot find it. Its print can be seen after the first winter. The ring is thus lost to all: anyway, its size would make it impossible for anyone else to wear it, except Jane, whose hands are also small. Particularly moving, Jane's insistence on a unique connection between her mother and herself is paradoxically alluded to by juxtaposition [9 and 10a] plus [10b] rather than explicitly stated; its poignancy results from its cryptic enunciation at the end of an account from which the narrator is "locked out" by others through the use of the passive voice ("I'm told"). The *fabula* could thus be [2d], [3], [5b], [2a + 2b], [1], [7a + 7b], [6b], [6a], [8]. The relation of events is further complicated by the retrospective phrase [2c] that negates the previous validity of [2a], through a considered, but failed, act [4a + 4b] whose temporality—conditional and simple present—matches the final truth [10a], which leads to [9] to the exception of [10b]. The content of the paragraph, with its internally disrupted—not to say chaotic—chronology, is further questioned, as the use of the past simple in a narrative otherwise related in the present tense might imply that the events related are imaginary or rather willed to be so.

The mixture of general statements, scenic pictures whose chronology cannot be established or whose occurrences cannot be numbered, and retroversion or anticipation with an equally vague time reference thus characterize the loose succession of paragraphs. The intentional inconsistency of the narration matches the lack of unity and relationships within the protagonist's family. Capers and somersaults between sentences and paragraphs point out the loose links between the characters, their estrangement from one another, and their own alienation from life. Like "disembodied voices" (*EW,* 126) on the radio, the information given never takes firm shape and has its own reflection in the stream where Jane and her mother wash their hair. Seemingly stringed, but inherently loose, the pieces of information are like "bubbles of soap [that] dance in place, as if rooted, then the roots stretch and break" (127). The information imparted, its selection and ordering, is like the mother's discourse on "her lack of roots" (127). Like Gallant devising a story, "to give the story greater power, or because she really believes what she is saying at that moment, she gets rid of an extra parent" (127).

Concerned with its own creation, the story thus reveals the artistic process that leads to its existence. Its message, it appears, is determined by, and inherent in, the selection and ordering—or rather disordering—of facts and events: the story can be summed up as a hotchpotch of facts and events imagined or really experienced, unexpectedly changing settings, and disrupted—not to say purposefully obscure—chronology. Loose structure (of a seemingly sequential relation) and generalized disconnectedness become synonyms.

Gallant once remarked that "style is inseparable from structure" (*PN,* 177), so that both the expression and presentation of events, feelings, thoughts, and conversations convey the message of fictional pieces. The correlation between presentation and message would seem to imply that firm textual strategies accompany accounts of well-structured lives. Yet, in Mavis Gallant's fiction, firm structural patterns frame disjunction. The main characters of her firmly structured stories end up totally alienated from their human environment, where they lead marginal lives. Their marginality emerges from the organization of materials, as if their arrangement firmly marks out the route to the discovery of human isolation. The apparent "firmness" of such stories conveys patterns of fragmentation, disconnection, or alienation.

Thus in a strictly chronological narrative such as "About Geneva," the firm pattern encasing the story patently highlights the characters' disconnectedness.[20] True, the external retroversions—"about Geneva," as the title indicates—could be said to disrupt the chronology, but in fact the story is based on those very retroversions: the story would not be if it were not for them. The story basically recounts how two grownups are fishing for information about two children's first stay at their father's in Geneva. Still in their innocent childhood days, Ursula and Colin go back to their *meublé* in Nice, where their mother and grandmother welcome them. Immediately, the adults start cross-examining the children for facts "about Geneva." The shifting focus of their inquiry contributes to the increasing detachment between the children and the adults while the implicit tension between the setups in Nice and Geneva adds to the chaotic relationships within the family. In its exposition of the struggle for power taking place between the father and the grand-mother-mother pair over the two children, the story lays bare, through the text's structure, the fortress of the children's minds and their resistance to infiltration even from close relatives.

The story's tripartite organization with flashbacks discloses the children's unwillingness to communicate, asserting their determination to rule their lives alone. Divided into three parts of unequal length, the narration discloses an episode in the family confrontation while reproducing the order of the *fabula*. Each part focuses on one character at a time, thus emphasizing how divided the family is. The first part gives precedence to the overbearing grandmother: "Granny" not only presides over the opening but also manipulates each character so as to hear just what she wants to. In about three pages (*EW,* 46 – 48), she manages to exert her control over the entire family and go against her daughter's express request not to be openly inquisitive nor to formulate criticism. By starting the first line with her name—that of a function, not an emotional relation[21]—the story immediately establishes her power over the family: from the very first minute, she causes the children and her daughter to have feelings of guilt. The family network is immediately highlighted as the children conceal their uneasiness and discontent through misbehavior while their mother fakes cheerfulness. The theatrical reception lasts a page and a half before they are allowed in, as if to signify its unwelcoming quality. The selection of minute details makes this explicit: "She [the mother] came in *at last,* drew off her gloves, looked around, *as if she,* and not the children, *had been away*" (*EW,* 46; emphasis added). In the lapse of time between their arrival and their entrance, the grandmother hardly allows her daughter to speak. Then suspicion and contempt alternate in a concert of voices whose soloist, the grandmother, sets the tone. Firing insidious questions and comments, she elicits information from the children and keeps the conversation going, in spite of the children's unwillingness to cooperate.

Unexpectedly, the spotlight is then turned on Ursula, whose revelations make up the second part of the story (*EW,* bottom 48 –bottom 49). But her revelations say less "about Geneva" than about herself. What she has gained from her stay abroad is her newly acquired literary inclination. Like her father, she has developed a genuine enthusiasm for what she is writing—a play called *The Grand Duke.* She has even already suppressed her memories of Geneva and replaced them with her fantasies: "Everything about the trip, in the end, [crystallizes] around Tatiana and the Grand Duke. Already, Ursula [is] Tatiana" (49). Whatever she says is waved aside, for she takes after her father, the other. "By the simple act of creating Tatiana and the Grand Duke, she [has] removed herself from the ranks of reliable witnesses" (50). And so she ceases to be the focus of attention in favor of Colin, whose memories are recorded in the third and final part (bottom 49–51). However, he too has already started erasing Geneva from his memories: " 'I fed the swans,' Colin suddenly shouted. . . . There, he had told about Geneva. He sat up and kicked his heels on the carpet as if the noise would drown out the consequence of what he had revealed. As he said it, the image became static: a gray sky, a gray lake, and a swan wonderfully turning upside down with the black rubber feet showing above the water. His father was not in the picture at all; neither was *she*. But Geneva was fixed for the rest of his life: gray, lake, swan" (50). His subconscious retains a static image without human figures: his gray picture of the place is indicative of his indifference to people. "Having delivered his secret, he [has] nothing more to tell" (50).

The revelations "about Geneva" thus reach an end, for Ursula is not a reliable witness, and Colin starts inventing. The focus slowly shifts to the children's mother, who, now alone with Colin, tries to figure out "why her husband [has] left her" (*EW,* 51). The incursions into her mind show how she has combined the various images of Geneva that her mother, daughter, and son have evoked in turn. Totally fixed, the picture nevertheless arouses her envy and resentfulness at being left behind. Her eagerness to know more might lead to another, though unlikely, revealing discussion with Colin. Her final doubts, just before the end, leave a bitter taste of disillusionment, corresponding to her relegation to a position of less than secondary importance: "[N]othing had come back from the trip but her own feelings of longing and envy, the longing and envy she felt at night, seeing, at a crossroad or over a bridge, the lighted windows of a train sweep by. Her children had nothing to tell her. Perhaps, as she had said, one day Colin would say something, produce the image of Geneva, tell her about the lake, the boats, the swans, and why her husband had left her. Perhaps he could tell her, but, really, she doubted it. And, already, so did he" (51).

Thus the purpose of the trip is disclosed in a final interior monologue that mirrors the utter dissolution of a family whose members cannot and will not communicate. The final sentence ("And, already, so did he") gives the story a circular character: Colin is about to close the door to communication, which has led the children to be sent to Geneva. Cut off from the others, he reproduces his father's pattern of isolation and transfers the process of alienation into the next generation: an alien to his mother, Colin is not any closer to his father, whom he "kills" in a Freudian sense by erasing him from all his memories. Slowly but surely, the revelations "about Geneva" disclose the vicious circle of the family estrangement. The seemingly linear narration ends up closing in with its external retroversions that emphasize the repeated patterns of alienation.[22]

The recurrence of short-lived attempts at communicating offers a frame clearly corresponding to the characters' role in the family. Authoritative, the grandmother holds the floor before Ursula opposes her in the name of her father, whose literary talents she has inherited. Rejected for its literariness, her response is further counteracted by Colin's, which is invented, as is the mother's picture of things. Like a whirlpool, the subsequent round of dialogues of the deaf awaits its turn to end up in the same awareness of the characters' disconnectedness.

Yet another pattern emerges in "My Heart Is Broken." The protagonist, Jeannie, sees her own experience reduced to a trivial event in the story's triangular presentation. Raped in the immediate narrative past, Jeannie is first subjected to the endless platitudes of an elderly woman who lives in the same road construction camp. When Jeannie's interlocutor, Mrs. Thompson, opens the dialogue by mentioning the effect the news of Jean Harlow's death had on her when she was about Jeannie's age, Mrs. Thompson probably unconsciously intends to neutralize the effects of the rape. She virtually puts her own experience and Jeannie's on a par in spite of the drastic emotional differences. Once the rape has been hinted at, Mrs. Thompson carries on lecturing Jeannie about her responsibilities in the crime. The emotional impact of the experience is thus nullified as a total lack of understanding separates the two characters onstage.[23]

The internal organization of paragraphs also echoes the indifference with which the rape is being met. The initial disclosure of Mrs. Thompson's reception of the actress's death mirrors the lack of continuity in her discourse and the irrelevance of her revelations:

> "When that Jean Harlow died," Mrs. Thompson said to Jeannie, "I was on the 83 streetcar with a big, heavy paper parcel in my arms. I hadn't been married for very long, and when I used to visit my mother she'd give me a lot of canned stuff and preserves. I was standing up in the

streetcar because nobody'd given me a seat. All the men were unemployed in those days, and they just sat down wherever they happened to
be. You wouldn't remember what Montreal was like then. *You* weren't
even on earth. To resume what I was saying to you, one of these men sitting down had an American paper—the *Daily News,* I guess it was—and
I was sort of leaning over him, and I saw in big print 'JEAN HARLOW
DEAD'. You can believe it or not, just as you want to, but that was the
most terrible shock I ever had in my life. I never got over it." (*EW,* 60)

The opening line gives the impression that the matter at stake is the
death of Jean Harlow. Yet halfway through the story, the actual reason
for the two women's conversation—or rather Mrs. Thompson's monologue—establishes a drastic contrast: Mrs. Thompson's shock is senti-
mental and even mawkish; Jeannie's is physical and emotional, though
suppressed. Mrs. Thompson's sterile and incoherent comments are
matched by the "canned stuff and preserves" her mother used to give
her. Like processed food, Mrs. Thompson's commonplaces should be
swallowed without much chewing, for they are insubstantial.[24] The reference to her new marital status at the time, more or less comparable to
Jeannie's situation in the narrative present, might seem to imply that
she finds her feelings equivalent to Jeannie's. In fact, the allusion establishes a close connection between Jeannie and the famous sex symbol.
This parallel amounts to negating Jeannie's severe and traumatic experience. And the allusions to the interwar years in Canada only add to the
gap between the two women's perceptions. Mrs. Thompson's transitional phrase, taking her back to the issue of their conversation,
increases the awareness of her comments' non sequitur while her "most
terrible shock" provokes a derisive smile in the readers.

Such long soliloquies silence Jeannie, whose minimal retorts and
careful handling of the nail polish bottle confirm her will to distance
herself from her unpleasant memories and from the nonsense Mrs.
Thompson is talking.[25] The descriptive passages that interrupt her self-
centered discourse not only give panoramic information that clarifies the
situation but also reinforce the gap between the two women. Whereas
Jeannie is pretty and appealing, Mrs. Thompson is a "plain, fat, consol-
ing sort of person, with varicosed legs, shoes unlaced and slit for comfort, blue dressing gown worn at all hours, pudding-bowl haircut, and
coarse gray hair" (*EW,* 60). Their friendship results only from their being
together in a place cut off from civilization. The description of the
Thompsons' interior also mirrors their superficial orderliness, contrast-

ing Jeannie's messy and slovenly approach. In short, the descriptive passages reinforce the clash between their outlooks.

Further contrasts are evoked through the attempt at discussing Jeannie's rape and its causes, offered in part 2, after the climactic revelation. The exchange of ideas is very much like a table tennis match in which Mrs. Thompson's weighty attacks force Jeannie to be on the defensive.[26] This prevents Jeannie from scoring any points, as whenever she attempts to strengthen her position, her adversary smashes back. Either aggressive or inquisitive, Mrs. Thompson is anything but comforting, contrary to her announced purpose ("I came straight over here, Jeannie, because I thought you might be needing me" [EW, 63]). In fact, her aggressiveness and inquisitiveness both correspond to her fear of hearing who the victimizer is, lest it should be her husband, whose delight at listening to bawdy songs marks him as the likely lecher.

Were it not for Mrs. Thompson's report of a conversation overheard just before the narrative present, the story might not be triangular in its structure. Starting on a low with Mrs. Thompson's remembered shock over the death of a Hollywood star, the story reaches its peak with the allusion to Jeannie's rape and then proceeds downward with Mrs. Thompson's reprimands until Jeannie manages to express her despair. The base of the triangle is drawn when Mrs. Thompson thinks of her own youth, "wondering if her heart had ever been broken, too" (EW, 66). The final consideration of her own past ironically takes the readers back to the laughable, "most terrible shock [she] ever had in [her] life" (60). Because throughout the story physical descriptions enhance the similarity between the two Jeans, Mrs. Thompson's friendliness toward Jeannie is made even more blatantly dubious. Punctuated by the motion of her rocking chair, Mrs. Thompson's own life's meaninglessness is perceived in her incapacity to understand and comfort Jeannie. She can barely cry out her despair over her utter isolation because social conventions muffle her own voice. The story opens with the news of a sex symbol's death—whose voice cannot be heard either—and ends with Jean's spiritual death. The two women die victims to the high-heeled, peroxided image imposed on them by a heartless and macho society. The image of the canned stuff holds for both.

Since Jeannie's response to the rape differs from what one would expect, she is not presented as a tragic, or even pathetic, character. But total desolation emerges from the mixture of trifles neutralizing the effect of utter misery and from dialogues made of a minor character's long soliloquies, barely answered by the protagonist's short and indifferent repartees. Thanks to the triangular development, Jeannie is aptly compared to a symbol whose reality shatters all hope.

If a triangular presentation can record dejection, a purely linear narration can accompany dissolution, emerging from the different stages in the characters' slow loss of identity. In spite of the various parts announced by temporal and spatial references, such stories have a smooth relation for their one and only narrative thread. "Orphans' Progress," for instance, follows a linear progression that nevertheless evidences dislocation, if not emphasizes its manifestation.[27] In fact, bar a long flashback, the linear structure accompanies the slow psychic disintegration of two young girls after their widowed mother has been refused custody for inadequate care. Marking stages in the girls' progress to total dissolution of ties, temporal and geographical references disclose the linearity of the *story*.

Carried out in stages, the disjunction implies the degradation of blood ties resulting from social restraint. The *text* (Rimmon-Kenan, 3; Bal, 5) seems to suggest that emotional misery comes with affluence. Although every new roof provides the girls with better material circumstances, every move engenders a further estrangement from each other and the past. Before the time span covered by the plot, the sisters felt their mother's warmth and loved her, slovenly though she might have been. They were then part of a nucleus and shared everything with her: her presence, her moods, her bed and dirty sheets, her language, and even the lack of food. Separation engenders an irrevocable, alienating process. From their filthy loft, they go to their grandmother, who is "scrupulous about food, particularly for these underfed children, and [makes] them drink goat's milk" (*HT*, 56). But the place is not heated evenly: the grandmother saves money by not heating all the rooms. At their grandmother's, the girls' past is negated. Defamatory rumors make them look back on it in a different light: their mother was not up to standard, "they were living under . . . unsheltered conditions" (57). Yet the girls never resented their conditions and have retained the memory of a warm and close relationship (so that the elder objects). On the other hand, "what they [remember] afterwards of their grandmother [is] goat's milk, goat eyes, and the frightened man" (56), that is, scrupulous nutrition, no contact, and fear—definitely not loving kindness. Back in Montreal, the girls are not given any chance to identify with the place or to feel at home, for the atmosphere and the surroundings are totally different. Their relatives' exhibited wealth and resentment cause fear and darkness to prevail in the girls' lives (59). And they themselves now even resent each other's company: they fight over the blanket on their bed.

After this, disconnection is carried on one step further at the convent school, where expressing feelings and making references to one's family ties are offenses. Humiliated for mentioning her mother to a fellow boarder and confusing her whereabouts, Mildred no longer relates to her mother: the term " 'Mummy' had meaning" (*HT,* 61) only until she got punished. Similarly, the bond of sisterhood is broken: no longer sharing a room, let alone a bed, the sisters stop being on the same wavelength. The school system parts them: during breaks, Mildred can only catch glimpses of Cathie, whose age is more appropriate to serious walks. Furthermore, Cathie, who prays for almost unknown relatives and outsiders, "[forgets] Mildred in her prayers" (61). After a seven years' separation, the girls no longer get through to each other (62). Restraining social norms have erased their deviant, yet warm, past life. "Natural," that is, instinctive and spontaneous, sisterly feelings cease to be part of their experience. Their identity is lost. The slow disconnecting process has reached its peak.

The linguistic environment, too, contributes to the girls' gradual loss of affective response and identity. Each stage in their peregrination means rejection of their previous command of language and shows that the process of unlearning coincides with further estrangement from their mother's influence.[28] After their easygoing bilingual upbringing with their French-Canadian mother, they become repeatedly aware of one linguistic intolerance after the other. Their silent appraisal of the status of language is first made clear at their grandmother's: "They understood, from their grandmother, and their grandmother's maid, and the social worker who came to see their grandmother but had little to say to them, that French was an inferior kind of speech" (*HT,* 57). Although the girls have now become familiar with the linguistic code prevalent in Ontario, their natural language remains French; spontaneous expressions of discomfort, for example, will come out in French until the girls recover enough self-control to switch over to English (57). That a foreign language can exclude affectivity appears in the combined announcement of the grandmother's death and of the girls' newly acquired ability to speak with an Ontario accent (56–57). The statement does not make any room for emotions: it denies their existence. Back in Montreal, they go through the same linguistic ordeal. The prevailing darkness adequately renders the devastating psychological impact of such narrow-mindedness, so contrary to their original bilingual upbringing. Finally, the punishment inflicted upon Mildred at the convent school for uttering three words in English, not in French, also contributes to her detachment from her mother. This only paves the way for her acceptance of being swallowed up in her new French-speaking family. As she is referred to as "Mildred's mother" (62), the new mother soon supplants the real mother. Mildred may well be back in a French-speaking environment akin to her mother's, but the pressures endured to adjust split her from her natural background and true origins.

Similarly, throughout the story, words referring to ignorance and revelations mark the process alienating both Mildred and Cathie from their mother.[29] Before being taken away from her, "they loved (their mother) *without knowing* what the word implied" (*HT,* 56).[30] But soon they are made to consider her in a new light, by virtue of social criteria: "They *never knew, until told,* that they were uneducated and dirty and in danger. *Now they learned* that their mother never washed her own neck and that she dressed in layers of woollen stuff, covered with grease, and wore men's shoes because some man had left them behind and she liked the shape and comfort of them. *They did not know, until they were told,* that they had never been fed properly" (57–58).

At this stage, the girls still contradict rumors (*HT,* 57). Objecting to the denigration of their lodgings, Cathie reveals other particulars of importance to them (such as their two cats, their mother's pictures, and their own drawings on the wall). Some affectional space was given everyone in spite of the material scarcity. But already the little girl does "*not remember* having screamed or anything at all except the trip from Montreal by train" (58). Once they have moved to the house of their cousins in Montreal, "they [do] not see *anything that* [*reminds*] them of Montreal, and [*do*] *not recall their mother*" (59). The children do not talk about her until their cousins try to frighten them; only then does Cathie speak about her. "Our mother wouldn't try to frighten us" (59), she says, still remembering their past feeling of security. A reverse feeling marks the ignorance and revelation of the meaning attached to the shears with which Mildred is "made to promenade through the classrooms" (60) as a punishment for having told a lie: "She *did not know* the significance of the shears, nor, it seemed, did the nun who organized the punishment. It had always been associated with lying, and *(the nun suddenly remembered)* had something to do with cutting the liar's tongue" (60–61). As to Cathie, she is so worried "about forgetting Mildred in her prayers" that she invents "a formula" (61): "Everyone I have *ever known* who is dead or alive, anyone *I know now* who is alive but might die, and anyone I *shall ever know* in the future" (61). In other words, the girls go from carefree and happy ignorance to the awareness of their mother's inadequate handling of their upbringing before becoming conscious of their own shortcomings and inability to have any meaningful exchange. Theirs is a story of initiation: brought about by knowledge, their initiation coincides with a kind of fall. As Christian theology has it, ignorance and innocence yield happiness, while knowledge and experience provoke unhappiness and evil.

On the stylistic level, abrupt transitions reinforce the existing disjunction. Take, for instance, the following passage:

> "To the day I die," said the social worker from Montreal to her colleague in Ontario, "I won't forget the screams of Mildred when she was dragged out of that pigsty." This was said in the grandmother's parlor, where the three women—the two social workers, and the grandmother—sat with their feet freezing on the linoleum floor. The maid heard, and told. She had been in and out, serving coffee, coconut biscuits, and damson preserves in custard made of goat's milk. The room was heated once or twice a year: even the maid said her feet were cold. But "To the day I die" was a phrase worth hearing. She liked the sound of that, and said it to the children. The maid was from a place called Waterloo, where, to hear her tell it, no one behaved strangely and all the rooms were heated. (*HT*, 58)

If the first sentence records Mildred's misery upon parting from her mother, it also insists on the shabby lodgings as opposed to the cozier, yet unheated, parlor where Mildred's feelings are considered. After the comment on the locale where the conversation takes place, the maid abruptly comes in, very much as she has come in and out of the room during the meeting. The narration then reverts to, and elaborates on, the temperature of the room, an annoyance that is however more than compensated for by the maid's overhearing an interesting phrase worth repeating. No sooner has she used the expression than another comment on the heating habits at the maid's original home base is voiced. The passage, with its almost exclusive use of the narrative present for loosely reported actions, has a striking impact. It reveals to the readers, as it must have to the girls, that as much importance is attached—if not more—to the temperature of a room and to the use of a new phrase as to the marks of a child's despair. There is simply no trace of compassion. The girls are made to understand that feelings are worth nothing compared with physical comfort and minor intellectual satisfactions.

Likewise, events are often announced and followed straight away by asides or retrospective explanations that come in to disrupt the chronology, reducing the impact of emotions. In this way, the death of the girls' grandmother is broken to them two pages before they actually witness it: expressions of suffering have no room owing to the interruption. Anachronies take the readers back to the period before the Ontario experience, then back to the Ontario period, before combining the recent and less recent past in revelatory speech presentation concerning the girls' acquisition of knowledge at the time. Insidiously, the affect (emotional response) is neglected in favor of external judgments based on material considerations. A similar distance is effected in the passage about Mildred's adoption: "Mildred was suddenly taken out of school and adopted. Their mother's sister, one of the aunts they had seldom seen, had lost a daughter by drowning. She said she would treat Mildred as she did her own small son, and Mildred, who wished to leave the convent school, but did not know if she cared to go and live in a place called Chicoutimi, did not decide. She made them decide, and made them take her away" (*HT,* 62). The readers are not allowed to rejoice over Mildred's new life. Immediately, an anachrony makes it clear that the adoption is meant as a balm for the aunt and adoptive mother, not for Mildred: she is only to replace her lost cousin. The following statement marks the lack of feeling involved in the transaction. And finally, the last step before the actual departure, Mildred shows she has become a master in the art of social interaction: for the sake of restraint, she remains aloof in a decision that involves her future—or rather the extension of her cousin's life. That she substitutes for her cousin is emphasized by her denial of her past when confronted with her original "dwelling." Restraint has first blurred her memories;[31] it ends up annihilating the past altogether. The abrupt ending, closing in on her past like darkness on the world, leaves no hope for the future. The disrupted organization of the superficially linear third-person narration wipes off affective responses, so much so that it negates the existence of the self. Based on a linear progression and punctuated by temporal or spatial stages, the story thus unfolds the characters' slow disintegration.

Mavis Gallant suggests in one of her scarce comments on her production that her stories come to existence spontaneously: "I wouldn't choose a theme and write about it. A story usually begins, for me, with people seen in a situation, like that. (Locks fingers together). The knot either relaxes or becomes locked in another way. . . . The situation has a beginning and as much ending as any situation in life" (iHancock, 45).

One may doubt, however, that her selection and arrangement of details is genuinely spontaneous, as more often than not, her fiction includes comments that can be read on two levels—the purely fictional relation of events and the metafictional interest in the process of creation. Besides, the preceding consideration of structural patterns has established a correlation between organization of materials and cumulative effect. In her fiction, loose textual arrangement emphasizes the absence of a coherent line of conduct in the characters' lives, while a firm frame corresponds to a structured pattern of disintegration in their experiences. In either case, the ultimate significance of their lives is reflected in the narrative pattern of the texts, itself mirrored in their self-informing pictures. To put it differently, the final effect gained by using a firm structure together with other specific devices is to enhance the general estrangement of the characters. Most of Gallant's stories have a circular twist to them—looping the loop—a circularity that only reinforces the isolation the characters are trapped in. Like lions in a cage, they are seen going round in circles with no hope of ever escaping.

As Gallant conveys her theme through the very construction of her stories, she implicitly subscribes to Lotman's views that the structure of any given text shows "how the artistic text becomes a medium of a particular thought or idea, and how the structure of [the] text is related to the structure of this idea."[32] The message conveyed through structural patterns is, in her case, pretty grim: nothing can be shared, life is to be lived alone, no hope remains. The general oppressive atmosphere that ensues gives rise to two diverging images. On the one hand, the unconnected episodes of the characters' biographies are like sketches of empty bottles hanging on a wall, purposeless and indifferent, so that if one falls, no one notices it. On the other hand, the progressive development of a given pattern paves the way for a vanishing sense of self, so that asked who they are, the characters only visualize a black pit for an answer. As the fictional world crumbles, the readers are left with the disheartening picture of beings whose broken image in the mirror they cannot restore.

Chapter Five

Ironic Markers of Disintegration:
From the Fifteenth District

Written in the seventies, the stories collected in *From the Fifteenth District* present a good example of the destabilizing effect afforded by Gallant's irony.[1] As the title story deals with ghost stories, hilariously subverting all expectations on the subject, the collection evidences the disruptive force with which this mode of representation imparts facts. With the clash between eastern and western views, "Potter" is also an easy target for Gallant's irony. But even less markedly ironic subjects like those dealt with in the other stories—"The Four Seasons," "The Moslem Wife," "The Remission," "Baum, Gabriel, 1935 –( )," "The Latehome-comer," "His Mother," and "Irina"—achieve complexity of meaning because of the playful contrasts between appearance and reality, between the said and the unsaid, or between the expressed and the decoded. In addition, most of the stories contain some form of mockery directed at the characters for their unawareness that other levels of values, or other possible, if not preferable, interpretations of their situations exist. Lying in the readers' awareness of it, rather than in the characters', irony's doubleness disrupts the readers' "notions of meaning as something single, decidable, or stable" by its inherent opposed levels of understanding—the superficial and the hidden level of understanding.[2] Set in the south of France or in Italy, Berlin, Paris, Budapest, or a small alpine town in Switzerland, the stories are peopled by characters with a dislocated sense of self, whose narrated lives display some discrepancy that forces the readers to question the received value of the represented.

In the title story, for instance, Gallant ridicules those who believe in ghost stories by reporting with pretended seriousness three cases of haunting; readers used to the author's sharpness cannot fail to see her wink when mentioning the "three *acceptable* complaints . . . lodged with the police" (*FFD,* 162; emphasis added). But the readers have yet to discover the baffling reversal of the usual relationship between ghosts and the living, for the ghosts complain about the living, who leave the dead no peace. The readers become conscious of the reversal only toward

the end of the first long, convoluted sentence giving the first com-
plainant's ample biographical details of fantastic nature: "Major Emery
Travella, 31st Infantry, 1914–1918, Order of the Leopard, Military
Beech Leaf, Cross of St. Lambert First Class, killed while defusing a
bomb in a civilian area 9 June 1941, Medal of Danzig (posthumous),
claims he is haunted by the entire congregation of St. Michael and All
Angels on Bartholomew Street" (162).

The three complaints in fact share much with a comedy of manners
deriding the ludicrous habits, petty fights, and demands of the living.
"Every year on the Sunday falling nearest the anniversary of his death,
Major Travella attends Holy Communion service at St. Michael's, the
church from which he was buried" (*FFD*, 162). Funnily, the ghost feels
the need to perpetuate a rite usually performed by the living in memory
of the dead, a need that puts the habits of the living into question, the
more so as he differs from the living in that he avoids mixing with the
crowd. The haunted, and not the haunting, ghost resents that "the congregation doubles in size" as the anniversary of his death approaches,
indirectly commenting on the unhealthy curiosity of the living. He further relates to "the opacity of the living, their heaviness and dullness,
the moisture of their skin, and the dustiness of their hair," all characteristics "repellent to a man of feeling" (163). The living therefore turn out
to be insensitive and disgusting. Poking fun at the request of evidence
for any declaration and the untrustworthiness of witnesses, the ghost
suggests calling on the former porter of his lodgings, "now residing at
the Institute for Victims of Senile Trauma, Fifteenth District" (163), to
testify to his shunning crowds while alive. *Ironie des ironies.*

Thrice as long, the second complaint takes a social turn. For one, the
complaint is set forth by a certain Mrs. Ibrahim, whose numerous prog-
eny project received ideas about her origins; for a second, the ironically
conflicting and slanderous versions of her death maintained by the doctor and the social worker throw light on social prejudice, confirming the
impression evoked by her name. The doctor's account depicts facts usually taken for granted, such as insalubrious and confined living conditions, the possession of "one or two cars" per family in spite of poverty
(*FFD*, 164), the waste of skilled work "lavished on . . . plastics and base
metals" (164). He lays himself open to ridicule by pretending that foreigners spread invented diseases with Latinate names, characterized as
hereditary. His account further ridicules the administrative red tape that
prevents a doctor from "administer[ing] drugs for the relief of pain"
(164) without the signature of a social investigator, the Ping-Pong game

between social welfare and hospitals, and the common assumption that foreigners should come after native citizens in social welfare distribution. The social investigator's account manifests animosity toward the doctor's repeating, or rather elaborating on, the people's lack of hygiene and the diseases it yields. Mrs. Ibrahim's account gives a toned down, not to say rosy, description of her death, where both the doctor and the social investigator offer their help, and where her husband, after a short moment of despair when she dies, abides by the rules of hospitality and offers a piece of his artifacts to the generous helpers. Less prejudiced, her version of the facts can nonetheless not be relied on for all its fantasized goodness.

The last complaint, that of Mrs. Carlotte Essling, is directed against "her husband, Professor Augustus Essling, the philosopher and historian" (*FFD*, 166), another victim of Gallant's raillery. His "lifelong examination of the philosopher Nicolas de Malebranche" requires the presence of a person, "preferably female, on whom [he] can depend absolutely, who will never betray [him] even in her thoughts" (166). Amusingly, this academic works on similar aspects of Malebranche's work (materialism and money) or on aspects all starting with the same letter (materialism, mysticism, money, and mortality). Funnily, his philosophical research does not reconcile him with death, and he is seen pursuing his wife's ghost, not Malebranche's, to get a message *de l'au-delà,* afraid as he is of dying, hence her complaint. She resents his insistence to call her an angel on the basis of imprecision; the student tells her teacher off for stylistic looseness! In fact, what she perceives as the stupidity of angels bothers her, as though she were intelligent. Yet in her refusal of an escapade with the vegetable wholesale dealer, she failed to call on the easiest excuse, her devotion to her husband and children. Now, to prevent her husband from pursuing her with her good life, she suggests threatening him, the very negation of the exemplary life she led. No one can be trusted.

Gallant's ironic perspective might well result from her experience of culture and language, based on diversity and heterogeneousness. Having been torn from her natural Anglo-Saxon Protestant background at the age of four to be raised in a French Catholic convent school and subsequently sent to numerous different schools according to the whims and the itinerant *trajet* of her mother, Gallant has a composite vision of life. Looking at once through two lenses (French and British), she cannot have one, and only one, view of things. Forever an exile on home ground, she perceives culture and language as double; rooted in her

upbringing, this understanding of their duality has resulted in disengagement, in a lightness of perception, making her look at things and
people from a dispassionate, and therefore ironic, angle. Her having
uprooted herself again at a later stage contributed to further estrangement, every new situation increasing the number of lenses through
which she looks at people. Since she mingles with both locals and exiles
wherever she lives, the perspective is constantly reduplicated. As a consequence, hers is "an irony that understands limitations and contradictions as often inevitable, and even necessary—and therefore eludes the
negative connotations usually evoked by the term" (Siemerling, 132).
This she emphasizes, in a way, by confiding that irony is "just a way of
looking at things . . . [My tone] is not laid on. It is the way I am, probably" (iHancock, 52). The conflicting juxtaposition of affirmation and
hypothesis in the last sentence brilliantly exemplifies one of the manners
in which the Gallantian tension between certainty and uncertainty,
intention and actualization, utterance and silence manifests itself.

Inherent in Gallant's character, irony is one of the most-discussed
devices in her work. Although the earlier critiques do not dwell on irony
as a predominant trope of reading, they already refer to it as "perhaps the
most important technical element in any Gallant novel" (Godard, 73)—
or story, one should add.[3] One of her latest critics, Barbara Godard,
rightly asserts that "at the centre of [Gallant's] literary concerns from her
earliest writing has been a preoccupation with the tension between
appearance and reality."[4] In addition, "indirection and allusion—two
major elements in Gallant's writing—work out their own ironic patterns
of revelation, sometimes counterpointing, sometimes heightening the
irony that undermines assertions by recasting them as merely apparent
certainties" (Besner 1988, 4).[5] Irony, Siemerling adds, is also "linked to
Gallant's view of the possibilities and impossibilities of human perception
of the self and others, and to the role of memory in this process"
(135 –36).[6] Put differently, "her fiction pronounces no universal truths—
it works by ironic indirection, by oblique angles of vision, and by the presentation of images in clouded mirrors" (Kulyk Keefer 1989, 21). This
statement, like the preceding ones, presupposes the readers' ability to
decipher. As with many of the techniques discussed before, Gallant's
ironic touch affects the reception of her stories, forcing the readers' active
participation to decode the dissociated layers of the text.

In keeping with her critical outlook, Gallant's style is certainly not
devoid of sarcasm. In *From the Fifteenth District,* she often makes fun of
the ludicrous features of an age or country or derides some ridiculous

trait in her characters.[7] In "Potter," for instance, she ridicules the self-centeredness and lack of perspective of Laurie Bennett, Piotr's Canadian lover: "Her idea of history began with the Vietnam war; Genesis was her own Canadian childhood. . . . He called his beloved 'Lah-ow-rie,' which made her laugh. She could not pronounce 'Piotr' and never tried; she said Peter, Prater, Potter, and Otter, and he answered to all" (*FFD,* 169). The initial parallel makes the readers smile at Laurie's intellectual limitations and inaccurate outlook on history. Her "confident unawareness of a contrasting appearance and reality" amuses the readers who know more about history than she does.[8] Taken together, the next two sentences make fun of her narrow-mindedness. On the one hand, her reaction to Piotr's mispronouncing her name shows her inability to understand that others might have differing cultural standards. On the other, she does not seem to fathom her own incompetence, since her problematic pronunciation of Piotr's name is presented from the point of view of a detached, scornful observer, alluding to Piotr's generous acceptance of all the misnomers.

In the face of this "ironic situation" (Muecke 1970, 37), the readers feel both amused and superior, for Piotr's acceptance implies an imposed change of identity. Indeed, the misnomers have a symbolic meaning of which Laurie is certainly unaware, which adds another layer of irony. By calling him Potter, Laurie alludes to the master of matter, to whose hands she pretends to entrust her life.[9] Funnily enough, the name suits him perfectly, as toward the end of the story, he realizes that his love for Laurie was only his creation, that he had created an image of Laurie with which he had fallen in love. As she too eventually understands that she cannot live without him, the name suits Piotr doubly.

The same holds true for his animal nickname, Otter. Once caught, the North American trickster "pleads not to be thrown into the water and drowned and then, being thrown in, swims away laughing."[10] An emotional destitute when he understands that Laurie is unfaithful to him, Piotr decides to write about their story, producing a "long wail, . . . a babbling complaint" (*FFD,* 201) that encourages his suffering from "bachelor's ailment" (198). Nevertheless, like the otter "who swims away laughing," he eventually sees the true nature of their relationship, which, in spite of his initial rejection of it, helps him keep aloof and contemplate his departure.

The change from Piotr to Peter involves no semantic alteration but shifts the identity from Polish to English. Like many monolinguals who have a liking for such shifts, Laurie is unaware of the personality split

they bring about. The change gives a previous passage further significance: "[H]e had long considered himself to be bankrupt—of belief, of
love, of licence to choose. Here in Paris he was shackled, held tied to a
visa, then to the system of mysterious favors on which his Polish passport depended" (*FFD*, 169). The passage reveals how, on account of his
Polish identity, Piotr depends on others, how much he lacks emotional
and physical independence. But because he acquires an anglicized first
name, he eventually changes and learns from Laurie the ability to
"[spend] a legacy of careless freedom with . . . abandon" (169). This
allows him, toward the end of the story, to see their relationship in its
true perspective. He somehow betrays her trust in the image she has of
him, calling to mind his homonym, the leader of the Apostles.

As to the last nickname, Prater, it reveals more about Laurie than
about Piotr. The one who forever talks excessively or pointlessly is Laurie, not Piotr. A poet and a university lecturer, Piotr nevertheless occasionally makes statements detrimental to his interests, when interro-
gated by the Polish police about his translation of a mad German poet
(*FFD*, 183) or when responding to social chitchat at a dinner party in
Paris (191). As he misunderstands the rules of the game, he cannot
anticipate the consequence of his words and becomes a prater rather
than an intelligent conversationalist.

In a comment on Laurie, the narrator highlights how unfair she can
be, stating as its cause the very source of irony: "If she took some forms
of injustice for granted, it was because she did not know they were
unjust" (*FFD*, 169–70). Typical of irony, her unawareness leads to hilarious situations: "Piotr was supposed to know *by instinct* every shade of
difference between Victoria, British Columbia, and Charlottetown,
Prince Edward Island, whereas he, poor Potter, came out of a cloudy
Eastern plain bereft of roads, schools, buses, elevators, perhaps even
frontier—this because she could not have found Warsaw on a map"
(170). Not only is her assumption laughable, for it implies knowledge
prior to any actual experience, but her own incapacity to stand the test
is mocked, the more so as the image she has of Poland reminds one of
the North American ignoramus who thinks that all places unknown to
him or her are necessarily the dwelling place of savages. Her lack of
basic intelligence, recorded in her incompetent reading of maps, is, of
course, ridiculed.

Gallant's mockery does not stop there. She goes on describing Laurie's conversational achievements, highlighting her basic ignorance.
When she first meets Piotr, she tells him, "If Solzhenitsyn were to walk

in here, I'd get right down on my knees and thank him" (*FFD,* 173). Surprised, Piotr asks her, "What for?" "I don't know," she answers. "I thought you might. . . . I was just trying to show you I sympathized" (173). Having no sense of ridicule, she makes such nonsensical comments "to please; it [is] [her] way of paying a compliment to someone she consider[s] clever" (176). Time and again, she exposes her ignorance, accounted for by her lack of "memory, except for her schooldays" (175). Caustically, the narrator compares her to "a blackboard wiped clean every week or so" (175).

To no one's surprise, Laurie's ignorance is matched by her stupidity: "It seemed incredible that a man of his education knew nothing about Bishop Purse School or its famous headmistress, Miss Ellen Jones. Bishop, whatever its advantages, had not darkened Laurie's sunny intelligence with anything like geography, history, or simple arithmetic. She had the handwriting of a small boy and could not spell her own language. For a time Piotr treasured a letter in which he was described as 'a really sensative [*sic*] person,' and Laurie herself as 'mixed-up in some ways but on the whole pretty chearfull [*sic*]' " (170). The combined voices that describe Laurie contribute to the derisive quality of the passage. At first, Laurie's voice is heard within the discourse of the narrator, effecting a clash of views: Laurie's incredulity at Piotr's ignorance is pitted against the narrator's enlightened recognition of its normality. The next two sentences render facts dispassionately, silencing Laurie's voice and exposing both Laurie and Piotr to ridicule. Her stupidity and lack of basic knowledge, conveyed obliquely, match her childlike handwriting and atrocious spelling; as she is made fun of, so is Piotr because, though well educated, he paradoxically cherishes her the more for her intellectual shortcomings, as if they guaranteed her innocence.

If Gallant subjects Laurie to stinging ridicule, she turns to Piotr with gentle irony.[11] Although she makes fun of his weaknesses, she does not pierce her description of him with sneering irony. She rather conveys through forgiving irony her understanding of the deprivation ruining his life. She makes the readers grasp why Piotr loves such a shallow being as Laurie, why her carelessness attracts him; the product of her education, her typical carelessness seduces him beyond comprehension because it opens up new horizons. In sharp contrast to the binding and alienating realities inherent in the Communist system, Laurie's neutral and privileged Canadian experience turns her into an easygoing being making no demands on Piotr, who in turn cherishes her unconditionally. Blinded with infatuation, Piotr does not decode Laurie's messages properly and fails to realize that all the postcards she sends him to Poland are written on trips she makes with another man.

Gallant maintains Piotr as the target of her charitable irony till the end. Finally managing to get back to Paris, he enjoys a blissful, though short-lived, reunion; on account of his sudden discovery of her impending trip to Venice with an unnamed friend, his passion turns into grief and jealousy strong enough to disconnect him from his own self: "His work, his childhood, his imprisonment, his marriage, his still mysterious death were rolled in a compact ball, spinning along the grass, away from whatever was left from him" (FFD, 186). His newly acquired knowledge makes him see, like Gallant, "the element of farce in every iniquity" (186), for he realizes his gift of Polish contraceptives was foolish. He suffers from all sorts of ailments—psychosomatic manifestations of his distress as ironically pointed out by a pushy admirer of his—until the relationship is restored with Laurie's pitiful return. But Piotr has to leave the country prematurely the day after Laurie returns to him, situational irony being at hand. His departure results from his French exchange's expulsion from Poland after "finding her students materialistic and bourgeois . . . [and trying] to fire them with revolutionary ideals" (205).[12] This farcical reversal of expectation is matched by another, Piotr's invention that after all he feels only tenderness for Laurie, an invention prompted by Laurie's need to be loved, which would trap him. The final sentences of the story pit his voice against the omniscient narrator's, creating a comic alternation of the truthful and the invented version behind Piotr's refusal to respond to Laurie's need: "An immense weight of blame crushed him, flattened him, and by so doing cleansed and absolved him. I was incapable of any more feeling than this. I never felt more than kindness. There was nothing in it from the beginning. It was only tenderness after all" (FFD, 212).

Gallant pokes fun at other characters in "Potter." Marek, Piotr's Polish émigré friend with strategic connections, has such a marginal position in Parisian society that each time he opens doors for Piotr, Marek fears that Piotr might blunder thereby enforcing exclusion for both from circles not usually open to foreigners. Before the exclusive dinner party given by a famous French hostess, Marek briefs Piotr with a comic sense of urgency: "Piotr was not to contradict anything, even if he knew it to be inaccurate; above all, he was not to imagine that anything said to him was ever meant to be funny" (FFD, 190). The content of the advice, of course, leaves no doubt as to the underlying sarcastic intention. Both Marek and the French elite are smiled at, the one for his desperate clinging to the other's favors that help him climb the social ladder, the other for not accepting other people's conflicting views. Similarly, Gallant offers an amusing picture of the doctor with whom Piotr stays; unhappily married to a man who spends his Sundays with his mistress and illegitimate daughter, the doctor hints at her loneliness, hoping to evoke a similar response from Piotr and to establish good grounds for a love affair. Hers is the predatory approach, and Gallant holds it in derision.

In "His Mother," Gallant directs her irony at the mother of an émigré and the circle of émigrés' mothers to which she belongs. Her attitude even before her son's departure is laughed at explicitly; Gallant obviously makes fun of the hidden discourse underlying most parent-child conversation by opposing the said and the unsaid:

> He was a stone out of a stony generation. Talking to him was like lifting a stone out of water. He never resisted, but if you let go for even a second he sank and came to rest on a dark sea floor. . . . How could she give up? She loved him. She felt shamed because it had not been in her to control armies, history, his stony watery world. From the moment he appeared in the kitchen doorway, passive, vacant, starting to live again only because this was morning, she began all over: "Don't you feel well?" "Are you all right?" "Why can't you smile?"—though the loudest sentence was in silence: Ask me how I am. (*FFD*, 214)

Built around the two middle, particularly short, sentences with their cry of love, the longer sentences contextually stress the doubtful truthfulness of the mother's feelings, particularly because of the initial metaphor and its elaboration. Their insincerity is confirmed by the final chopped-up sentence with the string of questions that explicitly conceal one statement, begging for attention; the shorter section of the final balanced sentence after the questions supposed to mark genuine interest forcefully points to the woman's self-centeredness.

Further contextual indices mark Gallant's ironic intentions: "After he left Budapest (got his first passport, flew to Glasgow, never came back) she became another sort of a person, an émigré's mother. She shed the last of her unimportant lovers and with the money her son was soon able to send she bought a white blouse, combs that would pin her hair away from her face, and a blue kimono. She remembered long, tender conversations they had had together, and she got up early in the morning to see if a letter had come from him and then to write one of her own describing everything she thought and did" (*FFD*, 214). The short triadic sentence in parentheses marks a series of facts seen as the cause for her to change costumes and take a different part in the societal play—that of an émigré's mother—with falsified memories attached.[13] The status thus acquired in itself justifies the drastic change from slovenly to dignified appearance, from attached to proudly single, that might have agreed with the son before his departure.

Gallant goes on describing the hilarious ranking system among the émigrés' mothers: "The aristocrats were those whose children had never left Europe; the poorest of the poor were not likely ever to see their sons again, for they had gone to Chile and South Africa. Switzerland was superior to California. A city earned more points than a town. There was no mistaking her precedence here; she was a duchess" (*FFD,* 215). Entertaining, the whole system of appraisal reduces emotions to naught. The same happens with letters and presents; according to their nature, they confer the receiver credentials of varying importance. A mother of a silent émigré, therefore, enjoys no status whatsoever; her son "might as well be dead" (216). Paradoxically, in spite of her credentials, the title character realizes she is not better off; although she does not think of hers as dead, a corrective statement—"but as a coin that had dropped unheard, had rolled crazily, lay still" (216) implies that for all intents and purposes "he might as well be dead."

Her own letters with descriptions of her dreams or of the town evidence the distance that separates her from her son. Her dreams resurrecting dead people echo the reality of her life, for though alive, her son is caught "between the dead and the living, a voice on the telephone, an affectionate letter full of English words, a coin rolled and lying somewhere in secret" (*FFD,* 223); her sadness, if not bitterness, makes her accumulate metaphors reflecting the absence of her son, indeed his inanimate presence. Cynical, she knows she is only "the revered and respected mother of a generous, an attentive, a camouflaged stranger" (223); initial and final qualifiers evidence an unwanted reality—she is an image, a mother on paper, not in actual fact. The descriptions of the town finish with a description of the émigrés' mothers' haunt and an anguished question asked as if the son would come to visit—"will you know me? I was your mother" (214). Contrasting the future and the past, the question and statement thereafter obliquely express her present anguished need of recognition and aimlessness owing to her lost role in her son's life.

Even in stories that are compassionate, some irony slips in, for Gallant confides to Barbara Gabriel that she "can't imagine writing anything that doesn't have humor. Every situation has an element of farce" (iGabriel, 24). Take "The Latehomecomer," a story originally planned for inclusion in *The Pegnitz Junction,* which discloses the ultimate annihilation of a young German man's identity through mingled references to his past, present, and future. The story's very opening alludes to the ironies of life: "When I came back to Berlin out of captivity in the spring of 1950, I discovered I had a stepfather" (*FFD*, 117). While he was in France, he received letters from his mother, who never bothered mentioning her second marriage. Hoping to meet Frau Bestermann, Thomas Bestermann is confronted with Frau Toeppler, a woman he mistakes for her mother. She has grown older and has lost some front teeth, so that she speaks with her hand cupped in front of her mouth, a fact repeated with insistence to make fun of her self-consciousness. Funny too, the description of the stepfather ridicules his morbid need to hold the floor: "His mouth hung open much of the time, as though he had trouble breathing through his nose, but it was only because he was a chronic talker, always ready to bite down on a word" (118). Likewise, when others have the miraculous chance to open their mouths, he punctuates their words with "Ah, yes, yes" (117), and his stepson soon makes fun of him (124). Sarcasm is employed in the comment about his Uncle Gerhard: "[I]t had taken him four years to become officially and legally de-Nazified, and now, 'as white as a white lilac,' according to my mother, he had no opinions about anything and lived only for his rabbits" (123), afraid of being spotted. While evoking a complex context of exchange, the statement points to contradictions; under threat, the opinionated suddenly loses the opinions that allowed him to threaten others—a pungent example of the hunted hunter.

In other stories, Gallant also playfully calls on irony to add different levels of meaning.[14] "The Four Seasons," for instance, deals with the exploitation of a young Italian servant girl by a family of English expatriates, the Unwins, placed in the context of national and societal degradation. Moved by the story the girl-turned-woman told her, Gallant once more obliquely mocks laughable traits, particularly those revealing the fascist potential of the characters. An obvious example, the Unwins' approval of the "order and peace" (*FFD*, 24) that Mussolini has brought to the country parallels their own exploitative behavior—manifest in their treatment of their servant. Subversive irony records their despicable attitude on learning who in the colony has Jewish origins and what fate awaits them: "The Unwins were proud that this had not taken place in their country—at least not since the Middle Ages—but it might not be desirable if all these good people [the Jews in the colony] were to go to England now" (26). Rather than questioning the grounds for this totalitarian expulsion, and perhaps preventing it or at least expressing concern, the Unwins think of their own advantage. Typical of their self-ish conservatism but in stark contrast with their philosophical views, they exert an insidious influence upon the church; though agnostic, and presumably indifferent to religious matters, they reject any suggestion of change in the way the church is run, even the most practical ones such as fixing the church clock for it to keep the time. Convinced that Mussolini wishes peace, the Unwins do not believe that he has ordered the deportation of Jews and ironically ascribe the change to the last per-son who could initiate such plight, namely the priest, for he has "preached about tolerance once too often. It [has] worked the Italians up" (27). The incongruous juxtaposition of the two statements, of course, ridicules their view and their defense of a fascist leader.

Further signs of the fascist potential can be found in the local popula-tion. Some, like the Italian chauffeur of the Marchesa, the Unwins' American neighbor, stick to the expatriates' hierarchical system of evalu-ation: having acquired a new status through his employment, the chauf-feur refuses to greet Carmela until he realizes that she too works for a family of the colony. Others exploit the distressful situation in which the Jews find themselves. Carmela's brother Lucio and his boss, for instance, make money by smuggling Jews out of Italy. Business as usual.

Several comic scenes alert the readers to Carmela's innocence. Not well versed in the English language, Carmela misinterprets the meaning of Mrs. Unwin's trivial comments, believing them "to have a malignant intent she [cannot] yet perceive" (*FFD*, 5) or feeling accused (6, 7). Like-wise, when Mrs. Unwin makes flower arrangements, the narrative voice echoes her naive perception of "the white roses she was stabbing onto something cruel and spiked" (6). Credulous, Carmela believes the neigh-bor's chauffeur's stories about the ghost of the Unwins' uncle wandering in the garden (9) and also, most likely, the reports "that vegetables grown in Italy [give] one typhoid fever" (7). Her keeping the iron tablets the doctor gives her against anemia also partakes of a naive mis-trust and a need to keep the bottle as a "personal belonging" (12). A tragicomic scene happens when she sees Dr. Chaffee in a group of refugees taken to the frontier: feeling guilty over the untouched tablets, she looks ashamed; mistaken by her look, the doctor "thinks that her reaction is born out of shame at her guilt and complicity in his deporta-tion, and so pardons her in a greeting that also, perhaps, suggests his dim recognition that they are each in their way victims of forces beyond their control" (Besner 1988, 103).

Unbeknownst to the members of the family, Carmela learns English, becoming capable of decoding signs she is not meant to perceive, of understanding the gist of their conversations, of reading the letters they leave behind. Similarly, her exposure to the colony allows her to perceive the expatriates' hierarchical system of evaluation; in particular, her awareness results from her own exposure to the rich neighbor's chauffeur's refusal to greet her until he realizes she too works for a family of the colony. The final, doubly comic scene in this distressing account of exploitation on a personal and a national level occurs over an ice cream Carmela eats just before being sent home. Engrossed in her ice cream, she witnesses the confidences of the priest and Mr. Unwin over their life disappointments. Misunderstanding the priest's vague question asked to make a diversion in Mr. Unwin's interminable list of grievances, Carmela confesses she has "just eaten her way into heaven," upon which the priest, mistaken too, says, "then I haven't failed completely" (*FFD*, 34). The story paradoxically ends with two positive images, a tower of cream, the memory of Carmela's one and only treat in four seasons of exploitation, and the blessing of the doctor, a memory retained from a previous misunderstanding. By comparison with these two powerful images, Carmela's exploitation and the final conversation exposing Mr. Unwin's selfish outlook retreat to the far past, ironically emphasizing corrective memory.

While revisiting the past, Gallant exploits reflexive repetitions to add layers of meaning to her fiction. In "Baum, Gabriel, 1935 –( )," both Gabriel and his friend Dieter Pohl get roles in films about the Occupation, respectively as Jewish victim and German soldier as befits their origins.[15] Both mediocre actors, they nonetheless ironically consider each film as an advancement in their careers, as if going up in rank in a film compared with real-life promotion; whereas "Dieter had begun as a private, had been promoted to lieutenant, and expected to be a captain soon" (*FFD,* 147), and becomes a colonel at a later stage, "Gabriel had no equivalent staircase to climb; who ever has heard of a victim's being promoted?" (150). A comic comparison of the film industry in two different decades throws light on the futility of it all: in the early sixties, though the actors "played deportation the way they had seen it in films" or "surrendered according to film tradition" (157), they could draw on the firsthand accounts of their parents because the films starred only "real Frenchmen, real Germans, authentic Jews"; in the late seventies, "even if one could assemble a true cast of players, they would be trying to imitate their grandfathers. They were at one remove too many. There was no assurance that a real German, a real Frenchman would be any more plausible than a Turk" (157). Considering the changes, Dieter wonders "if Gabriel might not care to bridge this stage of his Occupation career by becoming a surrendering officer, seen in the last episode instead of vanishing after the first" (154), turning the seventh art into a pragmatic affair no longer concerned with verisimilitude, let alone with the creation of masterpieces.

By playfully alluding to literary works and reflecting them in her writing, Gallant often reinforces the ironic treatment of character, event, or context.[16] In "The Moslem Wife," for instance, the opening paragraph sets the mood of the story by referring to "the house where Katherine Mansfield ... was writing 'The Daughters of the Late Colonel' " (FFD, 36), a story in which two sisters, after having been under the yoke of their late father, cannot enjoy their new independence.[17] Enclosed in the feminine sphere created by men, they cannot free themselves from the constraints imposed by the male-dominated world. The reference takes its full significance when the narrative ironically highlights that Netta Asher follows their model, albeit in a modern fashion, for she "lives as a 'Moslem wife' in Jack's shadow and in the shadow of the late Mr. Asher" (Besner 1988, 107). In What Is to Be Done? Gallant appropriates the title of Lenin's 1902 pamphlet and also parodies his ideas.[18] While his text advocates the creation of a revolutionary party to lead the working class toward communism and fight against bourgeois inclinations, her play mocks the petit bourgeois concerns of a revolutionary cell in Montreal in the 1940s. Added irony lies in the presence of women in the revolutionary cell, totally absent in Lenin's text, but reminiscent of Nikolai Gavrilovich Chernyshevsky's 1848 novel of the same title, which focuses on the "new woman" with a professional and political commitment.[19] Set against the context of World War II, Gallant's play parodies its Russian homonyms by portraying women who talk of independence while the men are at war but retreat to the old order when they return. Adding another reflexive dimension that contributes to the complexity of meaning, Gallant pokes fun at her own political engagement in wartime Montreal as an "intensely left-wing, political romantic" (iHancock, 39).

Gallant's playfulness also guides her subversive choice of titles. Equivocal, most of her titles mislead the readers, who can assign a correct meaning to a title only upon reaching the end of the narrative.

Mired in the contrast between the real and the expected content, the double—unstable—narrative enforces reflection. With its echo of journalistic usage, the title of "From the Fifteenth District" deceitfully leads the readers to imagine that the story will treat them to major news items; instead it pokes fun at their first impression as it embarks on a magic realist description of contention between ghosts and the living. Seen in the light of its title story, the collection acquires a new dimension; by revisiting the past in the light of a magic realist framework, the stories appear unreal, as if to force the readers to interrogate "the habits of mind inscribed by the past," to question the baser instincts of human beings. The title of "The Remission" also misleads the readers by evoking a welcome period of respite that eventually turns out to be torturous for all concerned. Likewise, the title of "His Mother" calls to mind dependent sons; yet the narrative discloses a mother dependent on her son, whose independence has paradoxically given her life meaning, no matter how shallow. In a similar fashion, titular conventions affect the firsthand reception of "Baum, Gabriel, 1935 –( )." Akin to entries in biographical dictionaries, the title seems to announce the profile of a renowned figure, yet the narrative portrays a mediocre actor who fails to act on the direction of his life. As to "The Four Seasons," the title echoes Vivaldi's popular descriptive concerti.[20] But although Gallant's story, like Vivaldi's music, is built on the temporal frame of the seasons' passing and recurrent motifs, the story deals with five, not four seasons. The exact passage of time, or seasons, is meaningless, for extratextual and intratextual information reveals that apart from the first three months, Carmela is paid in prewar currency after the war.[21] The four seasons would then refer to her unpaid employment. Rather than conveying the beauty of baroque music, the title reflects the fascist tendencies of all walks of life.

From the Fifteenth District does not stand out as an exception in Gallant's oeuvre. All her short stories and novellas present in semiserious tone the aberrations of the system in which, or by which, her characters live. Even stories that are heavily autobiographical, such as the Linnet Muir sequence, for instance, have ironic undertones revealing her awareness of the discrepancy between the real and the ideal, pointing to "the contrast of 'appearance' and 'reality.' "[22] The analysis of *The Other Paris* has emphasized the characters' need to idealize reality and revealed the discrepancy between the views of one set of characters and another. The discussion of the split levels of narration in "The Pegnitz Junction" and "The Old Friends" has shown how powerful the ironic use of intertextual and contextual references can be. In the stories rewriting history, human indifference, segregation, and disconnectedness emerge from the derisive treatment of the characters and their actions as well as from the constant references to history and its representation. As Blodgett notes, "it is as though the unfolding of her text were a game of I Ching played with both the self and history, each design projecting a certain significance only to be immediately modified by the next, everything in order and everything changing simultaneously at random."[23] The narratives are given an ironic twist by the hints to previous realities that the characters, consciously or unconsciously, erase from their memory, in their search for a truth that will set their minds at rest.[24] Gallant accommodates the present by reinscribing the past in such a way as to satisfy the needs of the characters; since the latter cannot cope with the traditional versions of the past, they are shown reinventing it. Contextuality adds a corrective subtext, no doubt ironic in impact, as it reveals the fundamentally subjective perception of the past, virtually made up from start to finish, to assuage the characters' feelings of guilt.

Such a depressing certainty can only be counteracted by a measure of irony that combines contradictory concepts. Gallant does this so adroitly that "people sometimes take seriously things [she means] as a joke" (iHancock, 52). I would argue that her ironic prowess essentially results from the dispassionate grounding of her stories in culture. Take her Canadian, French, and German stories, or her stories about British exiles on the Riviera in From the Fifteenth District, to mention but a few— they all bear on the essence of the characters' culture. Only the open-minded insider can decipher the double layers of meaning; the obtuse insider or the outsider is likely to take every word at its face value and miss the irony that "[engages] its critique from the inside of that which it contests" (Hutcheon 1992a, 13). Gallant indeed describes a world she knows well, a world of which she has firsthand experience or on which she has multiple perspectives. Her penetrating gaze fixes the ways in which people function within a system that is originally theirs (as in the stories featuring Canadians at home, and in the German and Parisian stories) or inherited by choice (as in the stories featuring Canadians and Americans abroad, exiles on the Riviera, expatriates in Paris). Never does she openly take sides; rather, she remains aloof, evaluating the extent of human aberration. Thus she describes from a detached perspective, supposedly neutrally, characteristics that turn out to be rather ludicrous; hers is "a complex narrative mode involving both implication in the story and critical distance from it" (LaCapra 1987, 174).

Endowed with the gift of irony, Gallant achieves a special effect when she makes fun, either teasingly or piercingly, of her characters, their views and situations. An expert in the art of polyphony, Gallant uses this device to pit one voice against another and also to undermine a situation while distancing herself from it. In this way, she can easily portray breaks of continuity in history, thereby creating tension: in her work, neither continuity nor stability exists, and one perspective never predominates. Her irony thus "deconstructs one discourse . . . as it constructs another," offering the possibility of putting two levels of meaning together and, as a consequence, causing split levels of discourse.[25] Gallant's stories could be compared to a picture and its negative. Shown both at once, the readers see that what is white on the one is black on the other, and vice versa. Owing to the superimposition, they perceive both the positive and the negative aspects of anything, sensing the ironic fusion of opposites. Such perspective is destabilizing; it offers no security. Everyone is constantly exposed to the ironic pen, offering at once a usually harmless surface reading and a deeper, often critical, reading. Grounded in two levels, the text never allows the readers to gain a firm footing; certainties are forever beyond their grasp. In this respect, Gallant's outlook is definitely postmodern, for as Hutcheon argues, "postmodern irony is suspicious of any . . . claim to transcendence, universality and power" (Hutcheon 1992b, 35); it never accepts facile resolutions, never takes things at their face value.

Chapter Six

Spatial Patterns of Displacement: *Home Truths*

Home Truths, winner of the Governor General's Award for 1982, best exemplifies Gallant's particular concern with the evocation of atmosphere. Usually giving scarce, but precise, descriptions of specific environmental aspects, Gallant captures more than ever the ambience of places in *Home Truths,* investing it with a clear function in the action. Rather than clinically describing every item of the locale as Balzac does with the boarding house of Madame Vauquer in *Le Père Goriot,* for instance, Gallant chooses to mention those specific details that enhance the impact of the locale's atmosphere.[1] Space indeed invades the action in the stories about Canadians at home or abroad, and more particularly in the Linnet Muir sequence, probably because it is the sublimated product of memory.[2]

Gallant's careful consideration of space is not unusual. However far literary history goes back, space has been an intrinsic element of fiction. In Genesis, for instance, the description of the landscape created evidences this tendency: "In the beginning, God created the sky and the earth, and the earth was without form, and void, and darkness *was* upon the face of the deep" (Gen. 1:1–2). By paying attention to the delineation of the setting in which the fictional characters move about, the anonymous author of these lines evokes a distinct atmosphere. To give another example, the Romantics color descriptive passages with purely subjective perceptions, so that consciousness, exalted by an almost mystical attraction for nature, finds its reflection in natural forces: the storm raging in the landscape, for instance, becomes a spatial correlative for the emotional turmoil of the character involved. The previous examples reveal how important a role space plays in the creation of atmosphere in fiction, as the attitudes of the narrator and the characters find an echo in the physical background of the fictional world with, or in, which they are involved. In addition, space intrinsically permeates the very language writers use to communicate. Indeed, in an attempt to escape the absurdity of life, humankind tries to impose order on it by determining linguistically the position of objects and beings.[3] As a result, "today's vocabulary allocates, at all levels of thought, a considerable place to *Space*" (Matoré, 13; translation mine). Language abounds in adverbs, prepositions, adjectives, verbs, deictics, and other parts of speech that impart spatial realities.[4] Spatial language, of course, largely rests on individual linguistic performance, varying in intensity according to individual perceptiveness, itself dependent on circumstances and temperament, and on psychological or ideological values attributed to spatial terms.[5]

In the Linnet Muir sequence, Gallant exploits spatial language to project the emotions and feelings of the protagonist. Combined with other stylistic devices, the spatial polarities on which her images call expose with precision local cultural phenomena: laying out the fictional landscape of the Linnet Muir stories amounts to determining the social, religious, and cultural limitations imposed on all the characters. This reality emerges from the narrator's recollections of her life in Montreal as a child and then as a late teenager, that is, in the 1920s and 1940s.[6] Linnet, the narrator-protagonist of the stories and a fictionalized projection of Gallant at the time (*HT,* xxii), gives a rather grim picture of her compatriots and their outlook on life, as if time had not erased the memory of the frustrations she (and thus Gallant too) experienced in her youth. Significantly, Linnet perceives the space in which the characters move about as shrunken, a concomitant of the local cultural, social, and religious oppressiveness; definitely not overwhelmed by nostalgia, Gallant exploits spatially laden language to throw an ironic light on those restrictions.

In the representation of the city, which is "not so much . . . a physical location as a psychological state," the spatial references are colored with numerous undertones.[7] Locations, if need be, are (re)constructed to fit emotions. For instance, while in New York, Linnet is longing for a heavily distorted Montreal:

> My memory of Montreal took shape while I was there [1]. It was not a jumble of rooms . . . but the faithful record of the true survivor [2]. I retained, I rebuilt a superior civilization [3]. In that drowned world, Sherbrooke Street seemed to be glittering and white [4]; the vision of a house upon that street was so painful that I was obliged to banish it from the memorial [5]. The small hot rooms of a summer cottage became enormous and cool [6]. If I say that Cleopatra floated down the Chateauguay River, that the Winter Palace was stormed on Sherbrooke Street,

that Trafalgar was fought on Lake St. Louis, I mean it naturally [7]; they
were the natural backgrounds of my exile and fidelity [8]. (*HT,* 223)

Linnet could not describe more clearly how memory works, how its
beautifying process involves spatial changes: "small" becomes "enormous," "hot" becomes "cool," a "drowned world" seems "glittering and
white," and movement renders common places magical.[8] The initial
verb "took shape" even points to spatial invention and spatial memory.
Once actual comparison cannot challenge the remembered object, place,
or person [2], memory embellishes it and even sets out to negate the
existence of "the jumble of rooms" in which the Muirs used to live,
opposing to it the pretended faithfulness of real memory—the memory
generating positive reminiscences. The following simple sentence [3],
with its apposed subjects and verbs implying the process of improving
memory, confirms the modifying impetus, as does the use of the comparative expressing an increase in quality. By comparison with the clarity of perception *du vécu hic et nunc*—that is, of the present experience—
the past becomes a "drowned world" whose haziness alters and modifies
things for the better; by referring to her expanding memory, Linnet
makes Montreal look small. Similarly, the achromatic purity ("glittering
and white") of the recollection [4] imparts Linnet's will to forget the
stronger chromatic, unpleasant, components of her past. Actual evidence of modification [5] follows to back up the argument: houses—
essential components of the urban landscape—are obliterated; yet they
"[bear] the essence of the notion of home," which amounts to bringing a
sheltering and reassuring warmth.[9] She equates her remembrances with
a memorial, with those funeral orations in which defects, weaknesses,
and shortcomings are left unmentioned or are beautified [6]. The long
balanced sentence [7–8] at the end punctuates the earnest yet illusory
perception of the past, as do the initial phrases "seemed to be" and
"became enormous." The first dramatic section [7], with its periodic
structure paralleling three that-clauses of pure geographic fantasy, post-
pones the main idea and stresses its importance: no harm is meant;
imagination is allowed license. The second section [8], a shorter, and
thus more powerful, main clause, restates the first one in objective,
explanatory, and abstract terms and no longer only in spatial visual
images: "exile" and "fidelity" merge to sharpen the nostalgic yearning
for an otherwise disillusioned world.

The sense of space and nature present in nostalgic descriptions marks
the magic quality of Linnet's recollection, its expansion into myth. Glit-

tering colors, magnitude, vegetation—these transform remembrances for the better: "Montreal, in memory, was a leafy citadel where I knew every tree. . . . Sherbrooke Street had been the dream street, pure white. . . . It was a moat I was not allowed to cross alone; it was lined with gigantic spreading trees through which light fell like a rain of coins" (*HT,* 235). The actual counterpart, it appears from the next quotation, lacks grandeur, indeed might as well not exist:

> One day, standing at a corner, waiting for the light to change, I under-stood that the Sherbrooke Street of my exile—my Mecca, my Jerusalem—was . . . *only* this. The limitless green where in a perpetual spring I had been taken to play was the campus of McGill University. A house, whose beauty had brought tears to my sleep . . . was a narrow stone thing with a shop on the ground floor and offices above. . . . Through the bare panes of what might have been the sitting room, with its private window seats, I saw neon striplighting along a ceiling. Reality, as always, was narrow and dull. (*HT,* 235–36)

Linnet exposes the shock of disillusionment by humorously contrasting the sordid reality with the magnificent picture of her memory, equated with mystic places of worship. Boundless expanse in unchanging, propi-tious weather materializes as grounds that the readers soon recognize as bounded and exposed to harsh weather. The magnificent house capable of moving Linnet to extreme emotions turns out to be an unqualifiable building, at the most cramped and unpoetic. Crude artificial lighting replaces warm and comfortable decorations. Only bleakness prevails, as marked by the derogatory adjectives "narrow" and "dull." The accumu-lation of confining terms related to the actual setting serving as a basis for memories is striking. The contrast between the "aesthetically com-fortable" character of her recollections and the spatial discovery that the word *city* means "drab, filthy, flat, or that city blocks could turn into dull squares without mystery" (*HT,* 292) shakes Linnet with dismay, as the cumulative disparaging adjectives emphasize.

The same correction of reality marks Linnet's memory of Dr. Chauchard's house. The only one to grasp her sensitivity and grant her marked favors, Dr. Chauchard is the person closest to her bar an old *bonne:* "The house he came to remained for a long time enormous in my memory, though the few like it still standing—'still living,' I nearly say—are narrow, with thin, steep staircases and close, high-ceilinged rooms" (*HT,* 302). The description of her recollection and of the actual house again shows the selectiveness—and even correctiveness—of memory. This confrontation of remembrance and its object confers fluidity to the perception of culture; the juxtaposition of what is and what might ideally be—the difference between the adult's perception of space and the child's naturally deformed remembrance of it[10]—thus, alternatively evoked, produces the undulating motion of self-inquiry. Significantly, the foregoing quotation also discloses a spatial reality, namely that Montreal's architecture in part illustrates the harsh principles of Presbyterianism. Houses with Scottish characteristics still stand in some areas: "[N]arrow, with thin, steep staircases and close, high-ceilinged rooms [they are] the work of Edinburgh architects and [date] from when Montreal was a Scottish city" (302). Their narrowness and height convey the Knoxian imperative that people should follow the narrow path and look upward "to open [their] eyes unto the heavens" so as to be "delivered from all fear, all torment and all temptation."[11] Because they are given no space to expand either physically or spiritually, they have neither free choice nor freedom to exist.[12]

In "Between Zero and One," the prevalent restrictions on emotional freedom, no doubt perceived by the narrator and protagonist if not by the other characters, are reflected in the topographical details. The decor in which the action—or rather inaction—takes place is described in spatial terms of restrictive psychological impact. Linnet makes revealing comments about the atmosphere at work: "I remember a day of dark spring snowstorms, ourselves reflected on the black windows, the pools of warm light here and there, the green-shaded lamps, the dramatic hiss and gurgle of the radiators that always sounded like the background to some emotional outburst, the sudden slackening at the end of the afternoon when every molecule of oxygen in the room had turned into poison" (*HT,* 240). The protagonist's associative memory has lost none of the irritating sounds, smells, colors, and heat. Rather than offering comfort in contrast to the harsh climate, the interior locale Linnet describes seems to enhance the inclement weather. In spite of occasional patches of shaded light, the pictures evoke a dark, stifling atmosphere punctuated by the infuriating noises of the radiators. These depressing images piled up in the loose sentence echo the characters' frustrations on account of the restraints affecting their meaningless lives.

When—if at all—will an "emotional outburst" liberate Linnet's colleagues? One can hardly imagine their lives without the slow-moving lift, a symbol for the exiguity, smallness, and limitedness of their world: "I climbed to the office in a slow reassuring elevator with iron grille doors, sharing it with inexpressive women and men—clearly the trodden-on. No matter how familiar our faces became, we never spoke. The only sound, apart from the creaking cable, was the gasping and choking of a poor man who had been gassed at the Somme and whose lungs were said to be in shreds. He had an old man's pale eyes and wore a high stiff collar and stared straight before him, like everyone else" (*HT,* 246). Imprisoned in life as in the lift with an iron fence preventing emotions from coming out, the characters follow the path society has designated for them. Linnet makes fun of the normative rules that dictate the slow pace of the flock. Communication between people who have not been formally introduced is impossible. The only person who departs from the norm is the gassed veteran from World War I, but then his is a message of oppression, a cry for emotional and physical freedom. Nevertheless, apart from his gasp for air and his choking, which may be seen as an incapacity rather than as a symptom of oppressive social norms, he conforms as appears from his stiff collar and the blank look on his face. Clearly, real communication cannot exist among citizens abiding by the local inhibitions that religion exacerbates. Whatever they do, they are overcome with their sense of sin, for man is "never able to fulfil the works of the Law in perfection" (Knox 1848, 107), so that they live in the terror of God, in the terror of the "plagues to fall upon [them] in particular for [their] grievous offences" (Knox 1864, 295).[13] Bearing the stamp of imported prewar British behavioral patterns, the characters have typically cool, shy, and repressed attitudes registered in the physical background.

With the subtle collage of random memories from her past life and extratemporal reflections on cultural issues, Linnet evokes a provincial world where emotions, rather than having a positive effect on mores, have to be repressed. As soon as she mentions crossing the border between the United States and Canada, spatial and human barrenness strike the readers: she discovers "a curiously *empty* country, where the faces of people [give] nothing away" (*HT,* 222; emphasis added). It soon appears, from the accumulation of comments in passing, that " 'like' and 'don't like' [are such] heavy emotional statements" (229) that Canadians keep "their reactions, like their lovemaking, *in the dark*" (230; emphasis added). The confinement in the dark of their shameful and unavowed self marks the national repression, predominant in all fields. Questioning her country's ban on spontaneous responses, Linnet eventually discloses the ironic advantages of composure, in a detached voice rather like that of an anthropologist assessing the value of social behavior in some far-off country:

Now, of course there is much to be said on the other side: people who do not display what they feel have practical advantages [1]. They can go away to be killed as if they didn't mind [2]; they can see their sons off to war without a blink [3]. Their upbringing is intended for a crisis [4]. When it comes, they behave themselves [5]. But it is murder in everyday life—truly murder [6]. The dead of heart and spirit litter the landscape [7]. Still, keeping a straight face makes life tolerable under stress [8]. It makes *public life* tolerable—that is all I am saying [9]; because in private people still got drunk, went after each other with bottles and knives . . . [10]. (*HT,* 227–28)

The initial balanced sentence [1] considers the impact of countenance in abstract terms and concedes it a beneficial function. The examples of advantages stressed by sentences [2–3] show the tip of the iceberg: they assert with insistence the importance of the facade and relegate feelings to a dark corner. The next purposefully short simple sentence [4] sets out a theorem that the narrator subsequently proves by reducing it to the absurd [4–8]. By first delaying and preparing the way for the main thought, namely the ability to behave in cold blood, the next periodic sentence alerts the readers to its assumed importance [5].[14] Linnet's statement in sentence [6], nevertheless, brings the reduction to the real crisis: murder. Playing the momentary crisis against murder in everyday life ironically punctuates the ridiculous attachment to apathy. The resulting waste invades the emotional landscape: a purely spatial image [7] involving no motion whatsoever ("litter the landscape") enhances the climactic message.[15] Crucial emotions expressed in terms of motion are therefore not just a characteristic of Linnet's narration; where other narrators spatially reflect feelings—whether manifested or masked—in the midst of action, Linnet discusses them theoretically, allowing abstraction. After establishing the waste in the emotional landscape [7], Linnet praises impassiveness [8] as if to tease the reader somewhat more: it "makes life tolerable under stress."[16] The concession, though, is short-lived [9]: it is immediately corrected and restricted to the italicized public life. And the correction emphasized in the restatement suddenly echoes a different voice. Linnet gets involved and remembers [10] violent—and thus energetic—scenes of private lives, and this recollection annihilates the hypothetical value of restraint and denounces it.[17]

Indeed, the numerous references to behavioral responses interspersed here and there show the negative effect of self-control. Most of the characters are about to lose their sanity from frustration and repression: "[T]he winter tunnels, the sudden darkness that April day, the years he'd had of this long green room, the knowledge that he would die and be buried 'Assistant Chief Engineer Grade II' without having overtaken Chief Engineer McCreery had simply snapped the twig, the frail match-stick in the head that is all we have to keep us sensible" (*HT,* 240). The cumulative spatial descriptions of depressing restrictive impact pave the way for the final metaphor pointing to the precariousness of people's psychological balance. In the case of Linnet's colleagues, their imbalance results from their education and its success in making them "invisible to [themselves]" (243). This spatial quality is reinforced because adults live in a "world of falsehood and evasion" (229) where everything is signifi-cantly "hushed, muffled, disguised" (230).[18] The overwhelming anger resulting from the agelong-inflicted "deprivation of the senses, mortifi-cation of mind and body" (245) is anything but surprising.

"Easily angry, easily offended" (*HT,* 247), married women are espe-cially prone to bitterness. These keep "[yelling]—to husbands, to chil-dren, to dogs, to postmen, to a neighbor's child" (263), an asyndeton reinforcing the harshness and violence of resentment. The epitome of what restriction and lack of opening both privately and professionally do to people is to be found in Mrs. Ireland, one of Linnet's colleagues. Named after the battered wife of England—the normative ruler whose inhibiting repression causes discontent—she is a battered wife, too. Her appearance also partakes of the general restraint: she keeps her hair braided in an attempt to control it, just as she constantly wears a scarf to conceal an aspect of her private life, namely the bruises her husband inflicts on her. In spite of all her degrees, she does not know any better than to explode in wrath at any moment; unapproachable, isolated Mrs. Ireland is an island, too. One can but appreciate the double pun con-tained in her name—an evocation of a fragile psychological and political landscape—and understand the sarcastic criticism of the still pervasive constraining British norms.

Whether it evokes past or present situations, Linnet's recollection of the local people deforms the picture negatively. She repeatedly empha-sizes in spatial terms the emptiness of her compatriots' lives and inciden-tally tries to determine the difference between men and women: "When I was young I thought that men had small lives of their own creation. I could not see why, born enfranchised, without the obstacles and con-straints attendant on women, they set such close limits for themselves and why, once the limits had been reached, they seemed so taken aback. . . . There was a space of life I used to call 'between Zero and One' and then came a long mystery. I supposed that men came up to their wall, their terminal point, quite a long way after One" (*HT,* 238). The images conjured up in this passage evidently reveal what Linnet thinks of the people around her. A posteriori, the vague reference to age intimates that the narrator is considerably removed from her childhood and teens. Indeed, it points to the distance between the time when Linnet, the protagonist, perceives facts and the time when Linnet, the narrator, relates them. From the start, men's lives are shown as exiguous of their own volition. Linnet's incomprehension of such a narrow choice—their "close limits"—is marked by the opposition between men being "born enfranchised" and "the obstacles and constraints attendant on women." Spatial polarities thus immediately allude to the inequality of the sexes as well as to the men's surprise at being limited.

Linnet considers life in terms of space and numbers, but they leave so little scope that it suggests how little she expects from life for anyone, including herself. She cannot decode the "long mystery" after One either for her age or for her sex. And yet, ironically, men do not seem to go beyond One, at least if one considers what the male characters do with their lives: "Why didn't they move, walk, stretch, run? Each of them seemed to inhabit an invisible square; the square was shared with *my* desk, *my* graph, *my* elastic bands. The contents of the square were tested each morning" (*HT,* 246). The initial question and its asyndeton enhance the lack of scope characteristic of men's lives: the succession of negated and noncoordinated verbs of motion reduces their range to virtually nothing. Indeed, the next comment defines their domain as "an invisible square," a most exiguous fortress in which they are locked up. The men carefully check their poor belongings each morning like a king threatened to be overthrown checking his armament in search of protection; not desirous of expanding, they merely protect their territory, indeed define *their space.* The irony, of course, lies in the totally selfish character of the endeavor stressed by the italicized first-person possessive pronoun.[19]

Nevertheless, an opening seems to lead to another secret room, one whose existence is immediately denied for fear of revealing one's feelings: "Sometimes one glimpsed another world, like an extra room ("It was my daughter made me lunch today"—said with a shrug, lest it be taken for boasting) or a wish outdistanced, reduced, shrunken, trailing somewhere in the mind: 'I often thought I wanted . . .' " (*HT,* 246–47). Emotions cannot come to the fore, as obviously reflected in the meaningless content of the reported speech: it simply reveals an insignificant scene in the life of a supposedly free man.[20] Further confirmation of the negative character attributed to emotions appears in the spatial comparison of this other world to "a wish outdistanced, reduced, shrunken, trailing somewhere in the mind": the uncoordinated participles reduce the opening to a microscopic hidden corner of the heart.

If men lead limited lives, women enjoy even less scope.[21] Their opportunities are painfully restricted by the "obstacles and constraints" hampering them. Linnet contrasts the men's spatial freedom with the enclosure her female fellow workers have to bear; theirs is the constricted space "between Zero and One," as marked by the space allocated to them: "A few girls equipped with rackety typewriters and adding machines sat grouped at the far end of the room, separated from the men by a balustrade. I was the first woman ever permitted to work on the men's side of the fence. A pigeon among the cats was how it sometimes felt" (*HT,* 242). The secretaries' remote and nonindividualized location in the room, the physical separation between them and the men, and the use of the word "girls" by a woman who has internalized the men's lack of respect for women all underline the hopelessness of their banishment. The final, strikingly short sentence with the reversed cliché stressing the foray into the animal world appropriately conveys Linnet's feeling of entrapment in a world that does not grant women any rights. Further descriptions of their situation in "the darkest part, away from the window" (255) confirm the minimal respect granted them. Linnet resents the separation and equates it to women being "penned in like sheep" (226) or "parked like third-class immigrants" (255)—two phrases denouncing the spatial constraints imposed on them and proclaiming Linnet's revulsion at their degraded status. She discloses that even outside work, "where women were concerned men were satisfied with *next to nothing.* If every woman was a situation, she was somehow always the same situation, and what was expected from the woman—the situation—was so *limited* it was insulting" (262; emphasis added). Considering the nonexistent respect for women at work, their humiliating reduction to an abstract concept of unchanging nature is anything but surprising.

The variations on the theme "a pigeon among the cats" illustrate "that there are two races, those who tread on people's lives, and the others" (*HT,* 244). Thus Linnet's first appearance at work arouses her male colleagues' resentment against her presence:

And so, in an ambience of doubt, apprehension, foreboding, incipient danger, and plain hostility, for the first time in the history of the office a

girl was allowed to sit with the men. And it was here, at the desk facing
Bertie Knox's, on the only uncomfortable chair in the room, that I felt
for the first time that almost palpable atmosphere of sexual curiosity, sexual resentment, and sexual fear that the presence of a woman can create
where she is not wanted. If part of the resentment vanished when it
became clear that I did not know what I was doing, the feeling that
women were "trouble" never disappeared. (*HT*, 243–44)

In this passage, the succession of periodic sentences increases the weight
of the final main clauses, whose offensiveness echoes the hostile male
discourse. As she sits opposite Bertie Knox, the fictional counterpart of
John Knox, whose teachings established "the divinely ordained superiority of men over women," the spatial confrontation takes on a further
dimension:[22] religion dictates the inferiority of women and justifies male
contempt. The piling up of feelings with overlapping meanings also
makes for a tangible perception of the atmosphere, so much so that the
readers shudder from revolt: the cumulative pinning down of male
antagonism to women reinforces its extent, indeed universalizes it.

Worse still in this antifeminist context, women's discriminatory
shouts sometimes join in. Although battered, Mrs. Ireland does not seek
support from other women; she makes their situation worse:

> "Girl?" [Mrs. Ireland] could never keep her voice down, ever.
> "There'll never be a girl in this office again, if I have a say. Girls make me
> sick, sore, and weary."
> I thought about that for a long time. I had believed it was only
> because of the men that girls were parked like third-class immigrants at
> the far end of the room—the darkest part, away from the windows—
> with the indignity of being watched by Supervisor, whose sole function
> was just that. But there, up on the life raft, stepping on girls' fingers, was
> Mrs. Ireland, too. If that was so, why didn't Mrs. Ireland get along with
> the men, and why did they positively and openly hate her . . . ? (*HT*, 255)

Mrs. Ireland's rejection of "girls" (the commonly masculine derogatory
term for women, which she has internalized) and the double metaphor
("life raft" and "stepping on girls' fingers") enhance the secretaries'
hopeless exclusion from professional recognition. Mrs. Ireland's revulsion, paralleled with male arrogance, only stresses the abominable reality made palpable through the relegation of the women to obscure and
remote areas. The first metaphor, concerning Mrs. Ireland's position "up
on the life raft," spatially proclaims the universality of the age-old dis-

crimination—whether women come first or last. The puzzling question as to why the men do not esteem Mrs. Ireland, their equal in intelligence and education—if not their superior—confirms the inequality, indeed poses its inescapability. The second image, showing Mrs. Ireland fighting for her own survival, just confines all the more the "girls' " scope for individual decision making and professional advancement.

No more welcome than women, children live in a confined atmosphere.[23] Their situation is so undesirable that Linnet sums up her own experiences as those undergone in the "prison of childhood" (*HT,* 225):[24] parents—or rather adults in general—are inflexibly strict with children, as if to punish them for some primeval sin linked with their actual birth:

> Halfway between our two great wars, parents whose early years had been shaped with Edwardian firmness were apt to lend a tone of finality to quite simple remarks: "Because I say so" was the answer to "Why?," and a child's response to "What did I just tell you?" could seldom be anything but "Not to"—not to say, do, touch, remove, go out, argue, reject, eat, pick up, open, shout, appear to sulk, appear to be cross. Dark riddles filled the corners of life because no enlightenment was thought required. Asking questions was "being tiresome," while persistent curiosity got one nowhere, at least nowhere of interest. (*HT,* 282)

Translated in visual images, the detached sociological comment on educational methods stresses the rigid reality of children's lives. No perspective is granted to children; the adults' final retorts allow no opening. Repressive threats and orders mar relations permanently, for children cannot be themselves or move about freely.[25] Any natural instinct has to be curbed: the breathtaking series of juxtaposed prohibited actions highlights the all-embracing ban on spontaneous reactions.[26] Overpowered, children do not even have a little bright corner to hide in: they are brought up in total darkness, with no possible escape or enlightening discovery. Parents' answer to their children's need to know the reason for a decision "seems to speak out of the lights, the stones, the snow; out of the crucial second when inner and outer forces join, and the environment becomes part of the enemy too" (*HT,* 293). Far from abating the children's wretchedness, the spatial analogy and the enmity of outer space exposes their predicament more acutely.

Exiled in the 1920s, children cannot aspire to a better position in the 1940s: "How much has changed? Observe the drift of words descending from adult to child—the fall of personal questions, observations, unnecessary instructions. Before long the listener seems blanketed. He must hear the voice as authority muffled, a hum through snow. The tone has changed—it may be coaxing, even plaintive—but the words have barely altered. They still claim the ancient right-of-way through a young life" (*HT,* 282). Invited to participate in the sociological inquiry, the reader soon discovers that adults still use their hierarchical authority (like God's in paradise) to sentence children to life imprisonment.[27] The apposition of drifting words and its asyndeton render the forcefulness with which adults exert their power; interestingly expressed in terms of space (the "drift of words *descending*" and the *"fall* of questions"), their control announces further cosmic imagery involving heaven and hell.[28] No longer addressed directly, the reader visualizes, indeed physically experiences, the "drift of words" as blanketing. The drowned out voice of authority thus aptly evokes an insignificant change: authoritarian vigor has withdrawn in favor of luring and lament.[29] Linnet further uses an eloquent image to define parental voices: "Being constantly observed and corrected was like having a fly buzzing around one's plate" (284). But adult conversations deal with "shut-in velvet-draped unaired low-voice problems" (293), a spatial image whose palpable quality cannot escape anyone. Clearly excluding children from their world, parents in the 1940s maintain the set rules and message of the 1920s. The content of their discourse remains the same; parental prerogative cannot be done away with—a hint at the universally abusive character of education.

Under the adverse circumstances, children feel miserable. Exemplifying the distinction Gallant makes between journalism, which "recounts as exactly and economically as possible the weather in the street," and fiction, which "brings to life a distillation of all weathers, a climate of the mind" (*SS,* ix), Linnet indirectly reports her own helplessness in the description of the time lapse *entre chien et loup:* "There was one sunken hour on January afternoons, just before the street lamps were lighted, that was the gray of true wretchedness, as if one's heart and stomach had turned into the same dull, cottony stuff as the sky; it was attached to a feeling of loss, of helpless sadness, unknown to children in other latitudes" (*HT,* 311). Embedded in the distressing atmosphere of winter twilight, children's despair becomes an inescapable fact, the more so as the loose sentence echoes their neglect and the emptiness of their lives:[30] they experience their inner space—"one's heart and stomach"—as equally revolting as their outer space—"the dull, cottony stuff [of] the sky." The source of Linnet's injured, indeed repressed, sensitivity, her depressing lot nevertheless bears fruit. Drop by drop, she filters her emotions as if through "the cottony stuff" of the sky, the spatial symbol of her unhappiness that will eventually engender her art.[31] Her childhood experiences indeed contribute to the pervading spatial imagery of her stories: her visual rendering of emotions colors the narration of her past anxieties.

Another cause for anguish, Linnet's childhood excursions to town with her father are remembered in terms of space: "These Saturdays have turned into one whitish afternoon, a windless snowfall, a steep street. Two persons descend the street, stepping carefully. The child, reminded every day to keep her hands still, gesticulates wildly—there is the flash of a red mitten. I will never overtake this pair. Their voices are lost in snow" (*HT,* 283). Memory turns numerous outings into one, assimilating them all with one spatial perception; achromatic, without a breath of air but enough snow to drown voices, this composite memory characteristically takes the walkers downward, for it recalls unpleasant moments. The red mitten flashing in the white surrounding—a striking color in the otherwise white, thus emotionless, landscape—stresses the child's vitality, confirmed by her erratic movements. But the image belongs to the past and cannot be retraced: time has changed the data—the father no longer is; the child has grown into an adult. Their voices, like their figures, are drowned in snow; past events belong to an inaccessible time when spatial and temporal components merge in haziness. The excursions often take the pair to a doctor or a teacher, with whom the child stays while the father runs errands or pays visits to friends. The subsequent meetings at the station traumatize the child for fear she should be late and miss both her father and the train.

Her dreams after her father's death also clearly translate her obsessive anxiety in spatial terms: "[A]fter his death, which would not be late in coming, I would dream that someone important had taken a train without me. My route to the meeting place—deviated, betrayed by stopped clocks—was always downhill. As soon as I was old enough to understand from my reading of myths and legends that this journey was a pursuit of darkness, its terminal point a sunless underworld, the dream vanished" (*HT,* 284). Darkness, abandonment, deviation, obstacles, declivity, all these dominate Linnet's dreams and pave the route of childhood, another descent into hell.

Movement is evoked throughout the sequence because Linnet moves back and forth between the past and the present, as the shift in tenses implies. Her past experiences—almost forgotten or at least removed from her—weigh on her in such a way that returning home is like embarking on a "journey into a new life and a past dream" (*HT,* 228): movement thus translates her eagerness to plunge into life. She even has "a sensation of loud, ruthless power, like an enormous waterfall. The past, the part [she] would rather not have lived, [becomes] small and remote, a dark pinpoint" (225). Life and its opportunities lie ahead: the energetic spatial simile expresses her hope for a better future. The past and its unpleasant reality disappear and, reduced to naught, cease to have an impact on her. "A gate shut on a part of [her] life" (221), she moves on with optimism. Thus in the stream of life with its inevitable hardships, she is heard saying, "Sink or swim? Of course I swam" (226), extending the preceding water imagery with the implicit determination to overcome adversity:

> My life was my own revolution—the tyrants deposed, the constitution wrenched from unwilling hands; I was, all by myself, the liberated crowd setting the palace on fire; I was the flags, the trees, the bannered windows, the flower-decked trains. The singing and the skyrockets of the 1848 revolution I so trustingly believed would emerge out of the war were me, no one but me; and, as in the lyrical first days of any revolution, as in the first days of any love affair, there wasn't a whisper of a voice to tell me, "You might compromise." (225–26)

Suggestive of the intense determination with which she fights, the extended metaphor leaves no doubt about Linnet's designs. The first section in the enumeration announces her will to change, indeed to purge the country of its despots in charge of wielding antiquated, yet cherished, dogmas. The second one symbolizes the individual character of her enterprise, and the third one pays tribute to her freedom, authenticity, openness, and evolution. "The singing and the skyrockets" proclaim her acute happiness, while the parallel between love and revolution rejects concessions. In short, the passage confirms her resolve to change things and not to let narrow-minded dicta undermine her self-confidence.

The rigidity with which everything is set comes out even in art. Unfortunately the local limitations take the poetical breath of any writer away: "I could write without hearing anyone, but poetry was leaving me. It was not an abrupt removal but like a recurring tide whose high-water mark recedes inch by inch. Presently I was deep inland and the sea was gone" (*HT,* 248).[32] An echo to the set of rules imposed on journalists (320–21) and flowing from a dried-up "intellectual bath" (320), the sea imagery aptly conveys Linnet's progressively declining literary inspiration. It also reverberates with James Joyce's imagery: inland, poetic inspiration perishes as paralysis prevails; at sea, paralysis is defeated by new, and unconstraining, horizons. Freedom of thought and lyric creativeness can be restored only through the rhythmic rocking of the waves.

But originality is not looked for in Canada. Linnet's audition with Miss Urn, whose name recalls Keats's ode and its celebration of beauty in static art (Jarrett, 177, n. 4), ironically illustrates Canada's attachment to old values: "Miss Urn received me in a small room of a dingy office suite on St. Catherine Street. We sat down on opposite sides of a table. I was rendered shy by her bearing, which had a headmistress quality, and perplexed by her accent—it was the voice any North American actor will pick up after six months of looking for work in the West End, but I did not know that" (*HT,* 250). The small space in which the audition takes place mirrors the narrow-mindedness of artistic demand. The location in town presents an ironic contrast: while evoking the actual street's sex shops, it also reminds the readers of prudish maidens venerating St. Catherine in the hope of finding a husband. The stress put on the spatial opposition that separates Miss Urn and Linnet also marks a contrast in their outlook. Free of taboo and open to novelty, Linnet reads a passage of Thornton Wilder's *The Skin of Our Teeth.* Her choice of a play then on show in New York is a first offense. That it is a "self-conscious" play, and therefore a challenge, rules it out in the eyes of Miss Urn, who favors Dodie Smith's unthreatening, cozy family play *Dear Octopus.*[33] To make matters worse, Linnet, on her different wavelength, misreads the second play, as she mistakes it for a parody. Genuine creativity is thus annihilated because bigotry and intolerance control art.

Open-mindedness does definitely not distinguish WASP Canadians. Strictly adhering to British norms, WASP Canadians have also adopted their model's imperialist attitudes. Whatever is not English is met with contempt and rejection as not "part of the Empire and the Crown" (*HT,* 245). Linnet defines their insularism in opposition to her parents' innovative approach:

> This overlapping in one room of French and English, of Catholic and Protestant—my parents' way of being, and so to me life itself—was as unlikely, as unnatural to the Montreal climate as a school of tropical fish. Only later would I discover that most other people simply floated in mossy little ponds labelled "French and Catholic" or "English and Protestant," never wondering what it might be like to step ashore; or wonder-

ing, perhaps, but weighing up the danger. To be out of a pond is to be in
unmapped territory. The earth might be flat; you could fall over the edge
quite easily. (*HT,* 305)

The comparison of bilingual, and at the same time biconfessional,
groups in Montreal to "a school of tropical fish" spatially establishes that
the "two tribes [know] nothing whatsoever about each other" (*HT,*
245). The localization of each community in "mossy little ponds"
extends the piscatorial and spatial simile. That they are labeled accordingly merely evidences the local ossification and fear of assimilation; no
one in Canada, according to Linnet, consciously tries to edge through
the tangles of moss toward the other pond.[34] The spatially laden image
she uses is further expanded in geographical terms. The passage implies
that Canadians, frightened to be left on their own, seek the security of a
group's label, contrary to any existential approach to life. Floating
rather than following a definite course, the spatial equivalent of "being"
rather than "existing" (Sartre, 73–102), they cannot possibly consider
opening themselves up, for their attachment to the community confers
them assurance, if not arrogance, and a feeling of superiority recalling
their forefathers' when they landed in Canada.

In a country characterized by its "national pigheadedness" (*HT,* 261),
outsiders have no access to real citizenship. Immigrants are easy to spot,
for origins can never be discarded in a society that abides by strict normative rules. As the narrator of "Jorinda and Jorindel" tells the readers,
"in Canada you have to keep saying what you are" (21). Immigrants are
so poorly received that if a Canadian woman of old stock marries an
immigrant, she had better keep her maiden name, at least if she wants
to succeed professionally. As Linnet explains: "In Canada you [are] also
whatever your father [happened] to be, which in my case [is] English"
(220). Accents, of course, can betray one's origins.[35] Linnet herself shows
how accents help classify the population in Canada: "I can see every
face, hear every syllable, which evoked, for me, a street, a suburb, a kind
of schooling. I could just hear out of someone saying to me, 'Say, Linnet,
couja just gimme a hand here, please?' born here, born in Glasgow;
immigrated early, immigrated late; raised in Montreal, no, farther west"
(239). Her ability to localize people's origins by their accents and to pin
them down to a type of education, area, or even street suggests the
importance of such markers.[36] As in all rural and provincial communities, it is of the utmost significance to know if one really belongs, what
landmarks one can claim.

When second-generation immigrants try to adapt, they fear to use their mother tongue lest it be held against them. Thus, in "Virus X," during a pilgrimage in Germany, Lottie still feels inhibited. "When the first words of German [cross] her lips, she [thinks] they [will] remain, engraven, to condemn her" (*HT,* 189): the sentence, with its spatial verb "to cross" and the past participle "engraven," evokes the unlikely, indeed impossible, concept of crossing over to another linguistic community. With regard to immigrants' attitudes to their European origins, Neil Besner mentions "half-forgotten, half-suppressed native tongues, cultures and countries" (Besner 1988, 129), an observation that definitely falls in with Lottie's "speaking the *secret* language" (*HT,* 189; emphasis added) while in Germany. Indeed, all her life, she has fought to belong and has thus erased outer signs of her origins. Like all new immigrants, she has realized that once part and parcel of the community, she must safeguard its cohesion and specificity by protecting it against intruders.

To complicate matters, some established Canadians cling to their original culture and cultivate their "foreignness," if not their feelings of superiority. Linnet remembers her father refusing the process of cultural integration out of pride of his origins, just as many British citizens living in the colonies. As Linnet recalls: "He was seldom present. I don't know where my father spent his waking life: just elsewhere" (*HT,* 285), most probably longing for his birthplace, as implicitly conveyed by the vague localizer. Indeed, after years of residence in Canada, this Englishman by birth dies more British than Canadian. But what applies to him should not necessarily hold for his offspring. Nevertheless, owing to the system, Linnet is considered an immigrant on two counts, for her return also turns her into a newcomer for those long established. Significantly, at the beginning of "In Youth Is Pleasure," Linnet reveals that her father's "death turned [her] life into a helpless migration" (219), a spatial image reflecting displacement. Thus both his birth and death contribute to isolate her from others and to take her on the road paved by outcasts. She ends up "being an outsider in her own home," for she has "neither the wealth nor the influence a provincial society requires to make a passport valid" (232).[37]

Similarly, the remittance man (a Briton banished young for some obscure disgrace[38] whom Linnet meets one summer and observes in an attempt to understand her own reality) retains his Britishness till death. Linnet's comments revealingly confirm his origins. "Frank Cairns was stamped, labelled, ticketed by his tie (club? regiment? school?); by his voice, manner, haircut, suit; by the impression he gave of being stranded in a jungle, waiting for a rescue party—from England of course" (*HT,* 265). Initially cut off from all his ties, he ends up totally isolated, for he "was raised to behave well in situations that might never occur, trained to become a genteel poor on continents where even the concept of genteel poverty never existed" (269). To her he is "a curio cabinet" (275) from which she takes everything out "piece by piece, [examines] the objects [and sets] them down" (275) once she has understood what it contains. She points out that remittance men are "like children, perpetually on their way to a harsh school . . . [and] sent 'home' to childhoods of secret grieving among strangers" (269).

This image curiously echoes Linnet's own experience: she was sent to a convent at the age of four "where Jansenist discipline still had a foot on the neck of the twentieth century and where, as an *added enchantment,* [she] was certain not to hear a word of English" (*HT,* 299; emphasis added). She too was totally cut off from her milieu and had to live by the rules of a world she could not relate to. Like the remittance man, who "would never live in England, not as it is now" (275), she feels "apart from everyone, isolated" (280). So when she hears that he died during the war, she rejoices that he will never "be forced to relive his own past" (280). One inevitably wonders how he could, for he had no identity; therefore no past can be ascribed to him. This is made explicit when Linnet discovers the story she once wrote (although she does not remember when) about the remittance man's mysterious friend—"a man from *somewhere* living *elsewhere*" (281; emphasis added). He is thus positively different from the remittance man—but also, as the vague localizers imply, a fiction, an abstraction without real substance, indeed a man from nowhere living nowhere.

The other immigrants she meets are equally trapped. They try to integrate by applying for citizenship, changing their names, and eating cornflakes. In "Good Morning and Goodbye," an immigrant has "changed his name to Paul because the other [the original] sounded too German."[39] But this does not bring him closer to the family he lives with. Later in the follow-up, "Three Brick Walls," while going back home, he shuns people and "[trembles] with a sweet loneliness that [requires] no people."[40] With a new name or not, he remains an outsider like all other immigrants. The same applies in "Virus X" to Vera Rodna, whose relatives dropped the end of their name "to make it less specifically Ukrainian" (*HT,* 176). Their enterprise is vain, for at any time, they may be reminded of their alien origins: they cannot shun the effects of xenophobia.[41]

To escape from such a stifling and incomprehensible atmosphere, Linnet turns to writing. "Anything [she cannot] decipher [she turns] into fiction, which [is] a way of untangling knots" (*HT,* 261), the complex knots of her identity. To the readers' delight, Linnet's suffering is transformed into art, the art revealed in the stories she casually narrates and defines through an extended spatial metaphor: "[E]very day is a new parcel one unwraps, layer on layer of tissue paper covering bits of crystal, scraps of words in a foreign language, pure white stones" (248). The readers follow Linnet's meandering path as she is looking for herself in others and opening the secret drawer of one character after another. But soon she is seen shutting it again promptly: she feels that she should not "[look] inside a drawer that [does] not belong to [her]" (234), nor "[put] life through a sieve" (281). Why she should not is in fact echoed by her recognition of the local smallness, the limits of an art bred by suggestions and inhibitions, and her latent awareness concerning her own self. Once she has grasped the emptiness of the immigrants' reality, she is no longer interested in them because they can teach her nothing new. By then, no one can serve her as a model to understand who or what she really is; she is another, different from others. For throughout her quest, she intuitively senses that in the end, she will only find "another variety of exile" (281). Her awareness curiously echoes Coral Ann Howells's reflection about Gallant's collection of Canadian stories: "The most disturbing home truth of all is that the condition of being dispossessed is as common in Canada as it is among Canadians abroad" (Howells, 94).

Estranged within her family, her hometown, and her country, Linnet finds her sole remedy in writing. Generated by her need to understand herself and anchored in her rediscovery of her native Montreal, her prose eventually discloses the multiple facets of her culture. It emerges from the three layers of memory and historical time involved in her narration: twice removed from her childhood, Linnet, the narrator, looks back on the memories of her childhood as a teenager. This contributes to the detachment with which she can extract the numerous components of Canadian culture, whose spatial reflection plays an important role in delineating local limitations.

Concerned with aspects of the three dimensions, the spatial polarities used divide the world essentially into high and low, up and down, above and below or beneath, leaving those related to length and width in the background, with sometimes a reference to lengthy routes or processes. The up-down polarity and its related expressions evoke images of survival and decline, as such enhancing the cultural pressures. Often linked

with Linnet's attitude to life, the concept "up" and its equivalents by
and large imply endurance and vital force or refer to an imaginary or
utopian reality, whereas the concept "down" and its corresponding
phrases, associated with obtuse behavior and drabness, point to dissolution and annihilation. Movement contrasts mobility with immobility,
going up with going down, floating with drowning, ascending with
falling: lack of movement characterizes restrained Canadians, whereas
movement and water imagery stress Linnet's free response and willingness to live unhampered. Similarly, just as colors typify Linnet's "inad-
missible" lively and affective response, the achromatic black, white, and
gray seem to invade the landscape of emotional repression, with the
exception of Linnet's distorted pictures of Montreal, where whiteness
acquires a mystic quality. Finally, Gallantian polarities involving measures and proportions comprise oppositions such as exiguous and vast,
small and big, narrow and wide, close and far, limited and limitless,
enclosed and open, fenced in and unfenced. Contrary to the first concept
of this binary opposition evidencing the local constriction and narrow-
mindedness, the second concept reinforces Linnet's desire to question
dogmas, to live freely and fully. In short, the positive pole of each spatial
binary opposition refers to either Linnet's desire to keep body and soul
together or to an imaginary or utopian reality; on the other hand, the
negative one emphasizes either reality's dullness or Linnet's fellow citizens' compliance with local intolerance. It thus appears from the spatial
imagery used in the Linnet Muir sequence that any group—be it social,
religious, or linguistic—refuses to accept any intrusion, let alone admit
the worth of a custom, attitude, or belief different from its own agelong
approved norm.

   If the use of spatial references is at its most effective in the Linnet
Muir stories—Gallant's *"recherche du temps perdu"*—this mode of apprehension of the fictional world is not restricted to the stories enacting a
fictionalized version of the past Gallant went through; most of the other
Canadian stories have to some extent a spatial character that corrobo-
rates the general disjunction to which they all converge (as already manifest in the examples referred to in notes). Apart from the examples in
the Linnet Muir sequence, several characters of Canadian origin find
themselves victimized or trapped in inextricable situations owing to the
rigid model of human relations they received as part of their education.

   The negative effect self-control has on human beings is highlighted
in "The Ice Wagon Going down the Street." Agnes Brusen, a Canadian
of Norwegian descent brought up to escape her humble background,

survives by conveying "the charge of moral certainty round her, the belief in work, the faith of undertakings, the bread of the Black Sunday" that tastes like "ashes in the mouth" (*HT,* 118). Nothing else is left, for as a Presbyterian Canadian, she can only succumb under the weight of "work and debt and obligation" (115); "the ambition, the terror, the dry pride" (118) with which she is imbued turn her into a blind "mole" (116), a symbol stressing Agnes's industriousness, pride, and ambition, no doubt, but also her blindness to worldly pleasures. "Small and brown, and round-shouldered as if she had always carried parcels or younger children in her arms" (116), Agnes, "the true heir of the men from Scotland" (118), arouses pity, not envy. Her attire betrays her observance; she owns two strict, dull outfits, a "brown tweed suit with bone buttons" (116) and "a navy-blue dress with changeable collars" (118). Thus presented, religious inclinations and their benefits lose their attractiveness—if they ever had any. When she discovers at a Carnival party that the educated people her parents have always admired are decadent and degraded beings (132), she loses all her illusions and ends up in utter isolation and despair. She contrasts these with the feelings she had when still at home. Her longing for solitude, and thus for emotional and physical latitude, she expresses in spatial terms: "In a big family, if you want to be alone, you have to get up before the rest of them. You get up early in the morning in the summer and it's you, you, once in your life alone in the universe" (132).

Her colleague, Peter Frazier, the protagonist, is equally trapped in a worthless life owing to his conviction that his aristocratic background entitles him to higher positions. His lack of success he attributes without tangible proof to maneuvers high up in diplomatic circles. Eventually, his wife's contacts with men in key positions all over the world determine his career, or lack of it: against his aspirations, he ends up doing demeaning clerical tasks. He projects his dissatisfaction in spatial terms: he lives "in a mild yellow autumn," remembers "the streets of the city dark, and the windows everywhere black with rain," and has memories of being with his family "as if they clung together while just outside their small shelter it rained and rained" (*HT,* 113). When brought together with Agnes Brusen in what could be compromising circumstances, he visualizes "how disasters happen. He [sees] floods of sea water moving with perfect punitive justice over reclaimed land; he [sees] lava covering vineyards and overtaking dogs and stragglers. A bridge over an abyss snap[s] in two and the long express train, suddenly V-shaped, float[s] like snow" (*HT,* 129). These images convey his fear of establishing closer relations with Agnes, with whom he has more in common than he actually thinks. Indeed, while commenting on the lack of assets passed on in Peter's family, the disembodied narratorial voice alludes to his envying the only branch of the family that has become rich, "the granite Presbyterian immigrants from Scotland" (114), for anything would have been better than his present situation. "If Peter can choose his reincarnation, let him be the oppressed son of a Scottish parson. Let Peter grow on cuffs and iron principles. Let him make the fortune. Let him flee the manse" (114). Although Peter's envy is related ironically in a cold and detached voice, that of the creator granting her subjects an illusory free choice, the parallel imperative sentence structures—an obvious pastiche of the biblical style—bring to mind the reality that he might have enjoyed a more liberated and rewarding existence with Agnes. For though no one would want its concomitants—Presbyterian "cuffs and iron principles," as well as what Gallant calls "that iron-clad Presbyterian hypocrisy" (iHancock, 55)—the reward at the end of the painfully educational day attracts Peter beyond the limitations imposed, but in the end he remains with his dissatisfaction and retains only the vision of Agnes's life while Agnes concludes that "Peter is lost" (*HT*, 134).

Other characters let themselves be caught in vicious circles. Forever entangled in unhappy love affairs, Sarah, the protagonist of "In the Tunnel," becomes conscious that each amorous interlude in which she is involved leads to her "walking on her grave" (*HT*, 106). The initial stages of her relationship to Roy Cooper, a middle-aged Englishman, spatially convey his strategy, one that is reverted at the end in a much more drastic manner: Sarah's future lover keeps "space between them" (76), then allows them "to be moving toward each other without ever quite touching; then . . . they [are] travelling in the same direction, but still apart. They [can]not turn back, for there [is] nothing to turn back to" (76–77). Never quite relating to her in a deep sense, Roy starts exploiting Sarah, letting her slave around until she sprains her ankle, whereupon he takes a distance out of intense disgust and refuses even to speak to her. "The shadows of clouds" on their last outing prefigures the ending, the more so as Sarah feels "a prisoner impaled on a foreign language, seeing bright, light, foreign eyes offering something nobody wanted—death" (98). As irreversible as the beginning of the summer romance with Roy Cooper, the inevitable ending frees Sarah not only from the agony of rejection, but also from the claustrophobic setting. Called the Tunnel, the low building in which Roy lives can only be a place out of which to flee; dark with its "long windowless room," "the house and its terrace seem microscopic" (78), leaving next to no space for emotional and physical openings. Indeed once Sarah leaves Roy she remarks that "she [is] out of the tunnel. . . . she [is] alive" (105), obviously conscious of the repressive influence of the place, and by extension of the relationship.

Other places have a repressive impact. In "Thank You for the Lovely Tea," "the lightless corridors . . . the dark classrooms and sweating walls, the chill, the cold, the damp" (*HT,* 5) of Ruth Cook's boarding school contribute to a dejected atmosphere. This makes Ruth write that "Life is Hell" (3) before the disastrous outing with her father's friend. Once out of the convent school's building, she also remarks that she is coming "out of jail" (8), a spatial image revealing her aversion and reminiscent of Linnet's consideration of the "prison of childhood" (225). The same holds true for one of the places the Collier girls are sent to in "Orphans' Progress." There oppression finds its expression in the prevalent darkness and blackness of everything around them: "Their lives were in the *dark* now, in the *dark* of ghosts, whose *transparent shadows* stood *round their bed*; soon they lived in the *black of nuns*. Language was *black*, until they forgot their English" (60; emphasis added). The prevailing gloom contrasts with the relaxed atmosphere under their distracted mother's care; whether or not attentive, "she was there," and "the children were close to her" (57).[42] Despite the scarcity of food and the erratic care their mother gave them, the girls value the warmth and closeness under her shabby roof much more than the adequate food and clean surroundings secured by relatives who show no feelings for the girls. Similarly, in "Virus X," Vera reproaches Lottie for her indifference, which she associates with Canada: "I always felt I had less right to be Canadian than you, even though we've been there longer. . . . I've never understood that *coldness*" (210; emphasis added). That coldness is also exemplified in "Jorinda and Jorindel," in which "Irmgard's father looks cold, and Irmgard, without knowing it, imitates his look" (27) for want of another model.

Human reactions can sometimes be expressed in terms of spatial perception. The annoyance of Gérard's family with the aging father's boring discourse during the family reunion in "Saturday" is projected through spatial oppression. "A chorus of silent English: 'Shut *up!*' [can be heard]. If only the old man could hear the words, he would see a *great black wall;* he would hear a *sigh,* a *rattle,* like the *black trees outside the windows, hitting the panes*" (*HT,* 44; emphasis added). Spatial images of nega-

tive impact involving sounds, dark colors, and building elements convey
the children's irritation at their father's senile reflections in the same
way as Linnet's description of the atmosphere at work reveals her state
of mind: "[T]hey feel as if ashes and sand were being ground in their
skins" (44). Similarly, Gérard's fragile psychological balance finds its
projection in the concern he takes over the position of objects: "He had
always given importance to his gestures, noticing whether he put his
watch or his glasses to the left or the right of a bedlamp. He always left
his coffee cup about four inches from the edge of the counter. When he
studied, he piled his books on the right, and whatever text he was
immediately using was at his left hand. His radio had to be dead center"
(37). Noticing a change in his attitude to objects and their spatial location, he expresses in nonspatial terms Matoré's rule concerning chaos:
"He saw, and had been noticing for some time, that his mind was not
keeping quiet order for him anymore and that his gestures were not
automatic" (37).

Just as in "Saturday" the boredom of Gérard's siblings during the
family reunion is projected spatially, in "The Accident," Shirley Higgins's perception of the locale reflects her emotions. When she shows
her bereaved parents-in-law where their son met his death, the topographical description—somewhat similar to that of Linnet's dreams as a
child—conveys Shirley's gloomy state of mind: "The *steep* street *under
rain* was *black* as oil. Everything was reflected *upside down*. The *neon* signs
of the change office and the pharmacy *swam deeply* in the pavement"
(*EW,* 101; emphasis added). Shirley's recollection of the village in which
her husband Peter died also involves dark colors: "The last Italian town
of our journey was *nothing*—just a *black* beach with sand *like soot*, and
houses *shut* and dormant because it was the middle of the afternoon"
(96; emphasis added). The description of the scene just before the accident also reveals how the play of light and dark colors prefigure his
death: "I saw things meaningless now. . . . Under the leaves *he seemed
under water*. A *black* car, a submarine with Belgian plates, parked at an
angle, *stirred to life*. I saw *sunlight from six points* on the paint. My view
became discomposed, as if the sea were suddenly *black and opaque* and
had splashed up over the policeman and the road" (98; emphasis added).
Just as with Linnet, the combination of declivity, darkness, and submer-
sion capture Shirley's predicament.

An echo to the Muir sequence, the other Canadian stories also convey
the local stranglehold through their narrator's and sometimes their
characters' perception of the setting in which the action takes place. As

with Linnet, spatial polarities expose the narrators' and characters' feelings and thoughts, reflecting their outlook on life and the local limitations. Gallant's consistent comment about Montreal holds for her fictional Canada at large: "All those small worlds of race and language and religion and class, all shut away from one another. A series of airtight compartments" (iHancock, 25). Enslaved by their blind obedience to social and religious rules, Gallant's Canadians can neither live nor let live. Those with scope flee from the place, as Mavis Gallant herself did in her twenties; the others stay behind and succumb to the weight of obligations and frustration. Their deep-rooted restraint and repression inherited from the first immigrants hamper communication and estrange them from themselves. Irreversibly inhibited, they have no future ahead: their bleak lives and their disappointing perspectives offer neither outlet nor compensation.

Based on material Gallant knows well, the Canadian stories imprison the characters in a distinct atmosphere related to her perception of the local restrictiveness. Nevertheless, spatial components contribute to the fictional message of her other collections and novels alike. In "The Other Paris," for instance, at least two kinds of spaces are represented: on the one hand, Carol Frazier experiences the real Paris as dull, gray, and colorless—a source of "confusion and loneliness" (*OP,* 30); on the other, she substitutes an idyllic picture full of colors, sunshine, greenery—"a coherent picture, accurate but untrue" (30)—to match her idea of love. In "Autumn Day," Cecilia Rowe, an overprotected young American woman, is "[sent] off to live thousands of miles away with a strange man" (33), her soldier of a husband: distance to her corresponds to a perplexing trauma. As they cannot find accommodation in Salzburg, they live on a farm. The farm's location, "out of town" (33), parallels the protagonist's sense of isolation just as the "small, cold and coldly clean" (38) room they have mirrors the couple's lack of communication. The title character of "Ernst in Civilian Clothes" also finds his own displacement reflected by the "thick winter blanket, white and gray" (*PJ,* 131). "Stiff with the cold of a forgotten dream" (147), he decides to start a new life; "he will invent his own truth" (147), one that will nevertheless not prevent him from feeling alien and stranded in a world that does not need him. In transit, as the title of the story evidences, Philippe Perrigny feels as if he were "shut up in a stalled lift with nothing to read" (*IT,* 44). Similarly, in "The Remission," terminally ill Alec Webb regrets his decision of going to the Riviera to die: "without compassion" (*FFD,* 76), the sun weakens his febrile body rather than offering some comfort, affecting his health just as it throws light on the decline of the British Empire. He is forced to stay "indoors, moving from room to room, searching for some gray, dim English cave in which to take cover" (76)—the spatial allusion to his desperate search for a personal and patriotic remission that can eventually only be secured through death.

The preceding examples of spatial components—a handful in a corpus offering many more—contributing to the stories' messages show how Gallant exploits space not only to delineate the scenery of her fiction but also to reflect her narrators' and characters' states of mind and outlook on life. Nevertheless, nowhere in her oeuvre does Gallant offer as systematic a picture of an oppressive world through spatial constituents as in the Linnet Muir sequence. The six interconnected stories indeed build up a tension based on the spatial restrictions sensed at all levels: the frustrations of the protagonist (and by extension of the author herself) find their projection in the enclosing landscape, the other characters' limitations in the narrowing boundaries of their minds and environment. The overwhelming disjunction resulting from the stories' fictional space thus turns them into a model for Gallant's illustration of human dislocation.

Chapter Seven

Text and Image:
Overhead in a Balloon

Overhead in a Balloon, Gallant's collection of Parisian stories, explores the mentality of her adoptive fellow citizens in the late seventies and early eighties with the sharpness of the best introduced social critic. From an insider's perspective, Gallant exposes the pettiness and superficiality of the artistic and literary world (patrons and creators alike) as well as of the petite bourgeoisie, the upper-middle class, and the impoverished aristocrats. Several of the stories are linked by the recurrence of certain characters: "Speck's Idea" and "Overhead in a Balloon" both stage Sandor Speck, the curator of an art gallery, and his assistant, Walter Obermauer; "Larry," "A Painful Affair," "A Flying Start," and "Grippes and Poche" all allude to a famous American patron of the arts, Miss Pugh, and the last three refer to the rivalry of a French writer and his English counterpart for the favors of Miss Pugh; "A Recollection," "Rue de Lille," "The Colonel's Child," and "Lena" deal with the first and second wives of a literary broadcaster whose recollections are convincingly told in the first person owing to the true feelings or fascination he had, or has, for both. Standing apart are two stories concerned with further established citizens: "Luc and His Father" reveals a son's failure to follow his father's model, and therefore career, by failing the entrance exam securing admission to one of the *Grandes Ecoles;* and "The Assembly" reports the prejudiced discussion of flat owners in a building after one of them has been molested. The stories prove Gallant's familiarity with French letters, art, architecture, mores, and prejudice over changing demography (most of which appears in *The Paris Notebooks*).[1]

With its emphasis on the world of art, *Overhead in a Balloon* lends itself to a discussion of the interaction between text and image, and the extra interpretative dimension that interrelation affords. An avid visitor of museums and galleries, Gallant often discloses her appreciation for art (though not for the artistic clique) through descriptions of, and allusions to, paintings and photographs, but she surpasses herself here as she captures the world of culture.[2] "Speck's Idea" and the title story, more than half of the book, highlight the value and purpose of art in Paris and represent art works that have an impact on the textual interpretation. But several of the other stories not directly concerned with art describe the visual in the decor, such as "Luc and His Father," "Larry," and "A Flying Start," for instance.

Gallant's awareness of the problems posed by the representation of images in fiction and their potential as a source of irony goes back to her years as a journalist and finds an echo in Linnet's ironical consideration of the caption for a picture portraying a bear and a boy eating a bun: "There is no trick to it. You just repeat what the picture has told you like this: 'Boy eats bun as bear looks on.' The reason why anything has to go under the picture at all is that a reader might wonder, 'Is that a bear looking on?' It looks like a bear, but that is not enough for saying so" (*HT,* 318). As Barthes would say, Linnet's comment on the picture "is a matter of a denoted description of the image."[3] But she goes beyond a mere denotation; she also takes the image's reception into account. Without any attempt at theorizing, she pinpoints the "terror of uncertain signs" (Barthes 1977, 39), which makes the presence of the linguistic message necessary. In other words, she emphasizes the taming effect of captions, leaving no freedom of interpretation to the readers, who, in this case, are not endowed with perceptiveness or, as Barthes would have it, needs the "*anchorage* of all the possible (denoted) meanings of the object" (39). Linnet goes on thinking about the mechanics of captions: "You have a space to fill in which the words must come out even. The space may be tight; in that case, you can remove 'as' and substitute a comma, though that makes the kind of terse statement to which your reader is apt to reply, 'So what?' Most of the time, the Truth with a Capital T is a matter of elongation: 'Blond boy eats small bun as large bear looks on' " (*HT,* 318). Both compression and expansion of the caption change the impact of the picture. Compression, in that it takes away the links between the various denoted elements of the composition, reduces the "anchorage," whereas expansion, that is, the exact pinning down of characteristics, increases it. The irony of the passage here lies in the use of "Truth with a Capital T" in relation to the caption that leaves the field least open to interpretation, that "appears to duplicate the image" (Barthes 1977, 26). Linnet's exposition of the problems of representation calls to mind Barthes's question: "Does the image duplicate certain of the informations [*sic*] given in the text by a phenomenon of redundancy or does the text add a fresh information to the image?" (33).

By specifically narrowing the scope of interpretation, the linguistic message suits the needs of society, "concerned to tame the Photograph, to temper the madness which keeps threatening to explode in the face of whoever looks at it."[4] The overqualifying caption, the elongating text, nullifies the potential effect of the image, prevents the image from affecting the readers in any personal way. The reductive quality of the linguistic sign directs the readers' attention to harmless concepts. As Barthes says, one "means of taming the Photograph is to generalize, to gregarize, banalize it until it is no longer confronted by any image in relation to which it can mark itself, assert its special character, its scandal, its madness" (Barthes 1981, 118).

As Linnet goes on discussing unscrupulous, lyric, or crazy captions, she further prolongs Barthes's observations. Rules obliquely emerge from the presentation of various plausible reactions to rejectable types of linguistic text. The implication is that the person in charge of "what goes under the pictures" (*HT,* 318) should not elicit reactions from the readers. The neutral, yet all-embracing, text suits the demand: "[I]t is not the business of 'reader' to draw conclusions. Our subscribers are not dreamers or smart alecks; when they see a situation in a picture, they want that situation confirmed" (320). For, as Barthes says, "when generalized, [the image] completely de-realizes the human world of conflicts and desires, under cover of illustrating it" (Barthes 1981, 118). Told "to admire a contribution to pictorial journalism" (*HT,* 320) in the back issues of *Life,* Linnet decides to rephrase the caption: "Boy eats bun as bear looks on. Note fur on bear" (320). The tautological addition to the already reductive text ridicules the task of the caption writer and of the readers. As Barthes would have it, the readers can only "subject [the Photograph's] spectacle to the civilized code of perfect illusions" delimited by the text, rather than "[confronting] in it the wakening of intractable reality" (Barthes 1981, 119).

Gallant's attitude to the first pictures of concentration camps falls within Barthes's second option, that of allowing the photograph to open up new vistas and to display reality in its true light. Asked to write the captions and a text of 750 words, Gallant decided that "there must be no descriptive words in this, no adjectives. Nothing like 'horror,' 'horrifying' because what the pictures are saying is stronger and louder" (iHancock, 39). What she sensed then is that "the Photograph is an extended, loaded evidence—as if it caricatured not the figure of what it represents (quite the converse) but its very existence" (Barthes 1981, 115). What actually came out in the special issue was a severely tampered-with version of Gallant's captions, full of "adverbs and adjectives smothering the real issue, and the covering article, which was short, was a prototype for all the cliches we've been bludgeoned with ever since" (iHancock, 40). When she inquired about the reasons for the alterations, she heard: "Culture! Our readers never went to high school and you're talking about culture? All the Germans are bastards and that's that" (40).[5] This reaction definitely reduces the pictures to some almost innocuous images of the concentration camps, indeed denies the universal lure of fascism. The text and the captions thus minimize a terrifying reality. But Gallant rejected, and still rejects, the lie: "But that wasn't that and it still isn't" (40). To her, the travestied version reads like the following dichotomy: the picture tells a story; the text smothers it. The text should enhance the photographic message, not tone it down; it should reflect, not limit nor distort, the message.

Gallant's early career as a journalist undoubtedly awakened her perception of the complex relationship between picture and text. Her fiction gives examples of double layers of text: Linnet Muir reveals that in Canada, as in other countries with split-up communities, the titles of art works are "identified in two languages" (*HT*, 299), even when they do not call for translation. Behind the doubly printed text, and the accompanying comment to the effect that a house "had on display landmarks identified in two languages . . . as if the engraver had known they would find their way to a wall in Montreal" (299), lies the ironic smile of the bilingual speaker. The physical presence of both titles, not only on the engravings, but specifically on the printed page in Gallant's book, ridicules the flat refusal to open one's mind to others, the cold refusal to understand others, even where no misunderstanding can exist.[6]

Descriptions of, or allusions to, images abound in Gallant's fiction and journalism.[7] Her story "In the Tunnel" re-presents a painting of Judas, after he hangs himself, and several paintings of Jesus in an abandoned chapel somewhere on the Riviera. As Mary Condé rightly notes, the painting of Judas "controls the narrative," "drawing together the story's themes of politics, nationality and cruelty."[8] The idea of punishment pervades the whole story, securing an inescapable link between text and image, the more so as the biblical reference inherent in the painting adds another layer of contextuality.[9]

Another example of pictorial control of the narrative can be found in "Bonaventure." Several engravings adorn the walls of the pavilion in which the protagonist, Douglas Ramsay, is put up: once again, the story is centered on the punishment of Judas as well as on the last photograph of the late artist Moser, looking "like a famous picture of Freud going into exile" (*HT,* 145). The visual reflects the insidious acts and words of Katherine Moser, the artist's widow, for in the narrative past and present, she is seen subjecting all around her to the idea of punishment. To mention but two key instances, Katherine imposed a severe diet in the countryside on Moser, who abhorred both healthy food and nature, and she inflicts on Douglas Ramsay exhausting excursions to force him to enjoy nature (which he equally abhors) and art. As Douglas realizes while visiting an exhibition of impressionist paintings (164) that, owing to ill health, the painters were dependent on their wives, Katherine snaps back that he had better rest, reproducing the pattern of relationship she had with her late husband. In fact, she mimics the overprotectiveness of the painters' wives and also reenacts the sacrifice of Douglas's mother, who looks after her invalid husband, a situation that plagues Ramsay.

Only when faced with the prospect of being left alone with Katherine "at the chalet [with] the incomprehensible language of birds, and the cat with its savage nature, and the cannibal magpies, the cannibal jays" (*HT,* 166) for a whole month does Ramsay manage to break the spell of punishment. At the pension to which he escapes from Katherine, he finds in a drawer a forgotten sketch "of a naked and faceless woman wearing a pearl necklace" (169). A reminder of the "headless statue of an adolescent girl ... [with] small breasts, slightly down-pointed" (164), which delighted him as an incarnation of Anne, Katherine's adolescent daughter, the drawing seems to anticipate Ramsay's final discovery: perhaps he was mistaken; perhaps he needs the nursing of a woman, whose identity has yet to be determined, as suggested by the featureless face on the drawing.

With the presence of Judas etched indelibly in the readers' memories, the text reflects the image, stressing the similarity between Ramsay and his spiritual father (the late Moser), between Ramsay and his biological father (spiritually dead owing to his wife's equation of chastisement with justice). The final words provide evidence that Ramsay's attempt to disclaim heredity, both biological and spiritual, has failed: he too will be trapped—indeed he has been all along—in a retributive system in which he cannot have the upper hand. The images in the text thus reverberate with punishment and retribution, two ideas that the text illustrates at different levels.

In other stories, oil paintings, photographs, and posters impress a sense of duty and obligation. In "Thank You for the Lovely Tea," for instance, oil portraits of dignitaries and donors adorn the walls of the Catholic convent school where Ruth is a boarder, and a photograph of the late king and queen hangs in her classroom, powerful reminders of the school's cultural, ethical, and religious values that turn the place into a prison. On an outing, beyond the reach of the system's stern-looking representatives—both living and pictorially represented—Ruth and her friends can revel in harassing her father's lover.

Conversely, one could argue that in "Luc and His Father," the oil portraits of public servants, a photograph of his father's graduating class, and a picture of his mother overwhelm Luc, a French youth, so much so that they exert a negative influence on him. The Jesuits who run the "examination factory . . . able to jostle any student, even the dreamiest, into a respectable institute for higher learning" see through him and warn his parents that they should see to his lack of adjustment.[10] Reflecting her husband's manly talk to Luc, the mother replaces the photograph of her husband's graduating class with a framed poster of Che Guevara, bought on the advice of a salesman according to whom Che Guevara "had no political significance . . . had become manly, decorative kitsch" (*OB*, 78). Ironically, the father objects to the photograph of Hitler tacked near his son's bed because "he [does] not want Luc quite that manly" (79).

Trying to escape his stifling background, Luc takes a fancy to a young woman he has met at political meetings. In the long run, the politically correct Jesuit counselor—he wears "a small crucifix on one lapel and a Solidarnosc badge on the other" (*OB*, 82)—having read his letters—equally correct in such an overbearing institution—manages to ruin Luc's chance of escaping his milieu, which is after all based on false values. Back home, after hearing of his girlfriend's engagement to a cousin, Luc receives one more pictorial message; another picture of his mother adorns his desk, "a charming one taken at the time of her engagement. She wore, already, the gold earrings. . . . Her expression was smiling, confident but untried" (98). The implication of the text leaves no doubt about the intended message; the photograph highlights Luc's parents' socially correct—though perhaps unhappy—choice of each other, emphasizing Luc's incorrect, hence unsuccessful, choice. A clear sign of wealth, the gold earrings, his mother's "talisman" (97), confirm the rightfulness of Luc's parents' claim, crowned by the smile. The radiance of the smile displays no sign of life's inscriptions, no unpleasant subtext of trying experiences (like her son's failure, for instance).

The last scene—the father's tête-à-tête with his son—stages the father's final attempt at taking Luc back on to the right path while disclosing the old man's melancholy perception of his son's romance. Showing his determination to forgo such foolish thoughts, he turns to his wife's picture. By stating, "I always admired that picture of your mother" (*OB,* 100), that is, by setting a model, he annihilates any hopes he might have cherished for a spontaneous, fully gratifying relationship for his son, indeed for humanity at large.

In "Larry," another father, the elder Pugh, checks on his son, the title character, during a short visit in Paris and takes that opportunity to advise him about marriage, in spite of his own erring married life. After a failed attempt as a sculptor, Larry looks after a large, opulent house in the Huitième Arrondissement for the summer. In the course of the conversation, Larry's father announces his intention to bequeath a portrait of himself to his son. Larry's remembrance of the painting—"[his father] appeared to be elegant and reliable, the way things and people are always said to have been when one looks back at them" (*OB,* 116)— points to its unreliability, indeed reflects a general tendency in the story itself. The narrative reveals everyone's unreliability, starting with the rich landlords, who pilfer from hotels, then Larry, who breaks into their liquor cabinet, and finally his father, whose "sudden inclinations" (114) pass before morals or his family's interest. Just after the narrative voice reports that "shutters [are] bolted, curtains drawn on the streets with art names: Murillo, Rembrandt, Van Dyck [*sic*]" (113), as if art were reduced to names, the father expresses his views of art: "I suppose you found out there wasn't much to art in the long run" (113). With its indirect allusion to the ill-valued worth of art, the statement reinforces the unreliability of the portrait; it is further confirmed by Larry's memory of the mark left when the father, walking out on his wife, took the painting off the wall—"a blank place on the wall" (117), probably the truest image of him. The father's worthlessness is incidentally substantiated by the allusion to the allowance his rich daughter and art benefactress, Maggie, pays him "to keep away" (113). Larry, who envies his half-sister's wealth, is outraged that she should leave her fortune to an arts foundation when he, the would-be artist, could benefit from her support.

"A Flying Start" gives a good picture of the maneuvers performed by other would-be artists to win the favors of Miss Mary Margaret Pugh, an American patron of the arts and the Maggie of the previous short story. Most of the story consists of a section of the memoir that the French author Henri Grippes writes to recapture with questionable reliability the period when his English rival, Victor Prism, was the protégé of Miss Pugh. Recalling Prism's hesitant steps to be admitted by his patron, Grippes focuses on the impression that "an oil painting of the martyrdom of Saint Sebastian" (*OB*, 124) made on Prism: "He thought of mile upon mile of museum portraits—young men, young saints pierced with arrows, with nothing to protect them from the staring of women but a coat of varnish" (124). Often represented as a beautiful youth wounded by arrows, the Roman martyr sentenced to be shot to death by archers for converting many soldiers in his cohort appears in the foreground virtually naked, as in Antonello's painting. The compelling observation of the painting results from Prism's projection in the pierced naked body of his own vulnerability, not to say ordeal, when braving Miss Pugh's analytical stare. Ever so often ill at ease with his pretended vocation, Prism cannot avoid catching a glimpse of the painting, a reminder of his predicament. Prism's obsession with the painting finds its *mise en abyme* in his unfinished novel staging his alter ego as the male character and Miss Pugh as the female character: "Christopher seemed to leave a trail of sawdust. There were arrow wounds everywhere. He did not know what other people thought and felt about anything, but he could sense to a fine degree how they thought and felt about him. He lived on the feelings he aroused, sought acquaintances among those in whom these feelings were not actively hostile" (125). Prism's plight comes to an end when another mental vision of "museum rooms full of portraits of St. Sebastian, with nothing for protection but a thin coat of varnish" (128) makes him think of the two schools of art conservation. Reviewing the claims of both—the one refusing to restore the original color, the other restoring it whether or not the painter had originally taken fading into account—he has a flash, draws "a blank sheet toward him" (128), the symbol of a new start, and writes: "Are we to take for granted that the artist thinks he knows what he is doing?" (128). Grippes notes that "at that moment, Prism the critic was born" (128). The juxtaposition of Prism's question and Grippes's statement no doubt conveys Gallant's sarcastic view of the literary critic whose sudden vision gives him or her a new vocation, but without the tools.

Funnily enough, Prism secures the favors of Miss Pugh when, asked to give an opinion of Picasso, he represents Picasso in a picture of the mind that helps him focus his anger at the unconceited yet frightfully rich painter whose money he could put to better use. Reminiscent of

Larry's feelings toward his half-sister, the young man's anger causes Miss Pugh to compare her half-brother to Picasso, not for his artistic talent but for his looks, which sentences him to sisterly oblivion. Ironically, Prism's visualization of the artist, rather than his works of art, deprives the question of its metonymy and art of its value.

The slippage from art to artists finds its reflection in "A Painful Affair"; Miss Pugh does "not believe in art, only in artists" (*OB,* 109). Miss Pugh's devotion to art is thus questioned, the more so as she considers that "in art deception is a rule" (125). The irony, though, lies in the contemptible controversy that separates her two protégés at the time of the commemoration of her centenary, proving that she should not have believed in artists either. Further evidence lies in the appraisal of her belongings that gives them "an aura of sham" (106); no matter what convictions Miss Pugh held, she was exposed to deception over and over again.

Deceit also flourishes in "Speck's Idea" and "Overhead in a Balloon," two stories that highlight ways in which art is consumed, used, disposed of, and discussed in an illusory manner.[11] "Speck's Idea" concerns the title character's attempt to bring fame to his name and his art gallery. "Overhead in a Balloon" stars Speck's Swiss assistant, Walter Obermauer, in his peregrination through life, religion, and art. In both stories, text and image weave a web of meaning where the image, consisting of real or fictitious paintings, book covers, and films, reflects the message of the story, which in turn conveys the characters' attitude to pictorial creation, and to art in general. By merging with, and in, the text, images and the imaginary create a meaningful network that throws light on the reception of art in both stories, and on the selfishness of human endeavor.

In "Speck's Idea," an initial picture of human and political desolation finds its textual counterpart in an imaginary article foretelling many ills if all carry on ignoring the situation. Prompted by this imaginary article, Dr. Sandor Speck, an art dealer seeking prominence and prosperity, looks for ways of bringing about a new era. He then conceives an abstract image without forms or hues by conceptualizing an exhibition based on the invention, on the intellectual creation, of the work and life of an artist—likely to catch on—whose existence he has yet to trace. In other words, the text is based on the presentation of images or paintings that may or may not exist. He eventually decides to display ideal culture—or at least what he believes it to be—by exhibiting the works of a mediocre painter. The text, however, shows that this painter's re-presentation to the world does not really aim to boost a new, more dignified culture, but rather to promote an unsuccessful art dealer. The whole point of the story, evidently, is to make fun of the mercantile art world and of the production of culture in a politically and financially minded society, as comes out through the numerous paintings, drawings, and decorations depicted. The actors of this *théâtre de dupes* are the artists who produce indifferent works and the consumers who believe they are buying art objects. In between stands the illusionist, Sandor Speck, who tricks artists about what they do, and their customers about what they buy.

At the core of the story lies the basic question of authenticity and validity of both text and image in and beyond the fictional world. The creation of the imaginary artist originates in an authenticated text within the text. The "disturbing article in *Le Monde*" is presented with exact references between parentheses—"(front page, lower middle, turn to page 26)" (*OB*, 8)—that confer on it a real character. A sign presumably from the real world, yet belonging to the fictional realm by its very presence in the story, the article, written "by a man who never [takes] up his pen unless civilisation [is] in danger" (8), is meant to unsettle its readers—and supposedly the story's readers too—by mirroring the contemporary decline of society:

> Its title, "Redemption Through Art—Last Hope for the West?," had been followed by other disturbing questions: When would the merchants and dealers, compared rather unfairly to money-changers driven from the temple, face up to their responsibility as the tattered century declined? Must the flowering gardens of Western European culture wilt and die along with the decadent political systems, the exhausted parliaments, the shambling elections, the tired liberal impulses? What of the man in the street, too modest and confused to mention his cravings? Was he not gasping for one remedy and only one—artistic renovation? And where was this to come from? "In the words of Shakespr," the article concluded, supposedly in English, "That is the qustn [*sic*]." (*OB*, 8)

The picture raised by the successive questions displays culture—fictional or actual, the readers may wonder—as endangered by the commercial and political strongholds that cannot take in values of a different nature. The content of the article curiously recalls a historical harangue: on 15 March 1848, Sándor Petöfi, a Hungarian poet, became a national hero by addressing a crowd in Budapest and preconizing a revolution, indeed calling to arms to save the world and humanity.[12] The provoking questions result in Speck's immediate reaction, ironically so, for by hitting on the idea of the ideal artist agreeable to all, he falls back on the very characteristics abused by the columnist. Indeed, by devising an all-purpose figure, he sticks to philistinism and mercantilism. But then the columnist's mutilation of Shakespeare's name and a famous line from *Hamlet* reveals his own incapacity to safeguard the world's cultural heritage. This inevitably raises doubts about the identity of the writer: it could easily be Sandor Speck himself, the modern transposition and homonym, at least where his first name is concerned, of the historical figure whose discourse is echoed in less violent, but nonetheless culturally equivalent, words. The problem of the article's authenticity and the identity of its author thus remains unsolved.

Remaining on precarious foundations, Speck then starts elaborating on the life of the "savior," inventing a series of data, which raise problems of choice over the appropriate representation. A discussion with a Lodge brother eventually leads him to dig out of oblivion a second-rate painter by the name of Hubert Cruche. His surname, an aptronym, immediately creates a multiple image in the minds of the readers; *une cruche* in French means a jug, jugful, or "fool." The first meaning alludes to his life being filled up with convenient data pouring from Speck's mind; the second stands for his work being poured out on to the market to satiate humanity's thirst for a renewed cultural message; and the third hints at his being cheated on two levels (an unsuspecting cuckold, he never questioned the motives behind the sale of all his production for a period of 16 years to his wife's lover; and posthumously he is used by Speck, who tries to gain personal recognition through him). His first name, Hubert, *le patron des chasseurs,* even suggests that without benefiting from it, he offers protection to the East European hunter Speck.

The analogy between Speck and a hunter is further clarified by the existence and name change of another fictional character, namely the protagonist of John Marlyn's *Under the Ribs of Death*.[13] This immigrant novel, published in 1957, shows how, in a vain attempt to integrate, Sandor Hunyadi changes his name to Alex Hunter. The parallel highlights Speck's fruitless endeavor and the ultimate reality that he too is a broken man. Apart from being a hunter, Speck also turns out to be a shopkeeper whose small-town mentality finds a reflection in his aptronym: it is appropriate that *Speck* means bacon in German, since Sandor Speck is the "butcher" of art. Incidentally, taken literally as a very small piece, mark, or spot, the name of Speck would reinforce the futility of the art dealer's enterprise, its worthless achievement. Alternatively, taken as an abbreviation, the name would suggest that the man

embodies speculation without being able to assimilate cultural and ideological data.[14]

Traces of culture, displayed in paintings, books, and art objects, show
that the cultural patrimony has an illusory quality. Nonexistent schools
of art, such as the Tirana School, are disclosed (*OB,* 3); blatantly fake
paintings appear in galleries (3, 7, 35); souvenirs and other consumers'
objects no longer refer to traditional values but to other, new, equally
conventional ones—the Pompidou Art Centre instead of the Eiffel
Tower, for instance (44); trivial letters marked by royal stamps are more
attractive than real art (28). All these take characters and readers alike
into a realm of meanness and decadence.

In such a context, Speck can safely adopt, and persist in, a purely
mercantile attitude. His approach to art encompasses only commercial,
speculative concerns: "He knew one thing—art had sunk low on the
scale of consumer necessities. To mop up a few back bills, he was showing part of his own collection—his last-ditch old-age-security reserve.
He clasped his hands behind his neck, staring at a Vlaminck India ink
on his desk. It had been certified genuine by an expert now serving a jail
sentence in Zurich" (*OB,* 35). Art becomes merely a commodity to be
sold in order to make a living. The oxymoronic disclosure about the
"genuine" Vlaminck adds to the debasement of aesthetic values. Other
allusions to dubious transactions (7, 14) reveal that where money is concerned, Speck does not shrink from any criminal offense, be it faking (7,
14) or stealing (3, 14) a painting, or even making something up from
start to finish such as an art school or even a painter (3, 8–11). Besides,
his recollections of the parting argument he had with his second wife
confirm Speck's commercial approach: "In her summing-up of his moral
nature, a compendium that had preceded her ringing 'Fascist's, Henriette had declared that Speck appraising an artist's work made her think
of a real-estate loan officer examining Chartres Cathedral for leaks. It
was true that his feeling for art stopped short of love; it had to. . . . For
what if he were to allow passion for painting to set alight his common
sense? How would he be able to live then, knowing that the ultimate
fate of art was to die of anemia in safe-deposit vaults?" (29). The comparison with an estate agency loan officer establishes the real nature of
Speck's job. He does not, in the least, care about the artistic quality of
what he sells; only budget matters concern him. The two questions
hinting at an unlikely weakness caused by genuine enjoyment prove to
what extent art has sunk low, not "on the scale of consumer necessities"
as Speck would have it, but at a more elevated, disinterested level where

art is appreciated for its own sake rather than tucked away for fear of robbers in search of marketable goods.

Because speculators have invaded the market, Lydia Cruche, the painter's widow, acts as a shrewd businesswoman, flinching at no stratagem available to raise the value of her inheritance. Rather than being a *cruche,* she takes after Croesus, king of Lydia, and cleverly tricks Speck into supporting her own financial hopes. Calling to mind two real artist widows, Lydia Cruche behaves like a leech sucking its prey's blood. Like Magritte's wife, she makes sure that all her husband's works will sell well, as she has already shown that over a period of 16 years she could manage to secure just that. Alternatively, like Utrillo's wife, who kept her husband as if on a leash because of his addiction to alcohol, Lydia is a tough opponent in financial transactions. By pretending to be a Japhethite, a member of a sect rejecting the graven image as creation rivaling God, and thus regarding artists as impostors, she feigns a lack of interest in a retrospective of her husband's works—in other words, she refuses the kind of meat Speck offers her, the better to chew afterward. Eventually, by calling on the services of an Italian dealer, she manages to put Speck in a weaker position—the hunter thus gets hunted by the very wife of the hunters' patron saint.

Of course, Speck suffers from the ups and downs of his enterprise. An art dealer, he expresses his emotions through visual images taken from books, films, and paintings and through mental images. Visual references to the landscape (*OB,* 5, 46) offer a transposition of his feelings, at times also compared with actual paintings (23, 43, 45). Even films or cartoons (5, 46) reflect some emotional state of mind, and a series of pictures evoking Parisian society and emerging from Speck's imagination, perception, or recollection (12–13) clarify his moods. An unexpected source of pictures, his emotions add up to the overall artistic parody. On leaving Lydia Cruche after his defeat and the wreck of his car, Speck has to take a bus back to central Paris. While waiting for the bus, he equates "the dark shopping center with its windows shining for no one" to "a Magritte vision of fear" (45), a metonymy that reflects Speck's feeling of betrayal. His feelings, expressed through imaginary or real artistic images whose source is made clear by description or allusion, contribute to the visual qualities of the text.

Similarly, political ideas are rendered through images. Although camouflaged under the innocent sounding name of Amandine—a name redolent of sweets or exquisite chocolates—the shop opposite Speck's gallery conveys a clear political message. The pictures, book covers, and other pieces on show clearly indicate that the shop owner favors the French fascist movement called Jeune Europe:[15] "On the cover of one volume, Uncle Sam shook hands with the Russian Bear over prostrate Europe, depicted as a maiden in a dead faint. A drawing of a spider on a field of banknotes (twelve hundred francs with frame, nine hundred without) jostled the image of a crablike hand clawing away at the map of France" (*OB*, 6). These sarcastic attacks on American hegemony, the power of the Soviet Union, and the greed of Jewish bankers were the usual fare of wartime German propaganda. At this stage, the readers may share the amused contempt of the implied author—not to say of the author herself—for such views, as the bookseller's name, Chassepoule (hen chaser), seems to point to his trivial pursuit.

As for Speck, he does not question such fascist ideals, for he refuses to take positions or to get involved. In fact, when he looks for a location for his art gallery, he looks for a "safe place" (*OB*, 1–2) politically. However, though he remains neutral, he does not altogether abstain from thinking of the multilateral political reception of his invented painter, thereby giving another poor picture of artistic endeavor: "Left, Right, and Center would unite on a single theme: how the taste of two full generations had been corrupted by foreign speculation, cosmopolitan decadence, and the cultural imperialism of the Anglo-Saxon hegemony" (9). Out of commercial motives, Speck struggles for everybody's agreement, which stresses the weakness of his political arguments. As Janice Kulyk Keefer remarks, "French politics is a crazy salad" (1989, 186) of contradictory positions, and its blatant leanings toward nationalism bear a strong resemblance to World War II right-wing opinions. The same applies to Speck's imaginary show, for which he dreams of enjoying everybody's approval, though he cannot avoid expressing his preference:

> He could see the structure of the show, the sketchbooks and letters in glass cases. It might be worthwhile lacquering the walls black, concentrating strong spots on the correspondence, which straddled half a century, from Degas to Cocteau. The scrawl posted by Drieu la Rochelle just before his suicide would be particularly effective on black. Céline was good; all that crowd was back in vogue now. He might use the early photo of Céline in regimental dress uniform with a splendid helmet. Of course, there would be word from the Left, too, with postcards from Jean Jaurès, Léon Blum, and Paul Éluard, and a jaunty get-well message from Louis Aragon and Elsa. (*OB*, 10)

The emphasis laid on people championing extreme right-wing ideas is inescapable: three sentences are devoted to Drieu La Rochelle—a man of letters who was to be executed by firing squad after World War II for collaborating with the Germans—and to Céline, whose major anti-Semitic and pro-German writings during the war earned him public condemnation and incarceration in Denmark. Only one sentence is devoted to left-wingers: the pooh-poohing way Speck speaks about them proves that he adds them as an afterthought to please everyone. In fact, the readers feel that he rather agrees with fascist ideas, especially in the light of the insult proffered by his wife on leaving him and his own disparaging remark to Lydia Cruche after she has tricked him into accepting her demands.

In the end, however, the readers wonder who has tricked whom, for Sandor Speck expresses his triumph in two powerful images in which the landscape reflects his elated mood and where the cartoon picture he imagines visually proclaims his victory as the hunter taming the wife of the hunters' patron saint and Speck's second wife, too: "He opened his eyes and saw rain clouds over Paris glowing with light—the urban aurora. It seemed to Speck that he was entering a better weather zone, leaving behind the gray, indefinite mist in which the souls of discarded lovers are said to wander. He welcomed this new and brassy radiation. He saw himself at the center of a shadeless drawing, hero of a sort of cartoon strip, subduing Lydia, taming Henriette" (*OB,* 46). Although this picture clearly establishes Speck's confidence, it still raises doubts as to the real intentions of Lydia Cruche, who could change her mind once again. For in the courting game on which Speck has embarked, no one knows who will get the upper hand, as the people involved in it have radically different interests.

In "Overhead in a Balloon," the paintings displayed by the text also illustrate an aspect of French culture, namely the general decline of upper-class Parisian society as further exemplified by the experiences of Walter, a lonely art gallery assistant. As he befriends a mediocre French painter with a chain-link name—the distinctive token of nobility—and eventually moves into the flat of the painter's family, Walter is con-fronted by the way in which French aristocracy establishes and main-tains—or rather cripples—human relationships. This unfortunate situa-tion, reflected in the paintings of his new friend "Aymeric Something Something de Something de Saint-Régis" (*OB,* 59), is a source of daily, though unconscious, suffering. Walter is indeed unable to decode

Aymeric's paintings, even though they suggestively disclose the social behavior of the French aristocracy, and by extension of his own family too: "Now he painted country houses. Usually he showed the front with the white shutters and all the ivy, and a stretch of lawn with white chairs and a teapot and cups, and some scattered pages of Le Figaro—the only newspaper, often the only anything, his patrons read. He had a hairline touch and could reproduce Le Figaro's social calendar, in which he cleverly embedded his client's name and his own. Some patrons kept a large magnifying glass on a table under the picture, so that guests, peering respectfully, could appreciate their host's permanent place in art" (49–50). The description "poses the problem of representation within the represented universe of the narrative . . . by embedding one Art form, that of the picture, within another, the narrative."[16] The embedding functions on different levels: it reflects, as Sturgess argues, the characters' environmental subordination (47), but it also mirrors their superficiality. While depicting done-up country houses, Aymeric confines his attention to their conventional facades and external signs of wealth, much in accordance with the accepted conduct of his family, whose affected politeness conceals their real nature and inclinations. Moreover, the actual presence of the patron's name and his own on the reproduction of Le Figaro textually and pictorially announces their eagerness to be publicized. Beyond mere publicity stands the ultimate necessity to bridge the gap left by their shallow and empty lives. The image of the magnifying glass to decipher the represented text metaphorically confirms the pressing need to inflate the values of the bourgeois patrons encoded—a meaningless endeavor that does not fool those capable of interpreting the signs. Aymeric's minuscule signature on his paintings—a combination of the pictorial and the scriptural— finds a verbal echo in the reference to his voice, which is described as a "signature that [requires] a magnifying glass; what he [has] to say [is] clear but a kind of secret" (52). The analogy offers a symbolic reinforcement of the aristocracy's ambiguous need to be seen, yet not ostentatiously.

Besides reflecting the characters' shallowness, the description of Aymeric's painting mirrors the story's structuring process, evidencing metafictional self-reflexiveness. The painting actually reveals what Gallant does when devising her story: she too shows the facade, the surface of things, its hotchpotch of disconnected details and her characters' lack of culture and obsession with fame and moving in the best circles. Her ironic vision "overhead in a balloon" gives the story her stamp as well as ridicules her characters, whose names are embedded in the description of a kind of vanity fair. The visual thus mirrors the organizational principle of the text, adding a further layer of complexity.

Further textual and visual intermingling occurs in the description of the inflated picture story about the art gallery: "It happened that one of the Paris Sunday supplements had published a picture story on Walter's gallery, with captions that laid stress on the establishment's boldness, vitality, visibility, international connections, and financial vigor. The supplement had cost Walter's employer a packet, and Walter was not surprised that one of the photographs showed him close to collapse, leaning for support against the wall safe in his private office" (*OB,* 50). The fictitious magazine article combines both modes of representation, whose fictional description ridicules the undertaking by verbally stressing the paradoxical message of weakness hidden in the pictures. Pictorial and scriptural presentations thus work at cross purposes, thereby adding an extra ironic layer of meaning. The irony culminates in the insight into the financial burden of the enterprise, whose foreseeable disappointing outcome manifests itself as only Aymeric, prompted by his gullibility, pays an eager visit to the gallery. He imagines the place as packed with anxious buyers: "The accompanying article described mobbed openings, private viewings to which the police were summoned to keep order, and potential buyers lined up outside in below-freezing weather, bursting in the minute the doors were opened to grab everything off the walls. The name of the painter hardly mattered; the gallery's reputation was enough" (50).

But his actual experience as sole visitor affords a contrast to this illusion, not only in terms of numbers but also in terms of the outcome: "Aymeric showed courteous amazement when he heard just how much a show of that kind would cost. The uncultured talk about money was the gallery's way of refusing him, though a clause in the rejection seemed to say that something might still be feasible, in some distant off-season, provided that Aymeric was willing to buy all his own work" (*OB,* 51). In spite of the basic differences between these two pictures—the one imaginary, the other real (as real as fiction can be)—both evoke financial transactions and a purely materialistic approach to art. Some artists are businessmen whose talent ceases to be of aesthetic value: they and others alike take a purely pecuniary interest in art. The comparisons of Aymeric to Degas and Picasso—implicit in one case, explicit in the other—can therefore not be qualitative; denoting a purely matter-of-fact concern, the analogies only establish a parallel to Degas for not being married and to Picasso for having added his mother's maiden name to his own. No artistic similarity can be discerned. All neglect quality; money rules all. At least both text and image convey this idea.

Other textual and visual elements confirm this view while stressing the loss on the human level. For instance, Aymeric's assumption "that a show, a sort of retrospective of lawns and *Figaros,* would bring fresh patronage, perhaps even from abroad" (*OB,* 50) highlights the artist's greed. On the other hand, such a retrospective would imply a vast collection of quasi duplicates—a reflection of French superficiality and ostentation. With these sets of doubles, triples, and quadruples, Gallant brings out in bold a peculiar aspect of art, namely that when artists have a good subject matter, they sometimes paint it over and over again—as exemplified by modern painters (such as Monet, Cézanne, Magritte, and Munch, to mention but a few) and ancient painters alike. In addition, yet another set of images comes to mind with the reference to the kind of country houses Aymeric is "called in to immortalize" (50): "a done-up village bakery, a barn refurbished and brightened with yellow awnings 'Dallas' had lately made so popular" (50). The allusion to *Dallas,* with its flashy ranches and mansions, not to mention the characters' decadent lifestyle, reinforces the mercantile perception of art and the deterioration of human relations it seems to involve.

The allusion to the film is far from coincidental, for the family watches the serial in semireligious silence on a television set with a display of buttons that act as so many barriers to true communication. A *mise en abyme* in an admittedly different genre—that of the New World—the serial illustrates the nature of relationships within the family circle.[17] Robert, Aymeric's cousin, even goes so far as to announce his wedding in the middle of an episode, as if he were talking about a trivial fact. This recalls similar utterances in *Dallas:* Robert's announcement taking place in front of "a bright, silent screen" (67)—the image of failed communication—echoes the hollowness of human relations conveyed by the television show. Robert's careless attitude to human relations is further visually exemplified in his finger drawings of the flat and its new boundaries once he has decided to evict Walter: " 'We will have to rearrange the space,' said Robert. He traced lines with his finger on the polished table and, with the palm of his hand, wiped something out" (70). A symbolic and ephemeral picture of exclusion, the drawing signifies the annihilation of human emotions and the need of living space; anyway, it cannot appeal to anyone from an aesthetic point of view. As such it recalls Robert's attitude when he conducts an explanatory session on the extended family's dreams: in godlike fashion, Robert decides what they mean, often offering a pessimistic interpretation of the animals and violent scenes that people Walter's dreams. The sacred interpretation is based on clues taken from a Bible-like book, whose text and images Robert uses to achieve his ends—instead of offering comfort to others.

Since art and religion no longer fulfill their function, they can neither offer visions of a better world nor bring comfort to souls in want of an ideal. Barthes sees a connection between the images that invade the world and human discontent: "What characterizes the so-called advanced societies is that they today consume images and no longer, like those of the past, beliefs; they are therefore more liberal, less fanatical, but also more 'false' (less 'authentic')—something we translate, in ordinary consciousness, by the avowal of an impression of nauseated boredom, as if the universalized image were producing a world that is without difference (indifferent), from which can rise, here and there, only the cry of anarchisms, marginalisms, and individualisms" (Barthes 1981, 118–19). Thus the mystically inclined Walter looks for a spiritual message in art, but in vain. His constant attempts at harmonizing art and faith lead him to the gradual discovery of their incompatibility: "Immersion in art had kept him from spiritual knowledge. What he had mistaken for God's beckoning had been a dabbing in colors, sentiment cut loose and set afloat by the sight of a stained-glass window. Years before, when he was still training Walter, his employer had sent him to museums, with a list of things to examine and ponder. God is in art, Walter had decided; then, God *is* art. Today, he understood: art is God's enemy. God hates art, the trifling rival creation" (*OB,* 60). Since Walter searches for an absolute in art but cannot find it there, he ends up expressing his aversion forcefully—somehow earnestly echoing Lydia Cruche's pretended rejection of the graven image, therefore bringing to mind other layers of textual and visual reverberations. A Puritan rejecting works of art, he reminds the readers of some Calvinists who objected to the worship of the holy images and destroyed them: "Virtually anything portrayed as art turned his stomach. There was hardly anything he could look at without feeling sick" (66).

An expression of his religious inclination, his physical disgust for visual arts also points to his inability to cope with life. Since most objects, beings, and situations have their reflection in art, nothing he ever witnesses or takes part in can ever please him. At some stage, in a discussion with Aymeric, he discriminates between art and Aymeric's paintings: " 'I hate art, too,' said Walter. 'Oh, I don't mean that I hate what you do. That, at least, has some meaning—it lets people see how they imagine they live' " (*OB*, 54). Walter's feeling of repulsion raises an interesting issue, namely that of art and its meaning. Art, according to him, has lost its significance. However, Walter finds Aymeric's superficial and idyllic picture of society meaningful—an arresting paradox if one considers that "Fine art is that in which the hand, the head, and the heart of man go together."[18] Besides, the picture Aymeric gives of society goes against Walter's profound wish to establish proper relations with others. His artistic delusion results from his desperate need to belong. Ironically, the human warmth he erroneously seeks in his adoptive family turns out to be a profit-making enterprise for the family and a devastating source of worries for Walter. The misreading of Aymeric's paintings thus suggests that Walter is a prey to the glamorous message French aristocracy conveys in art. A pedestrian character, Walter takes everything at its face value. Contrary to the expected reliability inherent in his Swiss citizenship, Walter Obermauer is a dropout who cannot adjust to the necessities of life. As his name indicates, he is the upper wall without retaining wall, ready to collapse at any excess of weight.

An exponent of materialistic society, Walter shows signs of a spiritual corruption whose origin can be traced to a purely mercantile approach to culture. Built in a slapdash fashion by contractors in search of money, the cultural edifice on which art rests offers no safe ground. Gallant underscores its devastating loss of significance through images reflecting aesthetic degradation.[19] The quest for beauty has been replaced by the mercantile operations of would-be artists and art dealers. In Paris, apparently, the middle ground between weak-willed artists and a gullible public is held by unscrupulous people, who fix the rules of the game as arbitrarily as the ministers of the most exotic religious faiths.

Unlike postmodern photography, which "defamiliarises the images that surround us" "through a demystifying use of irony," the paintings, drawings, and photographs represented in Gallant's fiction are not necessarily ironical in themselves.[20] They become so owing to the interaction between text and image. The irony thereby created is multiple, one mode of representation reflecting the other almost ad infinitum, obviously depending on the readers' ability to see further layers of interrelation. As written texts and images do not have only one interpretation, superimposed decoding adds to their riches. Their multiple readings enhance the ironic impact of representation, the visual reflecting the textual, and vice versa. Because Gallant describes and refers to images that tend to present a rigid message of retribution and punishment, or to reveal ungratifying relationships and unacceptable views, she emphasizes and derides the selfishness of human endeavor conveyed in her stories. Emerging from the interaction between text and image, the characters' innate talent for destruction reduces constructive ideals to nothing. By reinforcing the message of the text on which the image is superimposed, the visual enhances the readers' awareness of the self-inflicted, and therefore ineluctable, human degradation prevailing in Gallant's work.

Chapter Eight

Stylistic Reflection of Tension:
In Transit

Originally written in the fifties and sixties, the stories collected in *In Transit* are set in multiple places—Spain, Italy, Switzerland, France, Yugoslavia, and Finland—and are essentially peopled with displaced characters from French, German, American, English, Irish, Spanish, or Romanian origin. Mostly consisting of short third-person narratives (with the exception of "April Fish," "The Sunday after Christmas," and "When We Were Nearly Young"), the collection presents a variety of concise, sharply contrasted portraits; short and compelling, these stories were written by a stylist reveling in her craftsmanship. Wasting no word, Gallant conveys atmosphere with economy, excels at minimalistic pictures of scenes and characters' moods, evokes different layers of understanding through one image—in short exemplifies her expertise at effective and powerful word spinning. Pitiless in her descriptions, Gallant accurately delineates the trivial elements that make up human life. She discusses human problems from a distance with impassible detachment, coldly assessing the ins and outs of human relationships even when involved.[1] Aloof and cool, she passes no moral judgment on either characters or situations, leaving it to her readers to interpret events and look for plausible solutions; in the same vein, she avoids closure, leaving the outcome of her stories uncertain, as if for the readers to construct.

Far from being equivocal, the openings direct the readers' attention to the very core of the stories. Sharp and striking, they announce the development by allusion; in some stories, they establish the thematic disconnection from the start, before subsequent illustration. Witness the opening of "When We Were Nearly Young": "In Madrid, nine years ago, we lived on the thought of money. Our friendships were nourished with talk of money we expected to have, and what we intended to do when it came" (*IT,* 61). The cynical first sentence refuses pretense of heartfelt feelings, announces the materialistic bind straightaway, a connection reiterated in the nature of the friendship. The story then proceeds to show the shallow basis for so-called friendship, the ties dissolving once the protagonist-narrator does receive some money. "Careless Talk" also starts strikingly with an opening sentence that leaves little hope for real relations: "Their language—English—drew them together. So did their condition in a world they believed intended for men. They were Iris Drouin, the London girl inexplicably married to a French farmer (inexplicably only because other people's desires are so strange), and Mary Olcott, her summer neighbor and friend" (123). The opening reduces human relations with such devastating cynicism that it comes as no surprise that the story develops the impossibility of really trusting anyone. When Iris discovers that unattached Mary uses her confidences and makes fun of her to entertain guests, she walks out on Mary, pretending the need to attend to her husband and children whom she really loves. At the end, Mary's concern over Iris's reaction and desire to make up with her boils down to keeping her hobby going, namely the multiple chess games she plays with people as if they were pawns (140)—true relations do not exist.

A few more examples help to explain Gallant's striking exploitation of revelatory openings. In "The Captive Niece" she reduces relationships to mere conveniences from the very beginning: "Without the slightest regard for her feelings or the importance of this day, he had said, 'Bring back a sandwich or some bread and paté, will you, anything you see— oh, and the English papers' " (*IT,* 233). The story then reveals the tenuous grounds for Gitta and her lover's relationship, worse still his abuse of her and her subservience. Similarly, in "The Statues Taken Down," the opening manifests that in spite of blood ties, the children and father are as apart from each other as the moon and the sun: "Crawley turned his two younger children loose day after day in the Palais-Royal gardens, because he thought it would keep them amused, but they were not brought up to spend a whole afternoon sitting on iron chairs. . . . It was convenient for him to imagine they were close and inviolate and that he, the adult, was excluded, but all Hal and Dorothy had in common was their colouring, which was fair, and houses lived in . . . and journeys shared, and the American tongue" (161). Having established that the father cannot be bothered to look after his children himself, the story illustrates how he secures Dorothy's help to take care of Hal, as well as how he influences her to view him as a poor swallow caught in the nets of women when in fact *he* consumes them. Dorothy's incomprehension of adult facts yields to her gullibility, so that her father can count her in the number of women he uses. The contrast in outlook is therefore explicit from the start.

At other times, as Kulyk Keefer points out, the opening consists of an "utterly authoritative statement—declaration rather than observation—[that] compels assent" (1989, 67). "Questions and Answers" starts with an assertion that "Rumanians notoriously are marked by delusions of eminence and persecution" (*IT,* 173), which the story evidences through the relation of the pseudofriendship of Marie and Amalia. "Vacances Pax" begins with an indisputable sociohistorical fact: "Midsummer Night has always been a pagan festival, and the Christians did not change its nature by naming the day for St John the Baptist" (191). Universal in character, the festival is thereafter celebrated by an international holiday camp. But just as the opening suggests that historical changes make no difference, so the modern, postpagan concept of "One Europe" also proves illusory; indeed, the story stresses the prevailing disjunction of the holiday makers, who all stick to their national identity. The participants end up sounding "like the ingenious all-Europe programs in which the best drummer from Denmark performs from a studio in Copenhagen, along with a trumpet from Stuttgart, an electric guitar from Milan and France's finest clarinet. No musician can hear or see the other, for each is in his own city" (200–201). This comparison then leaves no doubt as to the ironic intention of the opening. As to "Good Deeds," it starts with a comment whose truth cannot be refuted, not by virtue of its universality or established knowledge, but because of the readers' lack of information about the subject: "Houses of widows on the French Riviera have in common the outsize pattern of flowers on the chintzes; there is too much furniture everywhere, most of it larger than life. The visitor feels, as he is intended to do, very small" (247). Such openings cut a stunning picture that cannot be forgotten thereafter, the more so as it reflects the crushing power of the main character, whose indifference to all astounds even the most insensitive reader.

Besides the openings' compelling statements and thematic foreshadowing and final paragraphs avoiding closure, Gallant has a style of her own resting on her respect for her native language, which she treats "like a delicate timepiece, making certain it runs exactly and that no dust gets inside" (*PN,* 189).[2] Her own discussion of style does not offer the magic recipe to good writing; it gives a general direction but shies away from particulars: "Leaving the one analysis that is closed to me, of my own writing, let me say what style is not: it is not a last-minute addition to prose, a charming and universal slipcover, a coat of paint used to mask the failings of structure. . . . Style in writing, as in painting, is the author's thumbprint, his mark. . . . It is, finally, the distillation of a lifetime of reading and listening, of selection and rejection. But if it is not a true voice, it is nothing" (176–79). Critics have responded to her fiction in a similar fashion; most "acknowledge Gallant's mastery of language and . . . the authoritative elegance" (Kulyk Keefer 1989, 35–36) and vividness of her style and consider its speechlike quality as its "thumbprint," but no one has drawn a map of her work's stylistic features.[3]

Confirming the generally unsupported critical comments, the following close examination of stylistic patterns in the title story of *In Transit* highlights Gallant's predilection for simple and compound sentences, fragments and elliptical structures, colloquial idioms, common core Anglo-Saxon vocabulary, and unaffected language; but it surpasses expectations by highlighting an essential feature overlooked so far: it reveals the tension at the core of Gallant's style and its reinforcement of the thematic enunciation. The analysis of "In Transit" indeed shows how meaning and message are tied by particular stylistic features as the oxymoronic "silent cry" that dominates the characters' perception of life finds its reflection in the selection and organization of words.[4] The analogies with paintings by Edvard Munch that emerge from the analysis somehow take the readers back to Gallant's consideration of style, exemplifying the common ground of writing and painting.

The story's first sentence immediately announces detachment through its connotations: "After the Cook's party of twenty-five Japanese tourists had departed for Oslo, only four people were left in the waiting room of the Helsinki Airport—a young French couple named Perrigny, who had not been married long, and an elderly pair who were identifiably American" (*IT,* 153). The opening reference to the party of Japanese tourists conjures up a world of outsiders taking snapshots of every sight but never relating to the local population. The mention of Cook's travel agency also stresses the impersonal character of the group, itself indistinguishable from the hundreds of tours that have followed and will follow the same path. The locale, "the waiting room of the Helsinki Airport," also evokes transition between one world and another. As a transitional place, the waiting room clearly suggests impersonal relationships, further strengthened by the picture of the only travelers left—an elderly American couple and a couple of French newlyweds—set apart by their distinctive nationalities and languages. The participial clause ("named Perrigny") and the nonrestrictive subclause concerning the French couple ("who had not been married long") in an otherwise uninvolved relation both imply omniscience and insist on the recent—perhaps still fragile—nature of the tie that binds the couple. As to the American couple, they are defined essentially through the adverb "identifiably"; though it does not indicate omniscience, it calls to mind common European prejudices about Americans. The whole sentence then reads as a factual description without involvement on the part of the narrator. As sharp and incisive as many others, the opening of the story thus creates distance by virtue of its objective and detached tone.

Once the parallel structure in the opening sentence has created a link between the American and the French couples, the story proceeds to illustrate the disconnection within each couple. Breach of unity causes each person to take a distance from his or her partner, as highlighted by a further parallel drawn through alternation of perspectives and fast succession of surprising, if not contradictory, images. The oscillation between omniscience and limited perspective—a recurrent feature of Gallant's fiction—also renders the picture hazy, simultaneously affording affirmations and hypotheses. The following passage illustrates this point very clearly: "When they were sure that the young people two benches forward could not understand them, the old people went on with a permanent, flowing quarrel [1]. The man had the habit of reading signs out loud, though perhaps he did it only to madden his wife [2]. He read the signs over the three doors leading out to the field: " 'Oslo.' 'Amsterdam.' 'Copenhagen.' . . . I don't see 'Stockholm' [3]" (*IT*, 153).[5] Besides deriding the man's habit, sentence [2] linguistically presents at once two perspectives of narration: the phrase "had the habit" presupposes unquestionable prior knowledge while the adverb "perhaps" in the subclause reminds the readers of the fuzziness of human logic.[6] On the contrary, in the preceding sentence, the adjective "permanent" discloses a fact not limited to the narrative present and implies one perspective, omniscient this time. By pointing to the ongoing quarrel between the two Americans, the paired adjectives "flowing" and "permanent" insist on the gap that separates them. The matter-of-fact rendering of his sign reading throws light on the futility of his activity. The discrepancy between the man's trivial reading of signposts and the woman's existential question as to the nature of their relationship is pathetic:

> She replied, "What I wonder is what I have been to you all these years." [1]
> Philippe Perrigny, who understood English, turned around, pretending he was looking at Finnish pottery in the showcases on their right [2].

He saw that the man was examining timetables and tickets, all the while muttering "Stockholm, Stockholm," while the woman looked away [3]. She had removed her glasses and was wiping her eyes [4]. How did she arrive at that question here, in Helsinki Airport, and how can he answer? [5] It has to be answered in a word: everything/nothing [6]. It was like being in a country church and suddenly hearing the peasant priest put a question no one cares to consider, about guilt or duty or the presence of God, and breathing with relief when he has got past that and on to the prayers [7]. (*IT,* 153)

Rather static owing to the nature of the verbs, the picture leaves little hope for improvement: virtually no verb of movement is used, and when one is, it denotes minimal or insignificant motion ("to remove one's glasses," "to wipe one's eyes") except where a particle deprives the verb of its physical motion and gives it a connotation of continuity or of mental activity ("to go on," "to arrive at a question," "to get past a topic," and "to get on to the prayers").[7] Verbs of perception or of mental activity ("to quarrel," "to madden," "to choose," "to see," "to look away," "to read," "to examine") abound in the first 29 lines, but significantly they do not imply shared perception but rather something trivial. The woman's line [1]—incongruous in such a setup—overheard and decoded by the Frenchman leads to a few sentences [5–7] of free indirect speech in the present tense projecting the American couple's situation. A comparison [7] funnily transposes the question to an altogether different register, religious this time, that marks the unpleasantness of the moment. Compared with "guilt or duty or the presence of God"—three oppressive Christian concepts—the question posed takes another dimension. Its answer to the effect that their relationship must boil down to "everything/nothing" (*IT,* 153)—an equation empty of meaning—intimates the hopelessness of married life. The combination of such antipodal concepts, indeed, nullifies the worth of the relationship, the more so as the indeterminate voice expressing its meaninglessness can be simultaneously that of the exasperated husband, of the French observer, or of the uninvolved narrator.[8] The husband's following repartee then confirms the absence of a deep bond: " 'In the next world we will choose differently,' the man said. 'At least I know you will' " (153). The play on pronouns gives weight to the expression of the man's deep resentment while prolonging the question of guilt. As such, the sentence offers three different readings: it means either "It's your fault; you've made the wrong choice; you should have known," or "The one *I* chose was different; *you* have changed," or else "*You*'re the one who no longer loves me; *I* still love you . . . I think."

The answer to the American woman's existential question obviously triggers the young man's wild imaginings about the American couple. While doing so, the Frenchman assumes the voice of duty, which, the readers later hear, he himself did not listen to in his first marriage when he walked out without a word:

> The wild thoughts of the younger man were [1]: They are chained for the rest of this life [2]. Too old to change? [3] Only a brute would leave her now? [4] They are walking toward the door marked "Amsterdam," and she limps [5]. That is why they cannot separate; she is an invalid [6]. He has been looking after her for years [7]. They are going through the Amsterdam door, whatever their tickets said [8]. Whichever door they take, they will see the circular lanes of suburbs, and the family car out-side each house, and in the back yard a blue pool [9]. All across Northern Europe streets are named after acacia trees, but they may not know that [10]. (*IT*, 154)

The young man's rambling guesses about the old couple presented as in a scientific report [1] merge short assertions [2 + 6 + 7] and elliptical questions [3 – 4] with factual details [5 + 7]: this mixture of sharp suppositions and statements on the couple's depressing raison d'être is matched by the monotonous subject-verb-object pattern of the sentences. The monotony of the sentence structures is then reflected not so much in the more complex pattern of the following sentences [9 + 10] as in the depressing uniform description of northern European towns. Punctuated by the couple's departure through an arbitrarily chosen exit gate, the announcement of the townscape uniformity is all the more somber as a polysyndeton amplifies it. This distressing picture partakes of sterile preconceived notions while echoing the impossibility of being happy in marriage.

Once again, Gallant writes short sentences followed by long sentences. Echoing, indeed reinforcing, the thematic tension, the style is particularly disjunctive. It actually reflects the strain affecting the relationship of the old couple; the short, harsh sentences correspond to the periods of tension between them, while the longer ones correspond to the periods of boredom.

The allusions to the Japanese and the comments about the American couple contribute to the atmosphere of dejection, but the story is really meant to bring out the frailty of the French couple. The narration indeed proceeds to unveil breaches between Philippe and his new wife in a discursive survey of past and present facts intermingled with the couple's exchange of ideas. The looseness of the relation, needless to say, serves a specific function; it substantiates Philippe's inability to truly relate to other beings, even to his wife:

> Perrigny was on his wedding trip [1a], but also on assignment for his Paris paper [1b], and he assembled the series on Scandinavia in his mind [1c]. He had been repeating for four years now an article called "The Silent Cry," and neither his paper nor he himself had become aware that it was repetitious [2]. He began to invent again, in the style of the Paris weeklies: "It was a silent anguished cry torn from the hearts and throats . . ." [3] No. "It was a silent song, strangled . . ." [4] "It was a silent passionate hymn to . . ." [5] This time the beginning would be joined to the blue-eyed puritanical north; it had applied to Breton farmers unable to get a good price for their artichokes, to the Christmas crowd at the Berlin Wall, to Greece violated by tourists, to Negro musicians performing at the Olympia music hall, to miserable Portuguese fishermen smuggled into France and dumped on the labour market, to poets writing under the influence of drugs [6]. (*IT,* 154)

The unexpected addition [1b + 1c] to the banal main clause [1a] informs the readers that instead of enjoying their honeymoon fully, the couple has to come back with an article for Philippe's newspaper. The parallel structure [1a + 1b] equates honeymoon to work trip, while the final independent clause [1c] insists on the overwhelming professional preoccupations, leaving no space for amorous delight. To put it differently, the comparatively long statement [1b + 1c] about the assignment— approximately two-thirds of the sentence—stresses the room this task takes and the little importance attached to the wedding trip itself. The love song is thus superseded by the professional singsong. Repetitious, the metaphoric openings of his articles ironically reflect Philippe's unconscious refusal to immerse himself in the culture he is supposed to describe: the narrator's comments on his attempts at rephrasing the beginning of his article [3–5] evidence Philippe's determination to look at others from the outside, as does his lack of awareness about his stylistic trick. Even the original title of the article that serves as a basis for all his writing—"The Silent Cry"—reveals, by virtue of its oxymoron, his desperate vision of life while mirroring his own situation.[9] In addition,

the title and its repeated use recall the multiple versions of Edvard
Munch's painting *The Scream,* which refers to human wretchedness.[10]
What Ulrich Bischoff says about the painting can easily apply to the
story itself, for the painting portrays "the fear and loneliness of Man in a
natural setting which—far from offering any kind of consolation—picks
up the scream and echoes it beyond the bay unto the bloody vaults of
heaven" (53).[11] The series of verbs denoting his intellectual endeavors—
"to assemble," "to repeat," "to invent," "to join," "to apply"—loses its
strength because of the gratuitous repetition of the four initial words of
his original article. The mock-epic apposed topics of diverging aspects to
which this phrase has been applied emphasize the futility of the Frenchman's vision, its lack of openness and originality.

As if to confirm Philippe's obtuseness, a paragraph about the old couple interrupts the broken relation of his journalistic achievements, offering a typically Gallantian abrupt transition to force the readers to find a
connection; in this case, abruptness highlights the analogy between the
French and the American couple:[12] "The old man took his wife's hand
[1]. She was still turned away, but dry-eyed now, and protected by
glasses [2]. To distract her while their tickets were inspected he said
rapidly, 'Look at the nice restaurant, the attractive restaurant [3]. It is
part outside and part inside, see? It is inside *and* outside' [4]" (*IT,* 154).
The first two sentences imply that the old people communicate only
superficially: just as the verbs related to the woman—"turned away,"
"dry-eyed," and "protected"—mark a conflict and even withdrawal, the
husband's gesture compares to that of the adult pulling a child along
while walking too fast for his companion to follow. Besides, the verb
characterizing the man's mental effort—"to distract"—once more
marks an unequal relation, in which he assumes the role of the adult,
and the woman that of the child whose "silent cry" reverberates. Even
his speech act is patronizing in tone and diction and is repetitive, as if to
ensure reaching his target. As the old man insists on the location of a
restaurant "part outside and part inside," the readers are reminded that
solitude—"the silent cry"—is everywhere, both around and within oneself, and that true communication comes from inside, too.

All the more striking for it, the reminder establishes a fact that
Philippe has not yet assimilated. He definitely shuns communion, even
with his new wife, as appears from his subsequent conversation with her
and their individual reflections alternating their voices:

Perrigny's new wife gently withdrew her hand from his and said, "Why did you leave her?" [1].

He had been expecting this [2a], and said, "Because she couldn't concentrate on one person [2b]. She was nice to everybody, but she couldn't concentrate enough for a marriage" [2c].

"She was unfaithful" [3].

"That too. It came from the same lack of concentration. She had been married before" [4].

"Oh? She was old?" [5].

"She's twenty-seven now. She was afraid of being twenty-seven. She used to quote something from Jane Austen—an English writer," he said as Claire frowned. "Something about a woman that age never being able to hope for anything again. I wonder what she did hope for" [6].

"The first husband left her, too?" [7].

"No, he died. They hadn't been married very long" [8].

"You *did* leave her?" said the girl for fear of a possible humiliation—for fear of having married a man some other woman had thrown away [9]. *(IT,* 155)

As a rule, Gallant records only the significant passages of a conversation and lets her readers infer the rest for themselves. For example, she lets them deduce from the wife's question [1] that the couple has been engaged in this conversation for some time. That it concerns his relationship with his first wife is evidenced by the use of the adjective "new" and the visual image of the withdrawn hand, marking detachment, if only momentarily [1]. It becomes clear from further questions [5, 7] and answers [2, 4, 8] that in an attempt to gauge the strength of their bonds, the girl has been questioning Philippe about his first marriage. Information is disclosed slowly so as to keep the readers wondering about the true nature of the conversation. Abstract terms—"concentration," "marriage," "unfaithfulness," "humiliation," "fear"—and verbs indicating intellectual attitudes—"concentrate," "wonder," "expect"—characterize this passage in the inquisitive mode, as if feelings had no hold. Philippe's expectation [2a] proves that theirs is anything but a long-standing relationship. His reply [2b] reveals his incapacity to accept part of the responsibility for his first marriage's failure and probably also his inability to strengthen the bond necessary for a successful married life: the use of the verb "to concentrate" not only wipes out the emotional aspect of the relationship but also shows his egotistic views about the role of woman in marriage. The restatement [2c] about her being "nice to everybody" indicates that he was not ready to let her devote time to friends (the wasteful generosity of his first wife, Shirley, is narrated in *A Fairly Good Time*). The revelations of [2b] and [2c] echo Browning's "My Last Duchess," in which the Duke of Ferrara complains about his first wife's inclination to give her favors unrestrictedly.[13]

Philippe's new wife's postulate [3]—"she was unfaithful"—an unpoetic and straightforward statement, is less an assertion than a proof of her willingness to find her past rival at fault, a person who can be labeled and morally blamed. By virtue of their juxtaposition and their missing links—one of Gallant's characteristic stylistic features—the three sentences in [4] make it obvious that Philippe wants to put the blame on his first wife: the reference to Shirley's first marriage, straight after the repetition of her lack of concentration, worsens her position and casts a judgmental eye on her morals. Besides, his repartee clearly has the expected effect, for Claire's surprised "Oh?" is followed by a question not formulated in the regular inverted order [5]—in the manner of informal questions in French—implying that she takes for granted that Shirley was old. Philippe's reply [6] contradicts this; at the time of the narrative present, Shirley is only 27. Her age allows Philippe to make an abrupt comment that reveals both his first wife's fears, her literary taste, and his inability to understand her. Ironically, his grudges show that unawares, he shares his first wife's literary world (Browning). Still pursuing her idea and prolonging her husband's stereotyped thinking, Claire's question [7] proves that only faithfulness and abandonment matter to her, as revealed by her further question [9]. Here the narrative voice, no longer neutral after the textual sign of a reported speech act, comments on the second wife's apprehensions.

With its alternating questions and peremptory statements, the following exchange of ideas makes her anguish only too precise:

> "I certainly did [1a]. Without explanations [1b]. One Sunday morning I got up and dressed and went away [1c]. I came back when she wasn't there and took my things away—my tape recorder, my records [1d]. I came twice for my books [1e]. I never saw her again except to talk about the divorce" [1f].
>
> "Weren't you unhappy, just walking out that way? [2a] You make it sound so easy" [2b].
>
> "I don't admire suffering," he said, and realized he was echoing his wife [3a]. Suffering was disgusting to her; the emblem of dirt was someone like Kafka alone in a room distilling blows and horror [3b].

"Nobody admires suffering," said the girl, thinking of aches and cramps [4a]. (*IT,* 155)

Philippe's answer [1a], with its emphasis on the stressed adverb, is pungently short. An elliptic addition [1b] punctuates the first sentence's sharpness and reinforces the violence with which the action is willed to be unemotional. The following polysyndeton [1c] emphasizes deliberate detachment: the succession of coordinated verbs of action reduces the breakup to the three actions mentioned, thereby negating any form of emotional involvement. The next sentence [1d] combines two types of complexity: subordination again marks the careful choice of the moment for the action to be performed, and coordination adds another verb of action with some indetermination later clarified by the phrase after the dash. [1e] only adds one aspect of his retrieval and the extent of his possession and intellectual activity. Apart from [1b] and [1c], these sentences characteristically start with the first-person singular pronoun, showing Philippe's self-centered outlook (confirmed by the repeated use of the first-person possessive pronoun in [1d] and [1e]), and his unwillingness to take his first wife's feelings into consideration—a sign of total indifference, indeed cruelty. The main clause in [1f] confirms his indifference and refusal of a confrontation and its inevitable explanation; the subsequent restrictive infinitive clause implies that he sees her only to accomplish the recovery of his freedom.

His new wife's question [2a] restores an emotional element by reverting to a more personal plane: the combination of feeling—"unhappy"—and action—"walking out"—shows her attempt at humanizing an event from which Philippe's discourse has erased emotions. Her next utterance [2b] emphasizes her own ingenuousness, rendered by the simple adverb of degree and the unsophisticated adjective. Philippe's retort [3a] again nullifies sentiment: the irony lies in his appropriation of his first wife's views, acknowledged in narrated monologue. Through his appropriation, the reactions once expressed by his first wife [3b] can be seen as his: this, in a way, closes the circle and confirms the readers' impression that Philippe obliterates emotions. His new wife's repetition and universalization of his statement at once brings it back to a more concrete level, for the narrated monologue, with its "aches and cramps," gives the statement a tangible counterpart—an ironic contrast after the sophisticated comparison with Kafka and his supposed delight in suffering. The obliteration of emotions through the initial combination of verbs of movement and action is eventually confirmed both concretely and abstractly. The irony lies in the transposition (abstract-concrete) that shows the new couple to be poles apart.

What could have led to a long argument turns into petty chauvinism and leads to the awareness that marriage sometimes rests on rather shaky grounds:

> "She had a funny name" [1].
> "Yes, terrible [2a]. She always had to spell it over the phone [2b]. Suzanne Henri Irma Robert Louis Emile Yvonne [2c]. It is not pronounced as it is spelled [2d].
> "Were you really in love with her?" [3].
> "I was the first time I saw her [4a]. The mistake was that I carried her [4b]. The mystery was why I ever married her" [4c].
> "Was she pretty?" [5].
> "She had lovely hair, like all the American girls, but she was always cutting it and making it ugly [6a]. She had good legs, but she wore flat shoes [6b]. Like all the Americans, she wore her clothes just slightly too long, and with the flat shoes . . . she never looked dressed [6c]. She was blind as a mole and wore dark glasses because she had lost the other ones [6d]. When she took her glasses off, sometimes she looked ruthless [6e]. But she was worried and impulsive, and thought men had always exploited her" [6f].
> Claire said, "How do I know you won't leave me?" but he could tell from her tone she did not expect an answer to that [7]. (IT, 155–56)

Much emphasis is put on Shirley's foreignness, her name unfamiliar to French ears (as opposed to the seven "really" French names used to help others spell it properly) and her attire out of line with French taste. The strikingly imposing accumulation of derogatory adjectives—"funny," "terrible," "ugly," "flat," "too long," "dark," "blind," "ruthless," "worried," "impulsive"—undermines the few positive elements in Shirley while throwing an ironic light on French chauvinism. The approved characteristics, presented in parallel constructions [6a–6b], are irreversibly lessened by revision after the contrasting connective "but." The parallel constructions in [4b] and [4c], with their alliterations, assonances, and ironic echo in "carried" and "married," "mistake" and "mystery," confirm the clash between two worlds with different priorities— the old one favoring elegance, the new one encouraging comfort. The narrow-mindedness of the Old World's representatives is given voice through the repeated phrase "like all the Americans," an expression of prejudice already present in the opening paragraph of the story. Ironi-

cally, after this discriminating passage, Perrigny's new wife's name—
Claire, a French name, of course—is mentioned for the first time. An
aptronym, it hints at her lucidity, limpidity, and clearness while reminding the readers of "the blue-eyed puritanical north" (*IT,* 154). After this
long critical description, Claire Perrigny reverts to her original anxiety
about the strength of her own marriage. The narrated monologue after
Claire's question seems to indicate that she regards Shirley's American
origin as the sole reason for the failure of Philippe's first marriage. As
the dialogue draws to a close, the readers can nevertheless assume that
Claire hardly believes that he could discard her, and she dismisses her
own question about the issue, having mistakenly gained confidence in
the strength of their relationship, as it appears later.

Indeed, the following section of the narrative reverses Claire's
assumptions, as it gives a glimpse of the couple's respective thoughts. As
they move on to their next destination, a long flashback reveals the
essence of their relationship. Each seems inspired by erroneous expectations of the other:

> Their flight was called [1]. They moved out under "Copenhagen," carry-
> ing their cameras and raincoats [2]. He was glad this first part of the
> journey was over [3]. He and Claire were together the whole twenty-four
> hours [4]. She was good if he said he was working, but puzzled and
> offended if he read [5]. Attending to her, he made mistakes [6]. In
> Helsinki he had gone with her to buy clothes [7]. Under racks of dresses
> he saw her legs and bare feet [8]. She came out, smiling, holding in front
> of herself a bright dress covered with suns [9]. "You can't wear that in
> Paris," he said [10a], and he saw her face change [10b], as if he had dark-
> ened some idea she'd had of what she might be [10c]. (*IT,* 156)

The short simple sentence [1] concerning the call for passengers fulfills
two purposes. First, it interrupts the conversation and allows Gallant to
get rid of unwanted speech acts. Second, it allows for a transition to a
different kind of information, one that is inward, as manifest from sentence [3] onward. Sentence [2] offers a parallel between the French couple and all the other tourists, such as the Americans and the Japanese,
funnily undermining the individuality of the French couple.[14] The verb
of motion takes the characters away from the location where the conversation was taking place, while the present participle shows them displaying external signs of possession reminiscent of Philippe's preceding
insistence on such belongings as "my records," and "my books." These

two lexical signals announce that the narrative moves out of the conversation. Gallant's readers recognize this kind of stage direction, for she often resorts to such transitional effects. The lack of an explicit link between the next simple statements [3 + 4] makes it obvious that Philippe repeatedly jibs at having to share every single minute of the day with the same person. The next antithetical sentence [5], consisting of two parallel complex sentence patterns, points to the tension about the use of his time: it has arisen as early as the first week of their married life, although some concessions have been made. The contrasting adjectives—"good" versus "puzzled" and "offended"—recall the binary contrast in the description of Shirley: less importance is attached to the positively acceptable than to the reprehensible, which might foreshadow similar communication problems, the more so as the phrase "if he said" meets approval.

The simple periodic sentence [6] announces, if not trouble, at least some incompatibility and reminds one of Philippe's "mistake" about his first wife, projecting contention and disharmony into his second relationship. The next periodic sentences [7 + 8], two concise factual statements without emotional impact, increase the sense of suspense as they draw an ironic parallel between Shirley and Claire: like sentence [6c] in the preceding quotation (p. 152), these two sentences refer to clothes and bare feet or flat shoes. They delay the illustration of Philippe's clumsy handling of his wife and alert the readers to the importance of the scene to be described in the development of their relationship. Together with the next picture [9], they form a sequence of silent pictures whose meaning has yet to be defined; Claire's smile over her choice of a dress full of suns corresponds textually to Munch's *The Dance of Life*, in which a blond woman in a white dress with yellow circles wears the smile of seduction.[15] The order in which the apposed present participles are presented in [9], with "smiling" before "holding," is significant because the first marks Claire's triumphant choice concerning the action presented by the second, just as *The Dance of Life* prefigures the interference of the blond woman "out to pick the blossom of love without being picked herself" (Bischoff, 47), to quote Munch's diary. Philippe's simple utterance [10a] involving a negative ironically cancels the expectation of its positive anticipated by the smile in [9] and signified by the coordinated picture in [10b] implying Claire's immediate disappointment. [10b] and [10c] project Munch's changed darker face in *The Scream;* the hypothetical clause introduced by "as if" shatters Claire's hopes for a new image of herself, and thus for a new self, defeating her identity. Tension thus prevails even at this early stage: the couple's potential strength finds itself shaken at the onset, a reminder of Munch's feeling of estrangement and wretchedness.

The instability is all the more serious as the subsequent silent picture involves Philippe's interest in another woman, albeit for a brief moment:

> In a park, yesterday, beside a tall spray of water, he found himself staring at another girl, who sat feeding squirrels [1]. He admired the back of her neck, the soft parting of her hair, her brown shoulder and arm [2]. Idleness of this kind never happened in what he chose to think of as real life— as if love and travel were opposed to living, were a dream [3] (*IT,* 157).

The first, centered sentence enables Gallant to sort out the subordinate elements more clearly while reflecting the natural order of the events: the initial place marker puts this scene on a level with the scene in Helsinki. Its time marker shows that another mistake, closer in time, was performed the day before the narrative present. Its stative verb "found," together with the reference to the water of life and the animal world, points to basic human instincts so that the fairy-tale scene evokes the dark, unconscious aspects of the psyche. Similarly, with its sensuous adjectives qualifying parts of the body, the description of the girl in sentence [2] reads like a description of Philippe's anima and conjures up sensual desires. But these are repressed, as if the quest for the self and its symbolic journey were doomed to failure: the next, loose sentence with its numerous abstractions [3] indeed conveys Philippe's inability to relate fully to another being, for he chooses to dismiss both travel and love from his life; in short, Philippe lives in transit.

Philippe's lack of concentration is further illustrated in the following passage. As he tries to direct his mind toward Claire, his thoughts immediately take him away from her and back to his first wife:

> He drew closer to his new wife, this blond summer child, thinking of the winter honeymoon with his first wife [1]. He had read her hand to distract her from the cold and rain, holding the leaf-palm, tracing the extremely shallow head line (no judgment, he informed her) and the choppy life—an American life, he had said, folding the leaf [2]. He paid attention to Claire, because he had admired another girl and had remembered something happy about his first wife, all in a minute [3]. How would Claire like to help him with his work, he said [4]. Together they saw how much things cost in shop windows, and she wrote down for him how much they paid for each meal of fried fish and temperance beer [5]. Every day had to be filled as never at home [6]. A gap of two hours in a

strange town, in transit, was like being shut up in a stalled lift with nothing to read [7]. (*IT,* 157)

The connotation of the verbs in the initial sentence manifests a contradiction [1]: one implies physical movement in one direction, namely toward Philippe's present wife, whereas the other, denoting a mental state, takes Philippe in another direction, away from her, back to his first wife. Further ironic contrast is offered by the complements themselves: "new" is opposed to "first," "summer" to "winter." By contrasting both the complements and the verbs, Gallant manages to show the inconsistency of Philippe's attitude, his attraction to different personalities, his indeterminacy. Sentence [2] also mirrors sentences [1 + 3] quoted on page 148: the repetition of the words "hand" and "to distract" imposes a comic parallel between the American couple and the couple that Philippe and Shirley once were, questioning the depth of the new relationship. Sentence [2] shows in its looseness how he paid and is still paying tribute to women. Strangely enough, the parallel structures enhance the pattern of his married life:[16]

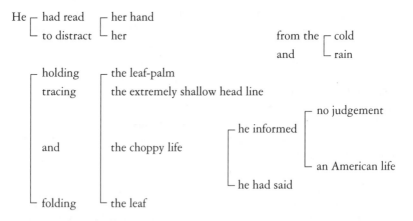

Because of the parallelism, reading and distraction become synonymous, so that Claire's previous resentment of Philippe's reading finds its justification. Both the cold, a symbol for lovelessness, silence, and death, and the rain, which intensifies solitude and wretchedness, appropriately complement the verb "to distract"; they confirm his predicament, his inability to relate. That danger is indeed lurking comes to the fore in the three present participles that linguistically follow the route of Philippe's first—and probably second—marriage: Philippe is seen grabbing, examining, and then discarding his wife after informing her of her short-comings in parentheses—that is, most probably, not explicitly.[17] The story about the failure of the marriage in *A Fairly Good Time* or even Philippe's comments on it in this story give a further dimension to the pattern described here. The objects of the participles, "the leaf-palm," "the extremely shallow head line . . . and the choppy life," as well as "the leaf," show a progression from the human body through an abstract concept to a vegetal element easily blown in the wind. The subordinate position of the reported speech also serves a purpose, that of stressing the Old World's prejudice about the New World—too young to think, too immature to have a smooth course. The next sentence, nonetheless, ironically reveals a representative, indeed a mouthpiece, of the Old World displaying the despicable characteristics ascribed to the New World:

$$
\begin{array}{lll}
 & \text{He paid attention to} & \text{Claire} \hfill (1) \\
because & \text{he had admired} & \text{another girl} \hfill (2) \\
\text{and} & \text{had remembered} & \text{(something happy about) his first wife,} \ (3)
\end{array}
$$

all in a minute   (1 + 2 + 3)

(1) = present, (2) = past combined with a possible future, (3) = past

The independent clause stands out by virtue of its function, but the con-nector with its effect/cause relation alerts the readers to the meaning-lessness of Philippe's attention to Claire. As the connector evidences, he turns to her out of guilt or duty (feelings he projected onto the Ameri-can [see quote on page 146]). Two extraneous actions, passive though they may be, have prompted his consideration. As to the complement of manner, "all in a minute," it is diametrically opposed to the independent clause and stresses his being "in transit," not there. The implication of the verbs combines the present with Claire, a possible future with another girl, and the past with his first wife, taken all together—a fur-ther sign of Philippe's dissatisfaction with any situation. The state of not being there causes the solitude and "silent cry" of the other, which again stresses the analogy between the American and the French couples. The next sentence [4], in reported speech with a modal (Gallant's favorite form) to convey Philippe's words, and the added distance secured by the transposition of the original pronouns "you" and "me" as "Claire" and "him," reveals Philippe's intention to distract Claire, to silence her anguish. As such, it offers a parallel to the American man's statement about the restaurant that is both inside and outside—his words are also meant to assuage his wife's existential misery. The next sentence [5], with its parallel independent clauses, also marks a pattern owing to the change in pronouns, namely that when they do something "together," *she* does something for him and not vice versa. The pragmatic character of this distraction and the reference to the type of food they eat takes away the spell that a honeymoon might cast. The adverb "never" in sentence [6] insists on the weight of "every day" and reinforces the feeling of obligation contained in the auxiliary "had to," implying that at home, things are different—for him. The meaningful parallel structure in [7] clarifies his outlook:

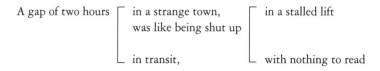

The parallel structures reveal a pattern in Philippe's life that reverberates beyond this specific situation, indeed beyond this story. It recalls other characters in stories by Gallant who experience hindrance in their movements, not only physically but also—and above all—mentally.[18] The inanimate subject of this independent clause objectifies Philippe, enhancing his inability to enjoy the present moment away from his usual background. The apposed place marker reveals how heavily a change of setting weighs on him; enclosure results, as marked by the quasi simile. The two complements punctuate enclosure, physically for the complement of place and intellectually for the complement of manner. In addition, the phrase "with nothing to read" implies the impossibility of occupying one's mind. Work, professional life, in short action— these make life, not the emotions and feelings of one's inner life. First pointed out by the American man, the concepts of "outside" and "inside" find their counterpart in the implications of this sentence, stressing once more the stylistic tension of the story. Writing and reading are Philippe's escapes: he can avoid seeing himself reflected in others (inside) and can safely devote himself to his egotistic concerns (outside). Security he cannot feel outside his familiar world: out of it, he is forced to face himself and look for his true self. Claustrophobia ensues from the necessity to face one's inner life and to share one's emotions.

In such a context, Claire's antagonism does not come as a surprise. Once again, parallel structures reflect her mood: "Claire would have given anything to be the girl in the park, to have that neck and that hair *and* stand off *and* see it, all at once. She saw the homage he paid the small ears, the lobes pasted" (*IT,* 157). The sentence can be transcribed as follows:

Claire would have given anything ⌜ to be the girl in the park,

                          to have that neck and that hair

             and | stand off

             and ⌞ see it,   all at once.

The parallel design exhibits her ambiguous attitude: she would like to have her cake and eat it, being as it were judge in her own case, being inside and outside, another instance of contrast, or tension rendered by the story's style. Like Philippe, who cannot just enjoy one aspect of life, she feels drawn from one extreme to another, from the need to be loved and to witness her own bliss. This again calls to mind Munch's *The Dance of Life.* As Munch explains, "in the middle the big picture I painted this summer, I was dancing with my first love; it was a memory of her. In comes the smiling woman with her blonde curls, out to pick the blossom of love without being picked herself. On the other side stands the woman in black, watching the dancing couple in anguish. She has been excluded, just as I was excluded when they danced" (Bischoff, 47–50). As the phrase "all at once" reverberates like the previous "all in a minute," the readers cannot overlook the two characters' lack of fulfillment, and the reference to the picture adds color to the concept of Claire's divided self.

Divided as she is, Claire manages to make the most of her inner displacement and turn the tables on Philippe, as shown in the first three sentences of the following passage: "She had her revenge in the harbour, later, when a large group of tourists mistook her for someone famous— for an actress, she supposed [1]. She had been told she looked like Catherine Deneuve [2]. They held out cards and papers and she signed her new name, 'Claire Perrigny,' 'Claire Perrigny,' over and over, looking back at him with happy triumphant eyes [3]. Everything flew and shrieked around them—the sea-gulls, the wind, the strangers calling in an unknown language something she took to mean 'Your name, your name!' " [4] (*IT*, 157). Whereas the first sentences show Claire as having the upper hand, sentence [4] linguistically represents (or re-presents) a Munch painting: the shrieks, the seagulls, the wind whirling things round belong to the picture of Claire's inner silent scream. The passage underlines the sense of anguish resulting from her divided self as portrayed in *The Three Stages of Woman;*[19] she has several identities, an old imposed image of Catherine Deneuve, her newly acquired identity as Claire Perrigny, and "some idea she [has] of what she might be." In addition to her identity as Claire Perrigny, she also envies Shirley Perrigny and the woman in the park, different faces of woman.

Later, although moved by Claire's childish pride over a mistaken triumph, Philippe feels contradictory emotions and is again reminded of his first wife: " 'They think I am famous!' she called, through her flying hair [1]. She smiled and grinned, in conspiracy, because she was not famous at all, only a pretty girl who had been married eight days [2]. Her tongue was dark with the blueberries she had eaten in the market—until Philippe had told, she hadn't known what blueberries were [3]. She smiled her stained smile, and tried to catch her soaring skirt between her knees [4]. Compassion, pride, tenderness, jealousy and acute sick misery were what he felt in turn [5]. He saw how his first wife had looked before he had ever known her, when she was young and in love [6]" (*IT*, 157–58). In colorful words, Gallant reproduces Munch's paintings: the first four sentences, with Claire's flying hair, smile and grin, her soaring skirt, dark tongue, and stained smile, go back to *The Scream, The Dance of Life,* and her "darkened . . . idea of what she might be"; sentence [5] enumerates the intense emotions present in *Separation* (in its different versions), *Jealousy* (in its different versions), *Despair, The Scream, The Dance of Life,* and Browning's "My Last Duchess," their literary counterpart.[20] With the last sentence, the readers are thrown back into the past and its pleasant memories. The story thus ends on an apparently happy note, but the happy memories take the readers back to a point in time out of Philippe's grasp. The mere allusion to Shirley in fact evokes Philippe and Shirley's failed attempt at communion and projects it on to all other relationships. The story thus reverts to its initial tension between man and woman while pointing to the disconnectedness inherent in Gallant's characters, reflected in Munch's *The Lonely Ones.*[21]

Structured in three sections, the story hinges on departures, emphasizing that relationships do not last, forever dissolve. The American man relaxes when his quarrel with his wife is stopped by their checking in at the gate, just as Philippe feels relief that "the first part of the journey [is] over" (*IT,* 156). With the repeated reference to groups of three—three nationalities (Japanese, American, and French), three exit doors at the airport, three girls (Shirley, Claire, and the girl in the park)—numerous paintings by Munch portraying three women, or the eternal triangular relation, come to mind: *The Three Stages of Woman, The Girls on the Bridge, Three Girls on the Jetty, Jealousy, Melancholy,* and *The Dance of Life.*[22] The story textually alludes to these paintings by turns. Although the quotes on pages 153 (lines 4–5) and 155 (lines 1–3 for both) show how Claire is filled with the anguished jealousy present in *Jealousy, Melancholy,* and *The Dance of Life,* they also contribute to a different reading of the quote on page 159, the direct consequence of the passage quoted on page 157, so that *The Three Stages of Woman* has its impact, too. At the left of the painting, a blond woman with "flowing hair [echoing] the flowing contours of the shoreline and the waves" (Bischoff, 44–45) represents Claire's no longer caring for Philippe's attention. The naked woman in the middle with a tree trunk appearing between her open legs, the natural seducer, stands for the girl in the park. The third woman, in black, corresponds to Shirley, whose long skirts and past glory find their manifestation in the skirt falling to the ground and the corpselike features. On the right, a male figure walking between two trees seems to be "an outsider turning away from the women" (46). The story and the painting thus complement each other, as each being is represented as cast-off at one stage or another. In general, Munch's paintings provide the atmosphere (angst, existential solitude, and death), as well as the setting (the sea, nature), the technique (the circles, the flying hair, the wavy movements), even the puritanical north.

Similarly, the reference to *The Scream* cannot be overlooked. Cross-references to the oxymoronic title of Philippe's articles, a clear textual transposition of the painting, stress the all too human sense of anguish. The American wife's question to her husband, Shirley's silent song of "My Last Duchess," Claire's repeated concern over other women are but a few examples of human wretchedness paired with a typically unsuccessful quest for identity. To crown it all, Gallant's stylistic strategies match the story's thematic disintegration. Lexical echoes and games, parallel and antithetical structures, abrupt transitions—all stress the stark reality behind the scene: at the core of the story, and of Gallant's work as a whole, lies total disjunction. Her fragmented perception and technique reflecting dislocation engender an overwhelming feeling of estrangement in a world that does not grant human beings any rights. Intrinsically "in transit," and therefore experiencing wretchedness or "acute sick misery," the characters can only join in the Gallantian chorus.

The previous analysis of stylistic devices has displayed Gallant's knack for making the most of contrasts, thereby sustaining "the inborn vitality and tension of living prose" (*PN,* 177). She clearly favors the opposition between terseness and repetitiveness, dynamic rhythm and slow pace, mono- or di-syllabic and polysyllabic vocabulary, parataxis and hypotaxis, asyndeton and polysyndeton, continuity and discontinuity, authoritative statements and expressions of doubt, hypothesis, or possibility, as well as oscillation between distance and proximity, past and present, abstract and concrete—all affording irony. The discussion of "In Transit" has also manifested other particularities. A past master in the art of allusiveness and indirection, Gallant suppresses feelings and urges the readers to find out emotions underlying the text; her predilection for missing links forces the readers to raise possible associations, while parallel structures and similes call to mind different levels of interpretation and unexpected connections. Although concise, her stories offer a rich texture of ambiguities and cultural subtleties. In addition, she excels at detached descriptions, cynical and caustic statements, and abrupt shortcuts. Paradoxically effecting and reflecting tension, Gallant's style matches the characters' disconnectedness, clearly illustrating that "content, meaning, intention and form . . . make up a whole" (177).

In Transit exemplifies that though written in colloquial English, in a relatively simple, everyday language of predominantly Anglo-Saxon origin, Gallant's stories are nevertheless characterized by an artful combination of contradictory strategies. The result is ambiguous, even puzzling. Feigning an apparent simplicity, she manages to convey tension through accepted linguistic and syntactic frames as if she distorted culture-bound norms. The structure of her prose establishes conflicting tendencies that correspond to the transitory state of the characters—and of the author herself, for that matter. As the stories feature exiles—whether geographical, social, or emotional—living in transit by choice or obligation, their style reflects their characters' displacement. Gallant's writing thus confirms one of Cluett's assumptions, namely that the "conscious and unconscious linguistic choices made by one writer . . . can have substantial interpretive [*sic*] importance" (18). In this respect, given a slight shift from Neanderthal man to exiles, Haliday's comment on *The Inheritors* applies to the fictional prose of Gallant. Golding, Haliday aptly argues, "conveys a vision of things which he ascribes to Neanderthal man; and he conveys this by syntactic prominence, by the frequency with which he selects certain key syntactic options."[23] In Gallant's case, the tension characteristic of her language and syntax typifies the problematics of displacement, its inherent disjunction, the tension that traps humans between two worlds.

Chapter Nine

Elegy and Intimacy:
Across the Bridge

Written in the late eighties and early nineties, the stories in *Across the Bridge* take the readers back to the setting of previous collections. Each story offers a bridge to a different temporal and/or spatial zone. "1933," "The Chosen Husband," and "From Cloud to Cloud" evoke the life of the Carette sisters in the Montreal of the thirties, late forties and early fifties, and late sixties and seventies, as if Gallant wanted to commemorate those eras and a place that marked her early experiences. "Florida" pictures the unstable marriage of Marie Carette's wayward son and a frail American in the seventies, while "Across the Bridge" exposes the tribulations of a young Parisian woman in the fifties before she gives in to a wedding of convenience. Set in Paris in the nineties, "Forain," "A State of Affairs," and "Mlle. Dias de Corta" delineate present and past episodes in the lives of political refugees and émigrés. Prolonging the topic of unwanted pregnancies touched on in "Mlle. Dias de Corta," "The Fenton Child" presents a Quebecois family's involvement with a foundling hospital and an adoptive family, taking the readers back to Montreal in the forties.

Where previous collections might have intimidated numerous readers on account of the all-embracing irony and the flawless excellence of the style, *Across the Bridge* elicits a different response, making it "one of the most engaging of all Gallant's work of fiction."[1] The stories remain as well crafted and ironic as ever, but the intimacy of vision draws the readers in, calling to mind their response to elegiac stories such as "The Four Seasons," "Bernadette," "Going Ashore," "The Ice Wagon Going down the Street," and the Linnet Muir stories. Clearly expressed rather than rendered obliquely as in previous collections, the emotional intensity of the stories fortifies a bridge between the characters and the readers. With earlier collections, most critics felt that "Gallant does activate in her readers both compassion and judgement; but she does not, somehow, allow the reader to feel secure in these responses" (Rooke, 25). Here, the readers' misgivings disappear, for Gallant describes a world close to her heart, namely the world of her past. From behind the scenes, she lets her warm nostalgia pour forth for characters whose world has vanished, creating a current that carries along the readers, whose response helps them "ward off anxiety in real life" and project "into the work a fantasy that yields the pleasure" they seek.[2]

Across the Bridge gives evidence of Gallant's compassionate understanding of victims, outsiders, and failures. She takes a particular interest in human relationships, particularly those between men and women. In "1933" and "The Chosen Husband," she takes pity on Mme. Carette, who, owing to her education, cannot escape her fate and will remain a widow in spite of her young age and her need of a serving escort. In "The Chosen Husband," Gallant pities the youngest daughter, Marie Carette, whose limited intelligence condemns her to a marriage of convenience with a man who accepts her only to escape being drafted for the Korean War. Likewise, Gallant allows Marie Carette to feel empathy for Mimi, the frail American wife of her wayward son, Raymond, and records the first embrace in her entire oeuvre: Marie is seen "enfolding Raymond's wife and Raymond's baby" (*AB,* 51), thus sealing a bond with pregnant Mimi. In "Across the Bridge," Gallant also shows compassion for Sylvie Castelli, who desperately but clumsily tries to call off her arranged marriage with Arnaud Pons on the imaginary grounds that a pen friend in Lille loves her and will marry her. The readers sense Gallant's concern for Sylvie's tribulations and eventual acceptance to marry Arnaud. Although the proposal on a bench calls to mind Georges Brassens's "Les Amoureux des bancs publics," the scene contradicts the song when Arnaud starts reading a newspaper left behind rather than gazing into their future or even kissing as the song would have it.[3] Sylvie's attempt to create an illusory bond by walking through rainy Paris all the while that the train is taking Arnaud back home is charged with such pathos that the readers cannot but feel concerned. For want of anything better, a stale romance awaits Sylvie.

The same holds for other family situations. In "Dédé" Gallant feels sorry for clumsy and dim-witted Dédé, rejected by his own family like Christian Rossi in the Gabrielle Russier Case (*PN,* 96–141).[4] With his awkwardness and limited brains, Dédé does not meet the standard of the family. To keep him at bay, his mother eventually buys him a small, self-contained flat in Paris, where his sister lives but never gets in touch with him in spite of her "still hoping for some reason to start loving [him] once more" (*AB,* 67). Dédé's nephew, Pascal Brouet, experiences the pangs of rejection on a smaller scale by being aware that his mother, for instance, "seem[s] to be listening, but the person he th[inks] he [is] talking to, trying to reach the heart of, [is] deaf and blind" (65). Similarly, Gallant shares Nora Abbott's pity, not for herself, but for little Neil Boyd Fenton, whose adoptive parents seem to take very little interest in him. Mrs. Fenton does not even show up when the baby arrives from the foundling home, and Mr. Fenton attends to his alcoholic thirst and his hunger rather than to the needs of his severely dehydrated son. Nora responds warmly to "this bit of a child" (173) and "the thought of [the baby as] a rebuffed and neglected toy touche[s her] deeply" (164); she worries about him even after she has stopped looking after him, perhaps because she rightly believes him to be her cousin and Mr. Fenton's illegitimate child, but also out of purely human concern, a far cry from the official parents' attitude. The Fentons' approach calls to mind the upper-middle-class lifestyle of the Castellis, for whom appearances should be safeguarded; thus when Sylvie leaves her father's car to meet Arnaud and attempt to glue together their relationship, she hears her father say, "Remember, whatever happens, you will always have a home" (101). But Sylvie realizes that this is "true but also a manner of speaking" (101), which helps to explain why she goes for a relationship that will not satisfy her.

Exiled, displaced, the other characters that Gallant depicts also deserve her compassion. Dominic Missierna, for instance, finds himself unrecognized after 24 years of research in linguistics conducted in the imaginary Republic of Saltanek. Gallant poignantly conveys his anguished hope that professionally "at least one conclusion might be named for him" (*AB*, 70) and that from his children "he would surely obtain the limited visa no one dares refuse a homeless man, a distinguished relative, not poor, needing only consideration" (71). Trying to get absolution, he justifies himself by noting that "he [has] been a featherweight on his children" (71), and since the people of Saltanek have rejected him, he "would live his six actuarial years on his own half-continent" (76). As to the title character of "Forain," though a native, he too compares to Gallant's displaced. Divorced, he rarely sees his daughter, who has moved down south with her mother and her new partner, so that Forain leads a lonely life. Having almost identified with the exiled authors he translates and publishes, he takes their lives under his wing and finds himself taking care of them, an undertaking that Gallant describes most warmly. The same holds for M. Wroblewski in "A State of Affairs," whose obsessive survey of past and present times helps him fill his utter loneliness. Because of his concern for his senile wife, whom he looks after, he "holds to his side of the frontier between sleeping and waking, observes his own behavior for symptoms of contagion—haziness about time, forgetting names, straying from the point in conversation" (138). As to the first-person narrator of "Mlle. Dias de Corta," she too expresses her solitude in a soliloquy that could alienate the readers for all its meanness; if it were not for her poignant entreaty of company from Mlle. Dias de Corta, the former tenant the narrator expelled, she would be classified among those characters Gallant criticizes for their failures. Her appeal to her tenant not to communicate, but simply to show up, most vividly records the narrator's deep need: "I prefer to live in the expectation of hearing the elevator stop at my floor and then your ring, and of having you tell me you have come home" (161). At this point, no reader remains unmoved.

Gallant encourages the readers' empathy most when her stories deal with death or its prospect. This collection broaches on this theme, whether minimally as in "1933," "The Chosen Husband," and "Mlle. Dias de Corta," or quite openly as in "Kingdom Come," "Forain," or "A State of Affairs." Disappointed with his life, "in part because he [is] no longer young, and it [is] almost too late for his competence, perhaps his genius, to receive the rewards he deserve[s]" (*AB,* 70), Missierna has asked for an insurance actuarial study. Like most people in the autumn of their lives, he sees a younger self in the mirror (74) but knows he is facing "his last adventure" and worries that he might have "lost his mixture of duty and curiosity, his professional humility, his ruthlessness" (74). In "A State of Affairs," Wroblewski explains to the bank clerk that "my death is my own problem" (146), as he would like to secure a small capital for his wife, should he die before her. Life fading away, his "acquaintances have vanished or moved away to remote towns and suburbs (everything seems far) or retired to a region of the mind that must be like a twisted, hollow shell" (133). As his life nears its end, he refuses to remember its hardships because "only someone pledged to gray dawns would turn back to examine them" and also because "there must have been virtues, surely" (136). As to Forain, he spends much time attending the funerals of the writers he has adopted and their relatives. As a publisher of translated Eastern European literature, "the destruction of the Wall . . . ha[s] all but demolished him. The difference [is] that Forain [can] not be hammered to still smaller pieces" (123), his professional end nearing every day.

Expressions of warmth, concern, and deep-felt emotions abound in Gallant's latest collection to date, encouraging the readers to feel for the characters rather than resisting empathy. As such, *Across the Bridge* could be compared to Alice Munro's *Lives of Girls and Women*, Isabel Huggan's *The Elizabeth Stories*, or Margaret Laurence's *A Bird in the House*.[5] But Gallant's collection differs in that she does not offer interconnected stories, bar the first four Carette stories, nor present autobiographical material. Although intimacy does not reduce Gallant's acute awareness of the sociopolitical context, it allows her to forgive her characters' idiotic behavior. Interaction between the readers and the text remains most rewarding because Gallant, more than other writers, leaves considerable gaps of indeterminacy, forcing the readers to fill them and supply the numerous missing links. As in previous works, Gallant merely sketches the characters, scenes, and circumstances. Allusions to the sociopolitical background of the stories force the readers to summon extratextual information to complete the picture. Both the stories' irony and their multiple voices and perspectives must be decoded to arrive at a clear vision. The difference, though, lies in the target of the stories' irony, which characteristically tends to be directed against the male characters, not against virtually all humanity, readers included.

At her best when she catches the weaknesses of her characters and makes fun of them, Gallant treats the readers with many a comic description. In "1933," for instance, the narrator laughs at the removal people who "kn[o]w only some forty streets of Montreal but kn[o]w them thoroughly" (*AB,* 3), a feat no doubt. Only through the distance that allows proper interaction with the text can the readers fully grasp the irony directed against the Carettes' landlord and neighbor, the only male character bar the removal men in "1933." The narrator derides his male prerogative just after his wife calls their dog in vain: "M. Grosjean had probably taken Arno for a walk. He made it a point never to say where he was going: he did not think it a good thing to let women know much" (6). Contemporary readers smile, for the prerogative calls to mind feminist debates and particularly the fight for equal opportunities, which M. Grosjean's attitude precludes. At a later stage, the narrator makes fun of his ignorance about the anxieties and sorrows of the women under his roof by juxtaposing the expression of his ignorance with an example of his insouciance: "Of course, M. Grosjean did not know that all the female creatures in his house were frightened and lonely, calling and weeping. He was in Parc Lafontaine with Arno, trying to play go-fetch-it in the dark" (9). But the situational irony does not erase the women's wretchedness, their helplessness; in fact it enhances it, encouraging the readers' empathy.

The alternation of mind reading and neutrally recorded facts characteristic of "The Chosen Husband" contributes to the readers' indulgent
smile at the whole situation. Never at a great distance from the
Carettes, the narrator smiles at their faults rather than deriding them.
This accounts for the unresentful allusion to Mme. Carette's social prejudice, so common in parochial circles. Having inherited a nice legacy
from a brother-in-law, Mme. Carette decides "to acquire a better
address" (*AB*, 11), and with it a more elevated self-image: "Before her
inheritance Mme. Carette had crept to church, eyes lowered; had sat
where she was unlikely to disturb anyone whose life seemed more fortu-
nate, therefore more deserving, than her own. She had not so much
prayed as petitioned. Now she ran a glove along the pew to see if it was
dusted, straightened the unread pamphlets that called for more vocation
for missionary service in Africa, told a confessor that, like all the prosperous, she was probably with no fault" (12). Recorded with elliptical
precision, Mme. Carette's modified self-image projects the arrogance of
the rich. Yet the narrator casts no criticism, as if accepting not quite
politically correct ways. Ensconced in her social group's preconceived
wisdom, Mme. Carette will ruin her daughter's life by refusing Marie's
choice of a well-behaved Greek for a husband. In fact, Mme. Carette's
biased attitude to marriage conditions her approach to her own life, contributing to her dissatisfaction: "Mme. Carette still felt cruelly the want
of a husband, someone—not a daughter—to help her up the step of a
streetcar, read *La Presse* and tell her what was in it, lay down the law to
Berthe" (14). Rather than carving her life, Mme. Carette remains dependent on male favors. Indicating both her pragmatic conception of marriage and her loneliness, the passage also alludes to Berthe's self-suffi-
ciency and independent, indeed nonconformist, thinking, more in
keeping with modern times. No harm is meant, and the narrator abides
by the vision.

In a like manner, the readers share the narrator's indulgent smile for
Marie's behavior, as if she were a sweet, naive relative: "Marie, who
spoke to strangers on the bus, once came home with a story about Fascist views; but as she could not spell 'Fascist,' and did not know if it was
a kind of landscape or something to eat, no one took her seriously" (*AB*,
12). Pointing to her dismal ignorance and everyone's acceptance of her
limitations, the passage also reveals the lack of political awareness of the
Carette family. The readers also smile at Marie's innocence and ineptitude. She misunderstands her sister's solicitude for her gallant choking
on a caramel in a most comic scene: "The Carettes looked away, so that

he could strangle unobserved. 'How dark it is,' said Berthe, to let him think he could not be seen. Marie got up, with a hiss and rustle of taffeta skirt, and switched on the twin floor lamps with their cerise silk shades" (19–20), funnily asking for silent approval thereafter. Instead of impressing the prospective husband, she acts like a child, "picking up cards at random, disrupting the game" (22). When her suitor vanishes, Marie preposterously suggests that her sister and herself should take the vows, totally unaware of, and even incapable of even envisioning, Berthe's involvement with men. Berthe "touche[s] her own temple, meaning that Marie had gone soft in the brain" (24), but the narrator remarks that had Marie seen the gesture, she would not have grasped its meaning.

As the narrator never embraces the perspective of the suitor, he becomes the target not so much of indulgent smiles but of irony. Unaware of being observed (*AB*, 15), Louis Driscoll is submitted to the Carettes' stares, and the narrator invites the readers to participate in the neutrally recorded scrutiny that nonetheless embraces the Carettes' angle of vision. The readers cannot but laugh when visualizing him "stopp[ing] frequently to consult the house numbers (blue-and-white, set rather high, Montreal style), which he compare[s] with a slip of paper brought close to his eyes" (16). A little later, the narrator, echoing the voices of Berthe and her mother worrying about the reliability of such a character, ironically notes that "a man with a memory as transient as his, who could read an address thirty times and still let it drift, might forget to come to the wedding" (16). Ironically merging the objective record of his appearance and the Carettes' reaction to it, the narrator pokes fun at the man: "It was too bad that he had to wear glasses; the Carettes were not prepared for that, or for the fringe of ginger hair below his hat" (16). Suggested indirectly between brackets, the women's criticism conveys Louis Driscoll's unstable position in the comparative assessment he is subjected to: "Louis meanwhile kicked the bottom step, getting rid of snow stuck to his shoes. (Rustics kicked and stamped. Marie's Greek had wiped his feet)" (17).

Before meeting with the family's acceptance, Louis goes through tests evaluating his worth. These tests ironically call interrogations to mind if only for the man's position in full light: "Berthe showed him to the plush armchair, directly underneath a chandelier studded with light bulbs. From this chair Uncle Gildas had explained the whims of God; against its linen antimacassar the Greek had recently rested his head" (*AB*, 18). Seated where others have sat before, Louis Driscoll is obviously going to be compared with them, unbeknownst to him, an ordeal to which the narrator points through a potent metaphor: "Of course he was at a loss, astray in an armchair, with the Carettes watching like friendly judges. When he reached for another chocolate, they looked to see if his nails were clean. When he crossed his legs, they examined his socks" (20). Echoing Linnet Muir's comments about people's accents, the consideration of the man's mastery of the French language evokes parochialism on two counts: "His French was slow and muffled, as though strained through wool. He used English words, or French words in an English way. Mme. Carette lifted her shoulders and parted her clasped hands as if to say, Never mind, English is better than Greek. At least, they could be certain that the Driscolls were Catholic. In August his father and mother were making the Holy Year pilgrimage to Rome" (18–19). Linguistic considerations and disguised reported speech convey Louis's suitability in the eyes of the Carette women. But even once he has established his authority in the family, he remains a target of mockery. After his death in "From Cloud to Cloud," reference is made to his treasured collection of autographs, which, in period of trouble, would allow his wife "to barter her way to safety" (35); in fact, his most famous signatures turn out to be fake, and the few authentic ones "too obscure to matter" (35).

Ironic situations abound in other stories. In "Forain," when an old lady falls on the steps of the church where a last tribute is paid for Tremski, the title character "in an attempt to promote Cartesian order over Slavonic frenzy, sen[ds] for an ambulance, then [finds] himself obliged to accompany the patient to the emergency section and to fork over a deposit. The old lady ha[s] no social security" (*AB,* 111). Criticism is directed here against the French sense of superiority, even though it may be unconscious. In the same way, the first time he meets Barbara Tremski, Forain decides he "would become Tremski's guide and father. He thought, This is the sort of woman I should have married—although most probably he should never have married anyone" (114). Forain's thoughts do not rely on logic; full of contradictions, they lead the readers to question his ability to guide anyone, let alone a man whose wife he covets. Gallant also exposes Dédé to mockery: "Dédé was too tall to ever be comfortable. He needed larger chairs, tables that were both higher and wider, so that he would not bump his knees, or put his feet on the shoes of the lady sitting opposite" (56–57). Acutely watchful, Gallant provides telling details for the readers to picture presumably recurrent incidents, provoking laughter. Funnily, contrary to all expectations, Pascal Brouet admires his clumsy uncle, whom everyone despises, so much so that when asked "what [he] will do, one day," Pascal, unaware of his blunder, answers, "I want to be a bachelor, like Dédé" (55). But then his father's profession does not seem so enviable, at least if one passes judgment on his propensity to fall asleep even in court: "[H]e would black out when he thought he wasn't needed and snap to just as the case turned around" (53–54). Where manners are concerned, M. Brouet is also made fun of; the minute food has been served, "there [is] no more conversation to be had from M. Brouet" (59), as if he were so famished that he must gobble the food up. His prestigious position in no way prevents Gallant from persecuting him with mockery.

Gallant further directs her mocking eye at academics, deriding the way they kill themselves for advancement, yet winning no recognition, let alone thanks (*AB*, 69). Described hilariously, Missierna's research sets the readers thinking about the relevance of academic investigations: "At the outset, in Saltanek, he had asked for a governmental ruling to put a clamp on the language: the vocabulary must not grow during the period of his field work. Expansion would confuse the word count" (73–74). This unreasonable demand from a linguist—he should know better than to try and prevent a language from changing and expanding—calls to mind Gallant's criticism of researchers: "With charts, graphs, and diagrams, [Gabrielle Russier] described how many times Robbe-Grillet or Nathalie Sarraute had employed the past absolute, the past perfect, or the imperfect when composing their novels. These studies, which are the fleas of literature and the despair of most writers—except those of France, who rather like them—are also important in a university career" (*PN*, 100–101). Gallant makes fun of Missierna's ability to "recite by rote the first test sentences he had used for his research" (*AB*, 73), the more so as they bear no relation to situations in a primitive society: "Now that you mention it, I see what you mean" / "There is no law against it, is there?" / "I am not comfortable, but I hope to be comfortable soon" / "Anyone may write to him. He answers all letters" / "Look it up. You will see that I was right all along" (73). The thoughts that obsess him after his lecture throw a comic light on his own approach: "He should not have mentioned in his lecture that the village children were of blank and unusual beauty. . . . It might induce plodding, leaden salacious scholars to travel there and seduce them, and to start one more dull and clumsy race" (75). He may not have seduced the village children, but he surely initiated a "dull and clumsy" investigation, spoiling their spontaneous reaction to language.

Had he taken time to ponder the villagers' wisdom, Missierna might have changed his own approach to life. But his obsession with words plagues him even after completion of his project: "What did they say when they thought 'infinity'? In Saltanek, in the village, they had offered him simple images—a light flickering, a fire that could not be doused, a sun that rose and set in long cycles, a bright night. Everything and nothing. Perhaps they were right and only the present moment exists, he thought. How they view endlessness is their own business. But if I start minding my own business, he said to himself, I have no more reason to be" (*AB,* 75). Rather than assimilating the notion the villagers impart, namely to accord primacy to the present regardless of the unknown lying ahead, he jumps to weird conclusions based on his obsessive need to record the vocabulary and structure of the villagers' language. Because Missierna is faced with his own nearing death, the recorded wisdom does not help him.

So used to meddling in other people's affairs, but not attending to his own (he hardly looked after his children, let alone got to know them), he sees the end of his career as a calamity, much like professionals without a hobby to fall back on for a rewarding retirement. Gallant pokes fun at his dealings with his family. Such disconnection prevails that he can think of his relations only in terms similar to his research: "What to take on the Christmas exploration? The first rule of excursion into uncankered societies is: Don't bring presents. Not unless one wants to face charges of corruption" (*AB,* 71). He has deformed his approach to people so much that he needs to convince himself that "[a] present from parent to child surely reinforces a natural tie" (71). Gallant then makes fun of his past unfair presents, causing no doubt much distress to his children: "When they were young, he used to bring one wristwatch and make them draw lots" (71), instead of showing attention to all and bringing them all a small present. His stale relations with his family make him approach them like a foreign country whose language might enlighten him. Thus he conceives his Christmas visit in terms of "exploration," requiring a set of formalities: "To enter one's family, he supposed, one needed to fill out forms. All he would have to understand was the slant of the questions" (72). Conditioned by the investigative procedures he has followed his life long, he concedes no part to feelings in his approach to his family. Thus Gallant warns the readers against academic pursuits that take life out of its context and end up warping the minds of those engaged in them.

Not content with casting an ironic light on academic endeavors, Gallant also derides societal phenomena. She pokes fun at the burgeoning of new organizations fostering the protection of the unlikeliest victims: "[J]ust after the First World War, a society for the protection of snails urged a boycott of mutilated shells—a prohibition that caused Saltanek great bewilderment and economic distress" (*AB*, 70). This preposterous boycott recalls the action of Brigitte Bardot, outraged by the inhuman manner in which seals are killed for their fur. That the protection of baby seals perturbed the arctic ecological balance and offended the Eskimos who relied on the product of their hunting for survival did not bother Bardot. In "Dédé" Gallant also mocks "the declining state of health and morality" of election candidates in France. The ironic statement that "some of these men ha[ve] to be found better than others, if democracy [is] not to come to a standstill" (59) raises the question whether, with the multiple cases of corruption reported almost daily, not just in France, democracy has not ceased to exist. In her survey of societal aberrations, Gallant also turns to education. In "Kingdom Come," she comments on the decline of education, fostered by the invasive influence of telecommunications: "Children in their collective vision now wanted buses without drivers, planes without pilots, lessons without teacher. Wanted to come into the world knowing how to write and count, or never to know—it was all the same conundrum. Or to know only a little of everything" (76). The assessment finds an illustration in "From Cloud to Cloud," in which Raymond "d[oes]n't mind learning but . . . hate[s] to be taught" (36). Infested by television, children aspire to stardom and mimic the stars, but without the tools, as appears in "Dédé": "The smaller boys, aged six, seven, tried to imitate Michel Platini, but they got everything wrong. They would throw the ball high in the air and kick at nothing, leg crossed over the chest, arms spread" (59). Education has such little influence on thinking that children "are born wondering if their parents are worth what the bus driver thinks" (73), epitomizing the ridicule of petit bourgeois mentality.

With such mentality burgeoning in real life, it should come as no surprise that Gallant's characters avoid certain unpleasant issues and escape history. The Carettes, for instance, seem completely disconnected from the world. Like Walter in "An Unmarried Man's Summer," they want "nothing but the oasis of peace" (*MHB*, 232). Ignorant of the world's geography, they cannot even imagine where on the globe the Korean War is being waged. They have, as shown, no notion of what fascism might be, yet they might have benefited from the information. It might have set them thinking and put a stop to their own reproduction of the movement's prejudices: initiated by Marie Carette's falling prey to the attentions of a well-bred man considered inadequate owing to his Greek origins, the search for the husband "of a right kind: sober, established, Catholic, French-speaking, natively Canadian. 'Not Canadian from New England' " (*AB*, 15) translates Hitler's theories of a pure Aryan race in Canadian terms. Although their personal discrimination bears no impact on society as a whole, its wide application could have as devastating implications as those of the Nazi movement. But if "literate people, reasonably well travelled and educated, comfortably well off, [can] live adequate lives without wanting to know what ha[s] gone before and happen[s] elsewhere" (*AB*, 117), as Tremski is recorded to have said in "Forain," the Carettes, with their insular perspective, are even less likely to connect events, to spot the flaws in their approach. To some extent, parents sometimes prevent their children from facing reality. As Sylvie Castelli realizes in "Across the Bridge," mothers "stand together like trees, shadowing and protecting, shutting out the view if it happens to suit them, letting in just so much light" (96), directing their children, rather than allowing their autonomous thinking.

Even highly educated characters escape history, ignore its lessons. In "Kingdom Come," well-traveled Missierna lives disconnected from reality, like Laurie in "Potter," who "refuse[s] to have anything to do with time" (*FFD*, 197): "[H]is life's labor—the digging out, the coaxing and bribing to arrive at secret meanings—amounted to exhumation and flight" (*AB*, 75). His analysis of the European sociopolitical structures ironically evidences the absurdity of human struggles: "Was there any cause to feel uneasy about the present moment in Europe? What was wrong with it? There was no quarrel between Wales and Turkey. Italy and Schleswig-Holstein were not at war. It was years since some part of the population, running away, had dug up and carried off its dead" (75). Written before the Bosnian war, the passage envisions tensions between unlikely places, ridiculing the fights for supremacy in those countries involved in such conflicts. Gallant implicitly blames the politically committed people who refuse to act responsibly, such as M. Brouet, the magistrate: "Sometimes he felt like washing his hands of the future," though to be politically correct, he would say, " 'But one cannot remain indifferent. This is an old country, an ancient civilization.' . . . 'We owe . . . One has to . . . A certain unbreakable loyalty' " (*AB*, 58), he would conclude with a fading voice. The passage recalls the question that haunted Gallant during and after World War II, namely how civilization had allowed extermination camps to emerge. It is precisely this lack of engagement, on the verge of disinterest, that facilitated the implementation of fascist discrimination. By abiding to such clichés, the leaders of civilization easily lapse into fascism without even an inkling of the disaster they provoke.[6]

Although Gallant's characters try to escape history, her readers cannot. Surveying the world around her, she refers to World War II (*AB,* 164), the Italian campaign (164), the Korean War (27), the Vietnam War (39, 50), and the German invasion of Poland (181), forever reminding the readers of human conflicts. Evoking the sociopolitical background of her characters, she mentions elections in France, the 1968 student upheaval, the abortion laws in France (149), the destruction of the Wall (123), the East-West dilemma (124), Prussia (133), wartime ghetto experience in Warsaw, the camps in Dachau (138), the German atonement (139), and Nansen passports for political refugees (139). Taking into account more than the immediate context of the characters, all these references contribute to a clearer, more precise delineation of the atmosphere.

Whether explicitly or implicitly, the allusions convey extratextual realities that widen the scope of the stories. Take for instance "1933." Purposefully set in the year Hitler was named chancellor and started establishing a brutal totalitarian regime, "1933" records desolation on a smaller scale at the antipodes, namely in the Carette family about a year after M. Carette's death. Tenuous, the parallel raised by the temporal setting calls to mind notions of living space. Forced to "move to a smaller place" (*AB,* 3), the family has to adjust to new circumstances, just like the Germans from all origins with Hitler's promise of more Lebensraum (living space) for all Aryans. The allusion thus brings in a whole variety of pictures that complement the story. With their evocation of a bygone past, the Carette stories demand complex interaction on the readers' part. As the narratives follow the evolution of the Carette sisters from childhood to the various stages of adulthood, they survey obsolete habits, enlightening for those readers not even born at the time, nostalgic for those who lived by the rules governing them. The same holds for the stories set in France, forcing the readers to face history in all its manifestations.

Just as Gallant draws the readers in by calling on extratextual realities, she often indirectly describes her own approach to the world. Like Wroblewski's friend in Warsaw, Gallant "is completely alert, with an amazing memory of events, sorted out, in sequence. . . . [She] would [and indeed does] find a historical context for everything: the new building and its mirrors, the naked model, the beggar girl with her long hair and the speck of diamond on the side of her nose" (*AB,* 133). Similarly, in "Kingdom Come," Missierna considers his options in life, comparable to Gallant's choice: "[H]e could watch Europe as it declined and sank, with its pettiness and faded cruelty, its crabbed richness and sentimentality. Something might be discovered out of shabbiness—some measure taken of the past and the present" (74). Gallant does precisely record the decline of Europe and Canada and describes their multiple facets, fostering the readers' enlightening comparison of past and present attitudes. And if she were to stop taking in the world and its representatives, that is, "if [she started] minding [her] own business . . . [she would] have no more reason to be" (75), like Missierna. By exposing the idiosyncrasies of human beings and the inconsistencies of societies, she does in writing and in a different context precisely what Arnaud Pons dreams of doing, namely to "expose the sham and vulgarity of Paris taste. . . . Conductors and sopranos would feel the extra edge of anxiety that makes for a good performance, knowing the incorruptible Arnaud Pons was in the house" (89).

Beyond the reflection of her approach to history, Gallant also lets the readers penetrate behind the scenes of her art. Metafictional allusions abound in this collection and reverberate beyond the stories they mirror. As she notes in "From Cloud to Cloud" that "the family's experience of Raymond was like a long railway journey with a constantly shifting point of view" (*AB,* 33), Gallant defines her own writing with its multiple perspectives even within one sentence. In addition, in "1933" she exemplifies the split perspectives within sentences by reflecting Berthe's split consciousness; while the latter immerses herself in her mother's grief, she is capable of standing at a distance and pondering over the scene: "Even while she sobbed out words of hope and comfort (Arno would never die) and promises of reassuring behavior (she and Marie would always be good) she wondered how tears could flow in so many directions at once" (8–9). Like the narrator at once involved and detached, Berthe perceives her own actions from the outside. Similarly, "Forain" gives a good example of Gallant's disconcerting combination of opposites: "Tremski could claim one thing and its opposite in the same sentence" (116), just as Carol Frazier in "The Other Paris" takes in two contradictory pictures at once—"the comforting vision of Paris as she once imagined" (*OP,* 30) and its real counterpart.

Gallant's writing further resembles Sylvie Castelli's approach in "Across the Bridge" as she begins "to show her feelings through hints and silences or by telling anecdotes" (*AB,* 95). Gallant rarely defines the

feelings of her characters, preferring to let the readers work them out for
themselves. Hints, silences, anecdotes, these enrich Gallant's oeuvre,
giving it its characteristic touch. Thus, while reading, the readers come
to perceive the profuse gaps of indeterminacy and to realize that their
activity "is like trying to read a book with some pages torn out. Things
are said at intervals and nothing connects" (97). The very interaction of
the readers with the stories, nonetheless, contributes to the "pleasure of
the text."[7] For as Wolfgang Iser notes, "the text's selective utilization of
the reader's own faculties results in his having an aesthetic experience
whose very structure enables him to obtain insight into experience
acquisition; it also enables him to imagine a reality which is a process of
experience, though it can never be real in a concrete sense."[8]

Given the parallels that can be drawn with Gallant's activity as a
writer, the readers may wonder whether the collection's treatment of
death and its prospect reflects the author's preoccupation with her own
mortality. "The chronicle of two generations, displaced and dispossessed" that "ha[s] come to a stop" (*AB,* 114) might refer to her own
writing as she faces the inexorable passing of time. *Across the Bridge* conveys her sense of urgency to bequeath ahead of time a vision of the
world that leaves room for feelings and emotions. The changed tone and
new intimacy of this set of stories might well be the privilege of age;
while in earlier works Gallant catches the characters' flaws with
admirable causticity, here she treats them with indulgence, fostering the
readers' sympathy for the characters' shortcomings. Gallant might well
want to share her feelings for a world that is anything but perfect, but a
world she nonetheless has enjoyed re-presenting with a profusion of
telling details colored by masterly irony. No longer needing to prove the
incisiveness of her vision, Gallant can sit back and delight in her characters together with the readers. Thus, when she remarks, "I still do not
know what impels anyone sound of mind to leave dry land and spend a
lifetime describing people who do not exist" (*SS,* x), the readers grate-
fully acknowledge the need to write that has driven her all along, for her
drive has afforded them infinite, supreme pleasures. And when she conveys the sense of an ending—"There is something I keep wanting to say
about reading short stories. I am doing it now, because I may never have
another occasion" (*SS,* xix)—the readers only hope that time will give
the lie to her statement. For the readers look forward to yet another
superb collection penetrating Gallant's world, whose emotional intensity emerges from the impeccably well structured and written stories.

Chapter Ten

Conclusion:
Fictional Worlds of Disintegration

In her eyes, irony flickers; in her heart, she hides the need to subvert human fate. Playing on the explicit and the implicit, Gallant has a "way of writing designed to leave open the question of what literal meaning might signify" (Muecke 1982, 31). Her irony deconstructs and constructs while "[activating] not one but an endless series of subversive interpretations" (31). In the first place, her ironic touch "works to distance, undermine, unmask, relativize, destabilize" (Hutcheon 1992a, 30); second, she opens up different readings of her fiction and the world whereby she enables the readers to confront history with its contra/dictions.

Apparent in her irony, the tension at the core of Gallant's vision also manifests itself through multifarious devices, among others in the contrastive structure and cumulative impact of her stories. Going from one extreme to the other, her range of patterns evokes the disjunction characteristic of the characters' lives. Whether tight or loose, the stories are constructed to emphasize the disconnection of the characters or their lack of a purpose in life, creating such a dark picture that the readers cannot decide which pattern is least oppressive. Both continuity and discontinuity are ill omens, neither implying a purposeful life for the characters nor suggesting the existence of a better lot. In either case, the readers can only stay at a distance, not wanting to identify with any of the characters, whether they follow as straight an itinerary as a colony of ants or as devious a course as a cat tormenting a mouse. Pushing the irony a little further, the stories' self-reflexivity magnifies the process of estrangement of the characters.

In a like manner, the voices heard—whether they echo the author, the narrator, or one or more characters—usually work one against the other, creating a set of diverging views. Generally dispassionate (with the exception of the autobiographical stories and elegiac stories such as those in *Across the Bridge*), the narrative voice records events as if clinically, but its cynical twist gives it a piercing quality that prevents the readers from identifying with the characters. No matter how desperate the characters' situation, no matter how distressing their voices, the readers remain at a distance. Even in the autobiographical stories, the narrator-protagonist adopts such a critical position that apart from the feelings she generates toward herself, she makes it hard for the readers to sympathize with the people she describes: she inscribes their idiosyncratic behavior in her narration so disparagingly that at best she fills the readers with dismay at the hint of their foibles. Her acute sense of the limited, indeed ridiculous, rules of conduct creates a gap that the readers, asked to participate in the anthropological survey, cannot possibly bridge for want of emotional involvement. On the contrary, in the elegiac stories, the readers feel closer to some of the characters because the narrator, sharing the viewpoint of the lucky chosen, imparts warmth toward them. But as the readers feel concern and sympathy for these characters, they cross a bridge that takes them to the dismal side of human life, one where beings forever experience desperation and alienation, both enhanced by the meaninglessness of their lives. When the characters try to convince themselves that life hides brighter prospects, as in "Across the Bridge," the readers aware of the lie cannot share their optimism.

Among the multiple voices heard, the historical allusions color the readings of Gallant's fiction in a most enlightening manner. Except for "Kingdom Come," Gallant does not invent sociopolitical events; she rather banks on the readers' knowledge of historical events, using them as theatrical background in which she places average characters. Like most stories delineating a political and social context, "The Pegnitz Junction" throws light on the author's desire to grasp the impact of sociopolitical events on the lives of ordinary human beings. The story's polyphonic quality emerges not only from the simultaneous voices of the author, narrator, and characters, but also from the context. Gallant's detachment encourages the interplay of intratextual and extratextual realities. The fictional picture of postwar Germany indeed calls on the readers' knowledge of cultural, historical, social, and political data. By controlling the decipherment of the novella, the intertexts impose other perspectives from which to look at the text. The reading of the world thus intimated casts a different light on traditional interpretations of World War II, allowing the readers to reprocess the past, to arrive at a better understanding of it, "having implications for the present and the future" (LaCapra 1989, 205). The same holds for stories concerned with the sociopolitical structures of France, Spain, even Canada. They tend to stress the aberrations of the system by which human beings live, calling for a re-visioning of the grounds on which we live.

Gallant's skillful mastery of voices results from a most sophisticated exploitation of language. By combining contradictory patterns, such as authoritative statements running counter to expressions of doubt, hypothesis, or possibility, she increases the polyphonic quality of her stories. This also applies to the shifts of perspective afforded by the unusual orientation of utterances with regard to space and time: she keeps changing the spatial and temporal anchorage, sometimes even within one sentence, producing clashes of viewpoints. These are multiplied when similes and metaphors add further points of reference by contextually bringing together different, often contradictory, situations. Gallant further manages to instill into her prose the tension inherent in her characters' lives by playing on opposite stylistic features. Here, she opposes a soothing, slow pace to a staccato rhythm, jumps from long sentences to harsh short ones, from colloquial loose sentences to more formal periodic ones, securing an oscillating motion of indetermination. There, she contrasts asyndeton to polysyndeton in a disconcerting, yet deliberate, combination of conciseness, speed, and forcefulness on the one hand, and slow, informal addition on the other. As she alternates continuity and discontinuity, she produces a disturbing discourse that forces the readers to look for possible relations between all the passages. Furthermore, by pairing words and presenting parallel structures, she alerts the readers to the manifold, sometimes even conflicting, facets of a character, action, or place. At other times, she sets abstract words against the more frequent use of concrete words, effecting a clash between banal reality and intangible qualities, often minimizing, even ridiculing, the issue at stake.

The same tendency can be traced in the description of fictional space. Gallant throws light on the setting in which the action takes place mainly through stylistic features. With the exception of positive spatial apprehension revived by memory, the global picture strikes one as rather gloomy because the characters' present emotions—mostly distressing—are reflected in the landscape. Such reflections characterize all the stories but find their epitome in the Canadian stories, more particularly in the Linnet Muir sequence. Emphasizing contrasts, spatial polarities point to an oppressive atmosphere, a projection of human anguish and sense of loss. To give an obvious example, the restrictive vocabulary and disjunctive style Linnet uses to represent people around her enhance their entrapment; on the other hand, a dynamic discourse and nonrestrictive vocabulary conveys her own willingness to get rid of taboos and dogmas. In either case, space is perceived as reductive and engendering unwanted tension.

Further disruption results from the interaction between text and image. A source of irony, the introduction of the image into the text destabilizes the readers, as the visual automatically generates new readings of the text. The various forms of representation discussed reveal a series of possible interrelations in which the text informs the image and vice versa. As text and image intersect, an ironic layer of interpretation emerges; becoming multiple, because each mode of representation mirrors the other, the range of interpretations expands, enhancing the ironic impact. Because of the repeated representation of images, Gallant's stories reverberate with the messages of the visual, which either confirm the message of the story or ridicule the superficial endeavors of the characters. Derision contributes to the vision, one that emphasizes the characters' self-centeredness, inhibitions, and materialism.

Together, the narrative strategies that Gallant exploits magnify the tension at the core of the characters' lives. Being exiles in their own country or in a land of adoption, they are forever beings "from somewhere, living elsewhere" (*HT,* 281). Theirs is a liminal position: on a threshold, they belong neither here nor there, for their exile would turn them into aliens should they return to their birthplace. Like Linnet, all they would achieve is a "journey into a new life and a dream past" (228), another form of exile.

To some extent, one might claim that the characters' liminality originates in Gallant's own position on a threshold between exile and belonging somewhere. The double lenses she acquired as a child— British and French, Protestant and Catholic—gave her an unusual outlook on people and the world, one that combines two conflicting perspectives. Her successive displacements in Canada and America as a child and teenager, and again at a later stage in Europe, made her aware of further contradictions. Generating superimposed pictures of any image, her eye developed like the lens of a sophisticated camera with multiple exposure: her composite photographs merge views from different angles and offer a manifold vision of the person she chooses to capture. Like the "Candid Camera" of television fame, she catches the incongruous, the contradictory, the conflicting in all.

To crown it all, one could also ascribe this tension to another liminal orientation/positioning/situation of hers, namely her wavering between modernism and postmodernism. Modernism would explain her traditional form of writing, which does not distort or transgress the culture-bound norms of syntax and language, and would account for her characters' quest for identity, verging on nostalgia for a past that they cannot recapture. On the other hand, the very disruption she affords by challenging and stretching the boundaries of all narrative techniques can be compared to the destabilizing modes of postmodernism: her intrinsic irony functions as a rhetorical and structural strategy, and her liminal characters, permanent exiles par excellence, have fractured identities. Furthermore, the stories' metafictional allusions, integration of art and life, intertextual intention, and required participation of the readers—all are inescapable postmodernist patterns of disjunction.

"Overhead in a balloon" rather than hopping "from cloud to cloud," the author sees through the characters' loss of self, their vanished "image on the mirror." Caught "in plain sight," "in the tunnel" "between zero and one," the characters are trapped in countless "varieties of exile," their "voices lost in snow." Exiles of the self, forever "in transit," they look for "the other Paris" as they drift "across the bridge," unless they are marooned at "the Pegnitz Junction" or at "the end of the world." As no one can "let it pass," the "state of affairs" can only be like "an emergency case" after an "accident." Aimlessly wandering in "the circus" of their deconstructing attempts to build themselves a nest behind "three brick walls," they are hoping for "better times" that will never come; there will be no "remission," only "a painful affair." Like an "April fish" deceptively promising "a flying start," any consideration of serious "questions and answers" is bound to end up in "careless talk." Therefore "the old friends" can never find a "lasting peace," the one always being the "alien flower" of the other, fearing "rejection." Since their "heart[s are] broken," because "acceptance of their ways" never emanates from anyone, the characters and the readers alike face the same reality: Gallant's short fiction hammers out the message that there is no Truth "With a Capital T." Fragmented worlds, such are the "home truths" of Mavis Gallant's short fiction. Nonetheless the "recollection" of "one morning in June" "by the sea" or of a "good deed" on "a day like any other" might brighten an "Autumn day" even if only "in youth is pleasure." News "from the fifteenth district" about "the cost of living" might then prepare characters, readers, and writer alike for "kingdom come."

Notes and References

Chapter One

1. Janice Kulyk Keefer, "Mavis Gallant: A Profile," in *Macmillan Anthology 1,* ed. John Metcalf and Leon Rooke (Oxford: Oxford University Press, 1988), 197; hereafter cited in the text as Kulyk Keefer 1988. Gallant bases her claim on her reaction after reading the biography of Katherine Anne Porter and repeats that people spend more time reading about Simone de Beauvoir's life than savoring her work.

2. She often wonders, "why should people trample about me when I don't trample about them? I have a right to privacy, which has nothing to do with creating an aura of secrecy." She adds, "I keep my private life private because my mother generated a lot of gossip over her love affairs. It seemed revolting to me. This is why I have always been very careful not to reveal information about things that I knew would not last" (conversation with Mavis Gallant, 6 December 1993; hereafter cited in the text as cSchaub 93).

3. The autobiographical character of both stories was mentioned in a conversation in January 1993; for a reference to the first story and its autobiographical elements, see Sheila Rogers, conversation with Mavis Gallant, *Morning Side,* CBC Radio, 24 January 1997; hereafter cited in the text as iRogers.

4. Mavis Gallant, *Home Truths: Selected Canadian Stories* (Toronto: Macmillan, 1981); hereafter cited in the text as *HT.*

5. Because of her mother, she moved around all the time, going from schools in Montreal and in Châteauguay to different schools in Ontario, then in New York, before ending up in a high school called Pine Plains in Dutchess County, on the Connecticut border, near Poughkeepsie (cSchaub 93).

6. Mavis Gallant, *The Selected Stories of Mavis Gallant* (Toronto: McClelland and Stewart, 1996); hereafter cited in the text as *SS.*

7. Alan Twigg, "Mavis Gallant," in *Strong Voices: Conversations with Fifty Canadian Authors* (Madeira Park, B.C.: Harbour Publishing, 1988), 105.

8. She once confided that she mixed with marginal people, not with bourgeois people, as the latter would not have provided her with material for her stories. They are *"si rangés, tellement comme il faut"* (so settled, so prim and proper) that they do not inspire her creativity (cSchaub 93).

9. By leaving her country, she joined the number of writers for whom exile proved indispensable for their writing, such as Anne Hébert, Mordecai Richler, Marguerite Yourcenar, James Joyce, and Ernest Hemingway, to name but a few.

10.   Mavis Gallant, "Fairly Good Times: An Interview with Mavis Gallant," interview by Barbara Gabriel, *Forum* 66, no. 766 (February 1987): 23–27; hereafter cited in the text as iGabriel.

11.   Her subsequent attempts to find out the real cause of his death—whether he died from tuberculosis or suicide—highlight the importance of her relationship to him.

12.   Gallant herself expresses the likely connection between her upbringing and her outlook on children's lives (Mavis Gallant, "Entretien avec Mavis Gallant," interview by Anne-Marie Girard and Claude Pamela Valette, *Journal of the Short Story in English* 2 [January 1984]: 89; hereafter cited in the text as iGirard-Valette). Among those devoted to children, one counts such stories as "Going Ashore," "Ernst in Civilian Clothes," "Jorinda and Jorindel," "About Geneva," "Wing's Chips," "Luc and His Father," "The Wedding Ring," to mention but a few. "Wing's Chips," "Autumn Day," "Rose" (*New Yorker,* 17 December 1960), "An Emergency Case," and some of the Linnet Muir stories, for instance, are written from the point of view of a child.

13.   Mavis Gallant, *From the Fifteenth District: A Novella and Eight Short Stories* (Toronto: Macmillan, 1979), 93; hereafter cited in the text as *FFD.* As Janice Kulyk Keefer notes, Gallant stresses in her work that "the terrors of childhood are rooted in the utter vulnerability of a child's position," (*Reading Mavis Gallant* [Toronto: Oxford University Press, 1989], 96; hereafter cited in the text as Kulyk Keefer 1989).

14.   Mavis Gallant, "What Is Style?" in *Paris Notebooks: Essays and Reviews* (Toronto: Macmillan, 1988), 176–79; hereafter cited in the text as *PN.* Her prefaces to *Home Truths* and *Selected Stories* also throw light on some aspects of her creative process.

15.   She has indeed reviewed books by or about Colette, Simone de Beauvoir, Günter Grass, George Simenon, Vladimir Nabokov, Jean Cocteau, and Luigi Barzini, to name but a few, in the *Times Literary Supplement,* the *New York Review of Books,* the *New Yorker,* the *New Republic,* and the *New York Times.* The *Paris Notebooks* contains several of her reviews published in the *New York Times Book Review.*

16.   All of the connected stories have been published as part of separate sections in the new *Selected Stories of Mavis Gallant,* except for the Paul stories— "Good Morning and Goodbye" and "Three Brick Walls"—published in sequence in *Preview* 22 (December 1944): 1–3, 4–6.

17.   In the preface to *Selected Stories,* Gallant explains that her writing as a journalist follows the same procedure as her creative writing, recording her inability to "move on to the second sentence until the first [sounds] true" (xiv).

18.   Conversation with Mavis Gallant, 16 January 1994; hereafter cited in the text as cSchaub 94.

19.   "I used to read as naturally as one drinks water." Gallant switches back and forth between English and French, even in midsentence, with bilingual interlocutors.

20. She has stressed her Canadian identity in her writing (*HT,* xiii–xiv) and in several interviews.

21. Postmodernism in Canada has found its supporters in both novelists and short-story writers, such as Bowering, Wiebe, and Audrey Thomas. Nonetheless, in the 1970s and early 1980s, Audrey Thomas, Dave Godfrey, Matt Cohen, Ray Smith, and Hugh Hood favored writing short fiction for its radical and politically interrogative nature.

22. I argue in this study that Gallant's seemingly modernist approach to writing misleads critics, who for a long time overlooked her fiction's postmodern trend.

23. Canadian internationalists include such critics as Alberto Manguel, Greg Gatenby (who organizes the Harbourfront International Authors Festival), E. D. Blodgett, and Michael Ondaatje. I am indebted to Frank Davey for his views on the trends of Canadian literary criticism expounded in his article "English-Canadian Literature Periodicals: Text, Personality, and Dissent," *Open Letter* 8, nos. 5 – 6 (Winter–Spring 1993): 67–78.

24. Peter Stevens, "Perils of Compassion," *Canadian Literature* 56 (Spring 1973): 61–70; Grazia Merler, *Mavis Gallant: Narrative Patterns and Devices* (Ottawa: Tecumseh Press, 1978), hereafter cited in the text; Geoff Hancock, ed., *Canadian Fiction Magazine* 28 (1978).

25. See the selected bibliography in this book. The same applies to theses: before the mid-eighties, a few M.A. theses and one Ph.D. dissertation were devoted to Mavis Gallant; since then, numerous others have examined or compared her work with that of other writers.

26. See for instance Michelle Gadpaille, *The Canadian Short Story* (Toronto: Oxford University Press, 1988), 38–56. Gallant's prominent position in the book clearly marks her, at least for those who share her views, as one of the forerunners of present-day Canadian short-story writers.

27. Janice Kulyk Keefer, *Traveling Ladies: Stories* (Toronto: Random House, 1990).

Chapter Two

1. Neil Besner, *The Light of Imagination: Mavis Gallant's Fiction* (Vancouver: University of British Columbia Press, 1988), 10; hereafter cited in the text as Besner 1988.

2. Chapter 3 examines Gallant's split levels of discourse and multivoiced narration, and chapter 5 discusses the sense of irony in detail.

3. William H. Pritchard, review of *The Pegnitz Junction, New York Times Book Review,* 24 June 1973, 4; Anatole Broyard, review of *From the Fifteenth District, New York Times Book Review,* 2 October 1979, 9. David Boroff, review of *My Heart Is Broken, New York Times Book Review,* 3 May 1964, 4; R. P. Bilan, review of *From the Fifteenth District, University of Toronto Quarterly* 49 (Summer 1980): 327. In this context, see also Kulyk Keefer's clear-sighted discussion of dissenting critics (1989, 35 –52).

4.   Constance Rooke, "Fear of the Open Heart," in *Fear of the Open Heart: Essays on Contemporary Canadian Writing* (Toronto: Coach House Press, 1989), 25; hereafter cited in the text.

5.   Wolfgang Iser, "The Reading Process: A Phenomenological Approach," in *New Directions in Literary History,* ed. Ralph Cohen (Baltimore: John Hopkins University Press, 1974), 133; hereafter cited in the text as Iser 1974.

6.   These blanks are what Wolfgang Iser calls "gaps of indeterminacy" in his article "Indeterminacy and the Reader's Response in Prose Fiction," in *Aspects of Narrative,* ed. J. Hillis Miller (New York: Columbia University Press, 1971), 9, 13 n. 8; hereafter cited in the text as Iser 1971.

7.   Mavis Gallant, "An Interview with Mavis Gallant," interview by Geoff Hancock, *Canadian Fiction Magazine* 28 (1978): 19–67; hereafter cited in the text as iHancock.

8.   A story favored by many, "The Other Paris" has been the subject of numerous critiques, among others by Besner (1988, 10–17), Kulyk Keefer (1989, 139–41), and Ronald Hatch, "The Three Stages of Mavis Gallant's Short Fiction," *Canadian Fiction Magazine* 28 (1978) [special Gallant issue]: 94–97 (hereafter cited in the text as Hatch 1978). The special Gallant issue of *Essays in Canadian Writing* (42, 1990) includes articles dealing with the story: Barbara Godard, "Modalities of the Edge: Towards a Semiotics of Irony, The Case of Mavis Gallant," 89–95 (hereafter cited in the text); and Winfried Siemerling, "Perception, Memory, Irony: Mavis Gallant Greets Proust and Flaubert," 138–43 (hereafter cited in the text).

9.   Mavis Gallant, *The Other Paris: Stories* (Boston: Houghton Mifflin, 1956); hereafter cited in the text as *OP.*

10.   This aspect of the readers' task calls to mind Thackeray's words as quoted by Iser (1971, 32): "I have said somewhere it is the unwritten part of books that would be the most interesting." Likewise it evokes Hemingway's "theory that you could omit anything if you knew what you omitted, and the omitted part would strengthen the story and make people feel something more than they understood" (Carlos Baker, *Ernest Hemingway* [Harmondsworth: Penguin, 1972], 165).

11.   Exceptions should be made for "Autumn Day," "Wing's Chips," "The Deceptions of Marie-Blanche," "Its Image on the Mirror," and "The Cost of Living" on account of their single angle of vision; nevertheless, their single perspective does not preclude gaps of indeterminacy and discontinuity.

12.   For an interpretation of the story and its structural pattern, see chapter 4.

13.   For a detailed analysis of memory's ghosts, see Besner 1988, 27–38. For a discussion of the narrator's questionable authority, see Donald B. Jewison, "Speaking of Mirrors: Imagery and Narration in Two Novellas by Mavis Gallant," *Studies in Canadian Literature* 10, nos. 1–2 (1985): 100–102.

14. Mavis Gallant, *My Heart Is Broken: Eight Stories and a Short Novel* (Toronto: General Publishing [New Canadian Classics], 1982), 155; hereafter cited in the text as *MHB*.

15. For an interpretation of the story and its structural pattern, see chapter 4.

Chapter Three

1. Gallant echoes Paul Ricoeur's view that "the more we are struck by the horror of events, the more we seek to understand them" (*Time and Narrative*, trans. Kathleen Blamey and David Pellauer, vol. 3 [Chicago: University of Chicago Press, 1988], 188; hereafter cited in the text).

2. This way Gallant's collection becomes didactic, comforting Hutcheon in her belief in art's "new engagement with the social and the historical world" (Linda Hutcheon, *The Canadian Postmodern: A Study of Contemporary English-Canadian Fiction* [Toronto: Oxford University Press, 1988], 1).

3. Dominick LaCapra, *History, Politics, and the Novel* (Ithaca: Cornell University Press, 1987), 205; hereafter cited in the text as LaCapra 1987.

4. See Besner 1988, 150–59; Hatch 1978, 101–3; Kulyk Keefer 1989, 171–77; Merler, 56–63; and George Woodcock, "Memory, Imagination, Artifice: The Late Short Fiction of Mavis Gallant," *Canadian Fiction Magazine* 28 (1978) [special Gallant issue]: 85–87 (hereafter cited in the text).

5. Merler (57–59) briefly discusses the polyphonic quality of the text.

6. Generally speaking, the readers' lack of involvement comes from Gallant's combination of voices—heard or unheard—and her inclination for a matter-of-fact style.

7. Susan Sniader Lanser, *The Narrative Act: Point of View in Prose Fiction* (Princeton: Princeton University Press, 1981), 4; hereafter cited in the text. See the various levels of perception, reality, and expression in the Linnet Muir stories: at times twice removed from the actual experience, the marked spatial components of the relation highlight the multiple layers.

8. "The Pegnitz Junction" thus fits Lanser's theory about the point of view (4) with its multiple internal relationships and its external constraints. Not exclusively Gallantian, this technique is nevertheless typical of Gallant's stories, as her fictional world is heavily laden with historical, social, religious, and political allusions.

9. Mavis Gallant, *The Pegnitz Junction: A Novella and Five Short Stories* (Toronto: Macmillan, 1982), 47; hereafter cited in the text as *PJ*.

10. The implied reader corresponds to "the audience presupposed by the narrative itself" (Seymour Chatman, *Story and Discourse* [Ithaca: Cornell University Press, 1978], 150; hereafter cited in the text; see also 149–51).

11. The most challenging experiment in Gallant's oeuvre, this unexpected mental ability finds no reflection in other stories. This peculiarity turns the critic's approach into a most rewarding task.

12.   Neil K. Besner also stresses the universal capacity for fascism. According to him, "the 'Fascism' Gallant creates in these stories is both more generally Western and more particularly human than a specifically German political, cultural or emotional aberration" (1988, 67). Present events, such as the recent turmoils in Bosnia, for instance, confirm this view, supplying further grounds for "dialogic interchange with the past" (Dominick LaCapra, *History and Criticism* [Ithaca: Cornell University Press, 1985], 139; hereafter cited in the text as LaCapra 1985). Incidentally, Norman Mailer exploits a similar technique to convey a comparable message in his pamphletarian novel *Why Are We in Vietnam?* (London: Weinfeld and Nicholson, 1969).

13.   Halfway between indirect and direct discourse, free indirect discourse tends to bring into play different voices, the narrator's and a character's, enhancing the polyphonic quality of a text (Brian McHale, "Free Indirect Discourse: A Survey of Recent Accounts," *Poetics and Theory of Literature* 3 [1978]: 249–50; hereafter cited in the text).

14.   Neutral omniscience characterizes texts whose omniscient narrators do not comment directly on the characters, events, or situations in their own voices but pass on judgment indirectly through value-laden descriptions (Norman Friedman, "Point of View in Fiction," in *The Theory of the Novel,* ed. Philip Stevick [London: Free Press, 1967], 123–24).

15.   A presence in absence, the implied author "instructs us silently, through the design as a whole, with all the voices, by all the means it has chosen to let us learn" (Chatman, 148).

16.   Norman Friedman's category "selective omniscience" refers to passages limited to the perspective of a single character (128).

17.   Announcing the representation of speech or thought, the inquit form identifies the speaker or thinker (for instance, "he said," "she answered," "she thought"). A frequent device in Gallant, the vague, or even absent, marker of a speech act or thought contributes to the polyvocality of her stories.

18.   Indirect discourse, mimetic to some degree, preserves the style of the original discourse (McHale, 259).

19.   In other stories, dashes and brackets introduce editorial comments. Examples of dashes abound in *Overhead in a Balloon* and most particularly in "Speck's Idea" (respectively 12, 15, 18, and 10, 24), whereas in the title story, brackets almost consistently announce editorial comments (50, 51, 55, 57, 59, 61, 63, 68–69).

20.   Merler (57) and Kulyk Keefer (1989, 172) compare her to a radio receiver.

21.   See Dorit Cohn, *Transparent Minds: Narrative Modes for Presenting Consciousness in Fiction* (Princeton: Princeton University Press, 1978), 11–12 and 21–57, and "Narrated Monologue: Definition of a Fictional Style," *Comparative Literature* 18, no. 2 (1966): 110.

22.   Similarly, in "Grippes and Poche," for instance, most of the conversations seem internalized for want of markers, though occasionally a declarative verb is used without inverted commas.

23. Roy Pascal, *The Dual Voice: Free Indirect Speech and Its Functioning in the Nineteenth-Century European Novel* (Manchester: Manchester University Press, 1977), 43.

24. Going a step farther, I would extend this remark to Gallant's oeuvre as a whole, for she consistently embeds one discourse into another through superimposed speech acts in which the implied author's presence cannot but be felt. On a slightly different level, Janice Kulyk Keefer even feels that "one cannot read more than a few of her sentences without adding to the fiction's list of characters an additional one: the superbly articulate author who situates and directs all" (1989, 63), a definitely pertinent remark.

25. Shlomit Rimmon-Kenan, *Narrative Fiction: Contemporary Poetics* (London: Methuen, 1983), 74–76; hereafter cited in the text. By opposition to the external focalizer, who is not personified and remains outside the represented events, the internal focalizer participates in the represented events as a character. Christine focalizes the people in the Kafkaesque scene at the castle from without, as their thoughts, feelings, and judgments remain unknown. Only their appearance, acts, and gestures are recorded. On the other hand, she becomes focalized from within when she records her feelings, thoughts, and judgmental appreciation of herself and others.

26. This applies to numerous narratives with allusions to the literary sphere, as for instance in *Overhead in a Balloon, A Fairly Good Time,* and *Home Truths.* See chapter 5 for the ironic reference to Katherine Mansfield's short story "The Daughters of the Late Colonel" in "The Moslem Wife."

27. Franz Kafka, *The Castle,* trans. Willa Muir and Edwin Muir (Harmondsworth: Penguin, 1962).

28. Allusions to other cultural traditions abound in the Linnet Muir stories, as Linnet, a keen reader and writer, mentions numerous books read at different stages in her life. From British children's books to "all the Russians" (*HT,* 265), to allusions to Chinese and Japanese literature, to British and American authors, a wide range of authors is evoked, not to mention journalism in Canada and its cultural norms. The scope of this study does not allow a review of the extent of the cultural voice, but its omnipresence cannot be overlooked.

29. Numerous stories are patched with historical references, often to World War II and the concentration camps, but not exclusively. Janice Kulyk Keefer's chapter "The Angel of History" (1989, 157–96) amply discusses how "Gallant's work is permeated by her engagement with history, her commitment to the imaginative exploration of the meaning of historical events, and her perception of history as lived experience" (162). Allusions indeed abound and color her narratives with a definite historical sense.

30. In all the other German stories, recurrent allusions lead the readers into the deeper meaning and origins of the war.

31. Gallant's abstention from using value-laden adjectives or descriptive words (iHancock, 39) while writing the captions for the pictures of the camps reverberates in her stories. What her stories, just like the pictures, are saying is "stronger and louder" (iHancock, 39), for her deliberately neutral

descriptions of facts. She leaves it to the readers to sense and assess human inclinations.

32.   Primo Levi, *The Truce,* trans. Stuart Woolf (London: Abacus, 1987).

33.   The italicized words in the following extracts recur, particularly in other passages trying to recapture feelings, impressions from the outside, as if recorded by an observer attempting to understand facts and events. Hypothetical, though not confirmed, observations are part of the detached mode of narration, as if the implied author willed the text to retain as many open options as possible. In the Linnet Muir sequence, childhood recollections, past feelings, and impressions confronted with present awareness of their incorrectness result in the use of such words.

34.   Franz Kafka, *The Trial,* trans. Willa Muir and Edwin Muir (Harmondsworth: Penguin, 1953).

35.   In general, Gallant's characters show a deep awareness of origins and consequently exclude those not belonging to their group. Her Canadian stories highlight the clear-cut compartments of their multicultural society. The stories set on the Riviera or in Paris also point to racial and social segregation, to differences in behavioral patterns owing to origins, welfare, and the like.

36.   Numerous stories allude to politics, whether to left- or right-wing opinions, or to someone's political adherence, or to one or another regime. Almost all the stories of *Overhead in a Balloon,* for instance, are graced with political allusions.

37.   Social concerns are present in most stories, as if Gallant were still weighing in her mind the social inequalities she witnessed as a journalist. Origins, upbringing, education, social class—these subjects preoccupy characters in virtually any collection.

38.   Neil Besner (1988, 160–61) makes a similar point in relation to the division between Christine and Herbert, where Christine voices her dissatisfaction with their physical situation, their relationship, and all that has gone wrong in their culture.

39.   Crystal clear, the information resounds like Nazi propaganda; ashen or muddy, it evokes the conditions in which the inmates of concentration camps ended. The repeated allusions to ash and fire obliquely refer to the past atrocities that haunt Gallant's German stories.

40.   Charlotte Sturgess ("Voices of Time in 'The Pegnitz Junction' by Mavis Gallant," *Visions Critiques* 6 [1991]: 68) makes a similar point, though based on another approach.

41.   Metafictional concerns characterize Gallant's fiction. She often refers to the act of creation within her stories, novellas, and novels, or to look at it the other way around, her narrative texts often self-consciously expose the artificiality of fiction (Robert Martin Alter, *Partial Magic: The Novel as Self-Conscious Genre* [Berkeley and Los Angeles: University of California Press, 1975], x) and implicitly offer a theory of the creative process.

42. According to Neil Besner, the end opens up "the possibility of a new direction, out of the destructive and repetitive cycles suggested throughout the story" (1988, 169). In spite of the positive message of Christine's story to Bert, Ronald Hatch maintains that Christine's lack of action is "a retreat to the realm of the mind, of reason, when the requirement is a confrontation with the present moment" (1978, 103). Hatch thus has a totally opposed, and therefore utterly pessimistic, view of the end.

43. The same concert was given twice, the first in what used to be West Berlin on 23 December 1989, the other in what used to be East Berlin on 25 December 1989. The highlight of the concerts consisted in the alteration of the refrain's last verse: instead of "Freude schöner Götterfunken," the choir pointedly sang, "Freiheit schöner Götterfunken."

44. Dominick LaCapra, *Soundings in Critical Theory* (Ithaca: Cornell University Press, 1989), 205; hereafter cited in the text as LaCapra 1989.

45. Fictional though they may be, Gallant's Canadian stories nevertheless evoke the grim realities of cultural, social, and religious life in Canada before the sixties. Similarly, the Riviera stories conjure up a world of displaced persons trying to evade their country either for health or for financial reasons, the latter reminiscent of tax evaders at all times. Reconstructing their small world in their new country, they reflect their own country's idiosyncratic system: by their very attitudes and deeds, they lay bare its social class structure and its insuperable subdivisions. The same applies to the Parisian stories with their telling details about French culture, society, and politics that reverberate the cultural, social, and political atmosphere from the fifties till the late eighties.

46. See Ronald Hatch's interpretation of the story in his article "Mavis Gallant and the Expatriate Character," *Zeitschrift der Gesellschaft für Canada-Studien* 1 (January 1981): 139–41.

47. Mavis Gallant, *In Transit* (Markham, Ont.: Viking-Penguin, 1988), 211; hereafter cited in the text as *IT.*

48. His situation, though typical of latehomecomers, cannot but remind the readers of Linnet Muir's feeling an outsider in her hometown as she returns from a long stay in New York.

49. Like Willi, the title character of an uncollected story (*New Yorker,* 5 January 1963, 29–31), Thomas "has kept his old national ideals alive" (Ronald Hatch, "Mavis Gallant and the Fascism of Everyday Life," *Essays in Canadian Writing* 42 [Winter 1990]: 15) and cannot adjust to his fellow countrymen's rejection of fascist ideals.

50. The repeated allusion to a "smell of burning" typically refers to the past atrocities that haunt Gallant's German stories.

51. For the sake of clarity, committed acts are italicized and contemplated acts are boldfaced.

52. Frank R. Palmer, *Modality and the English Verb* (London: Longman, 1979), 103.

53. Not only this scene offers a shift of perspectives, but also the story at large. Over and over again, the angle from which events are seen changes, and the voices heard are alternately Helena's, the commissioner's, the interviewer's, a proud German representative's, and the readers'.

54. Less distance is to be found in stories where the first-person narrator is a close projection of Gallant herself (the Linnet Muir sequence, "When We Were Nearly Young," "Wing's Chips," or "The Wedding Ring," for instance): the narrator manages to establish a voice to which the readers can relate; even better, the readers feel close to the narrating voice.

Chapter Four

1. The stories appeared in the *New Yorker* respectively on 27 June 1959, 11 July 1959, and 29 August 1959.

2. "The Accident," *New Yorker,* 28 October 1967, 55–59; reprinted in *A Fairly Good Time,* 230–45; reprinted in *The End of the World and Other Stories,* 95–105.

3. Even if the original publication order had been kept (that is, inverting the second and third scenes), the temporal frame would have been disrupted, though less so, at least on the surface level.

4. Besner 1988, 55; for a detailed analysis of the novel see 50–59. See also Karen Smythe, "*Green Water, Green Sky:* Gallant's Discourse of Dislocation," *Studies in Canadian Literature* 14, no. 1 (1989): 73–84, and "The Silent Cry: Empathy and Elegy in Mavis Gallant's Novels," *Studies in Canadian Literature* 15, no. 2 (1990): 118–22 (hereafter cited as Smythe 1990).

5. Mavis Gallant, *Green Water, Green Sky: A Novel* (Toronto: Macmillan, 1983), 3; hereafter cited in the text as *GWGS.*

6. Kulyk Keefer 1989, 79; see also 79–83 for a detailed analysis of the novel. Wishart has a penetrating insight, noting that Flor, and by extension her mother too, is "a floater" (Kulyk Keefer 1989, 97), someone out of her own environment, always away from home.

7. For an analysis of visual effects as structural devices, see Lesley D. Clement, "Artistry in Mavis Gallant's *Green Water, Green Sky:* The Composition of Structure, Pattern, Gyre," *Canadian Literature* 129 (Summer 1991): 57–73; hereafter cited as Clement 1991. For an analysis of mirrors and their structural impact, see Donald Jewison, "Speaking of Mirrors: Imagery and Narration in Two Novellas by Mavis Gallant," *Studies in Canadian Literature* 10, nos. 1–2 (1985): 94–100.

8. For other interpretations of the novel, see Besner 1988, 58–66; Kulyk Keefer 1989, 83–88; Linda Leith, "The Scream: Mavis Gallant's *A Fairly Good Time,*" *American Review of Canadian Studies* 18, no. 2 (Summer 1988): 213–21; and Smythe 1990, 128–33.

9. Janice Kulyk Keefer makes a similar point (1989, 86); so does Barbara Godard (73).

10. Godard contends that the "communicative exchange between mother and daughter" is a *mise en abyme* of "the instance of enunciation, that is the production, reproduction, and reception of the text" (72–73).

11. For an analysis writing the unwritten, see E. D. Blodgett, "The Letter and Its Gloss: A Reading of Mavis Gallant's *A Fairly Good Time*," *Essays in Canadian Writing* 42 (Winter 1990) [Mavis Gallant Issue]: 173–90.

12. Mavis Gallant, *A Fairly Good Time: A Novel* (Toronto: Macmillan, 1983), 4; hereafter cited in the text as *FGT.*

13. A similar disconnectedness is found in "Jorinda and Jorindel" and "Malcolm and Bea."

14. Mavis Gallant, *The End of the World and Other Stories,* New Canadian Library 91 (Toronto: McClelland and Stewart, 1974), 126; hereafter cited in the text as *EW.*

15. Alexander Pope, *The Works of Alexander Pope,* vol. 2 (New York: Gordian Press, 1967), 137–38. Although the original intention is different, the accumulation of unrelated objects has the same effect as Lautréamont's praising the beauty of "la rencontre fortuite sur une table de dissection d'une machine à coudre et d'un parapluie" (quoted from "Les Chants de Maldoror" in *Oeuvres complètes d'Isidore Ducasse, Comte de Lautréamont* [Paris: Agence Centrale de Librairie, 1938], 6: 3).

16. As Kulyk Keefer rightly points out, "the conspicuous absence of connections between incidents and emotions points to their presence offstage, as it were: poignantly inaccessible to the characters" (1989, 71).

17. Gérard Genette, *Narrative Discourse,* trans. Jane E. Lewin (Oxford: Blackwell, 1980), 35–36.

18. Mieke Bal, *Introduction to the Theory of Narrative,* trans. Christine van Boheemen (Toronto: University of Toronto Press, 1985), 59; hereafter cited in the text.

19. Numbers and letters between brackets mine. Each sentence (number) is a unit composed of one or more verbal components (letter) that refer to a point in time and thus help reveal the order in which the events happen.

20. "Thank You for the Lovely Tea" is another of those stories that could have served for the study of this structural pattern.

21. The adults are all referred to as functions, not as individuals with essential characteristics. Their names evoke "their relations to each other within the family hierarchy" (Besner 1988, 23).

22. Winfried Siemerling finds that "the story offers a carefully constructed picture of a maze" (146).

23. At this stage, a graph with the essential components of the narrative might be useful to clarify the triangular pattern:

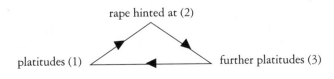

rape hinted at (2)

platitudes (1)   further platitudes (3)

24. Mrs. Thompson is indeed "an emotional and intellectual pauper" (Bernice Schrank, "Popular Culture and Political Consciousness in Mavis Gallant's *My Heart Is Broken*," *Essays in Canadian Writing* 42 [Winter 1990]: 68).

25. The references to the nail polish indeed punctuate Mrs. Thompson's gibberish in the first part before the allusion to the rape as if to brighten things and suppress retrospective considerations of the crude act.

26. Most of Mrs. Thompson's harangues are substantially longer than Jeannie's replies.

27. In the same vein, "Bernadette" unfolds smoothly as the title character anxiously counts the days she has not menstruated. Parallel to her concern, her employers' attitudes are seen to evolve as the wife decides to interfere with Bernadette's life. The wife interferes so much that Bernadette's pregnancy becomes a family affair.

28. As Kulyk Keefer remarks, their "emotional dislocation" is attributed to the "symbiosis of language and memory" (1989, 15).

29. For an enlightening interpretation of the voices heard in an earlier version of "Orphans' Progress," see Michel Fabre, " 'Orphans' Progress,' Reader's Progress: Voice and Understatement in Mavis Gallant's Stories," in *Gaining Ground: European Critics on Canadian Literature,* trans. Eva Schacherl and Michel Fabre, ed. Robert Kroetsch and Reingard M. Nischik, Western Canadian Literary Documents 6 (Edmonton, Alberta: NeWest Press, 1988), 150–60.

30. Italics mine. The same holds for the subsequent quotations.

31. As Grazia Merler puts it, she has "[learned] to blot out all memory as a way of protecting" herself (28).

32. Juri Lotman, *The Structure of the Artistic Text*, trans. Gail Lenhoff and Ronald Vroon (Ann Arbor: Michigan Slavic Contributors, 1977), 6.

Chapter Five

1. For an analysis of all the stories in this collection, see Donald B. Jewison, "Children of the Wars: A Discussion of *From the Fifteenth District*," *Commonwealth* 9, no. 1 (Autumn 1986): 112–20; for a detailed analysis of "The Remission," see Kulyk Keefer 1989, 89–95; for a detailed analysis of "Irina," see Rooke, 27–40, and Hatch 1978, 92–114.

2. Linda Hutcheon, introduction to *Double-Talking: Essays on Verbal and Visual Ironies in Contemporary Canadian Art and Literature,* ed. Linda Hutcheon (Toronto: ECW press, 1992), 13; hereafter cited in the text as Hutcheon 1992a; for a synthetic and limpid definition of irony in its different actualizations, of its related forms and of its rhetorical devices, see 32–38. For an interpretation of Gallant's subversive use of the preface in *Home Truths* see also Karen Smythe, "The 'Home Truth' about *Home Truths:* Gallant's Ironic Introduction," in *Double Talking,* 106–14. For an analysis of irony in "Bernadette," see Michael Darling, " 'Voices Lost in Snow': Verbal Irony in Mavis Gallant's 'Bernadette,' " in *New Directions from Old,* Canadian Story Tellers 1, ed. J. R. Struthers (Guelph, Ont.: Red Kite Press, 1991), 74–86.

3. Peter Stevens, "Perils of Compassion," *Canadian Literature* 56 (Spring 1973): 68.

4. See Godard (72–99) for an enlightening discussion of irony in *A Fairly Good Time,* "Good Morning and Goodbye," "Three Brick Walls," "The Flowers of Spring," and "The Other Paris."

5. Besner devotes a whole article to the four opening paragraphs of "The Moslem Wife," showing how important irony is in Gallant's work.

6. See Siemerling (131–53) for a discussion of irony in "Grippes and Poche," "The Other Paris," "About Geneva," and *Green Water, Green Sky.*

7. For a detailed analysis of "Potter," see Besner 1988, 94–99.

8. D. C. Muecke, *Irony* (London: Methuen, 1970), 35; hereafter cited in the text as Muecke 1970.

9. Ad de Vries, *Dictionary of Symbols and Imagery* (Amsterdam and London: North-Holland Publishing Company, 1974), 373.

10. J. C. Cooper, *Symbolic and Mythological Animals* (London: Aquarian, 1992), 171.

11. Gallant exhibits gentle irony toward characters for whom she feels compassion, such as Carmela in "The Four Seasons," or Molly, James, and Will in "The Remission."

12. Incidentally, while the French exchange harangues her students, Piotr is being aggressed by his students, who are convinced that he is a fascist, since only fascists are allowed to leave Poland. This comic reversal of the lecturer-student balance adds another dimension to the clash between the East and the West, as portrayed by Laurie and Piotr in their love affair.

13. The omission of coordinators in the elliptical triadic sentence renders the forcefulness of his escape palpable, justifying the drastic change in her, a sort of poetic mirroring.

14. For a discussion of the story, see Woodcock, 74–91, and Besner 1988, 99–104.

15. Gallant often alludes to films, whether real or invented, as in "A Recollection," "Lena," "The Assembly," "Overhead in a Balloon," "An Autobiography," and "Saturday," to give a few examples.

16. A favorite device of hers, allusions to books, literary or informative, real or invented, recurs in her oeuvre. "Grippes and Poche," "A Painful Affair," *A Fairly Good Time, What Is to Be Done?,* "The Pegnitz Junction," "The Hunter's Waking Thoughts," "A Day like Any Other," "Bernadette," "Its Image on the Mirror," "An Unmarried Man's Summer," "The Ice Wagon Going down the Street," and several of the Linnet Muir stories come to mind.

17. For an analysis of history's influence on individuals, the role of memory, and the story's structural organization, see Besner 1988, 106–16.

18. Mavis Gallant, *What Is to Be Done?* (Dunvegan, Ont.: Quadrant, 1983). For a feminist interpretation of the play, see Kulyk Keefer 1989, 121–25; for a discussion of the relation between the play and its Russian homonyms, see Godard, 96–97. Vladimir Ilich Lenin, *What Is to Be Done?:*

Burning Questions of Our Movement, in *Selected Works in Three Volumes,* vol. 1
(Moscow: Progress, 1976), 92–241; no reference to either editor or translator.

    19. Nikolai Gavrilovich Chernyshevsky, *What Is to Be Done?,* trans.
Benjamin R. Tucker (New York: Vintage, 1961).

    20. The musical echo has a self-reflexive value, for Vivaldi's famous con-
certi are the first 4 of a set of 12 violin concerti entitled *Il Cimento dell' armonia e
dell' inventione (The Contest between Harmony and Invention),* whose title reflects
the very contrast afforded by Gallant's ironic treatment of her material.

    21. "They paid her very little at first, and then nothing at all. . . . The
family came back to their villa after the war and paid the girl in pre-war francs.
Do you know what that meant? A few cents" (iHancock, 53).

    22. D. C. Muecke, *Irony and the Ironic* (London: Methuen, 1982), 44;
hereafter cited in the text as Muecke 1982.

    23. E. D. Blodgett, "Heresy and the Other Arts: A Measure of Gal-
lant's Fiction," *Essays on Canadian Writing* 42 (Winter 1990) [special Gallant
issue]: 3.

    24. Borges's story "Tlön, Uqbar, Orbis Tertius" clarifies such a modifi-
cation of the past by mentioning that "in all memories, a fictitious part occupies
the place of any other. We know nothing about it with any certainty, not even
that it is false" (in *Fictions,* trans. Alastair Reid [London: Calder and Boyars,
1965], 33; hereafter cited in the text as Borges 1965). This helps to explain the
similar perception of life that has allowed archaeologists "to question and even
modify the past, which nowadays is no less malleable or obedient than the
future" (Borges 1965, 29).

    25. Linda Hutcheon, "The Power of Postmodern Irony," in *Genre, Trope,
Gender: Critical Essays,* ed. Barry Rutland (Ottawa: Carleton University Press,
1992), 16; hereafter cited in the text as Hutcheon 1992b.

Chapter Six

    1. Honoré de Balzac, *Le Père Goriot* (Paris: Librairie Générale
Française, 1961), 19–25.

    2. Bachelard's theories and Proust's experiments have shown that
besides being time bound, memory is an essentially spatially laden component
of spiritual life.

    3. George Matoré, *L'espace humain: L'expression de l'espace dans la vie, la
pensée et les arts contemporains,* Sciences et techniques humaines 2 (Paris: La
Colombe, 1962), 16; hereafter cited in the text. To go back to the biblical
example quoted before, virtually the entire first chapter of Genesis illustrates
the need to master chaos by imposing order on it, by determining specific
spaces for all, the animate and inanimate alike. The same holds for the creation
of polarities ascribed to God, such as light and dark, land and water, heaven
and earth. Whether one considers that human beings are molded after God or

that God's existence is a construct of beings in need of a frame, the story of creation of all primitive peoples betrays a human tendency.

4. See Jean Weisgerber, *L'Espace romanesque* (Lausanne: L'age d'homme, 1978), 10 (hereafter cited as Weisgerber) and Matoré, 29. The English language is particularly rich in phrases such as "to move forward," "to get out," "to march out," "to throw up," made up of particles with a definite spatial character. But numerous other words convey spatial realities, as in phrases such as "to fall ill," "to come down with flu," "a long time ago," "far from the truth," which we tend to use without thinking of their spatial quality.

5. To go back to my previous examples, in the phrases "to fall ill" and "to come down with flu," downward movement has a negative connotation. But in the phrase "to fall in love," the value attributed to the same downward movement becomes positive, unless used in a sarcastic manner to refer to a person known for his or her amorous inclinations having fallen in love again. Similarly, "going up the ladder" may be acclaimed or despised on ideological grounds. This points to the flexibility of spatial perception, resting very much on personal outlook. Take for instance adjectives such as "small" and "large." "Small" may be sensed as limited, restrictive, oppressive. It would definitely be so to a claustrophobic person for whom "large" connotes unrestrained space, openness, unlimitedness. But the same qualifiers would acquire a totally opposed connotation in the mind of an agoraphobic person for whom "small" implies security and "large" danger. Another example might clarify the idiosyncrasy of spatial perception: whereas most people not living in the capital go up to London, the place with all sorts of treasures and activities unavailable where they live, people living in Oxford or Cambridge go down to London and up to Oxford or Cambridge, a remainder of an old attitude that valued learning more than urban pleasures.

6. The stories set in Canada are *pré-Révolution Tranquille,* that is, a period unshaken by the cultural changes non-British or western European immigrants have brought about. Not out of dishonesty, but out of a lack of assimilated firsthand experience, Gallant's picture of Canada thus overlooks the new multicultural nature of Canadian society, particularly in cities such as Montreal, Toronto, and Vancouver (Janice Kulyk Keefer, letter dated 27 July 1991). Personal conversations with Mavis Gallant make it obvious that she still sees Canada as it was—or almost—when she left the country in 1950. Needless to say, that does not detract from the stories' worth, but the readers should be aware of the standpoint chosen.

7. Mary Jarrett, "The Presentation of Montreal in Mavis Gallant's 'Between Zero and One' and of Toronto in Margaret Atwood's *Cat's Eye,*" *Etudes Canadiennes* 29 (1990): 174; hereafter cited in the text.

8. Weisgerber includes temperatures, sounds, smells, and lighting in the qualitative categories that contribute to the perception of space in fiction, although they are not, strictly speaking, spatial elements (18).

9. Gaston Bachelard, *The Poetics of Space,* trans. Maria Jolas (Boston: Beacon Press, 1964), 5.

10. This calls to mind Piaget's remarks that a child's awareness of space differs strikingly from an adult's: overwhelmed by what he or she senses as the enormous dimensions of the adult world, the child may well remember a radically strained environment.

11. John Knox, *The Works of John Knox,* ed. David Laing, vols. 2–4 (Edinburgh: Bannatyne Club, vol. 2, 1848; vol. 3, 1854; vol. 4, 1864), vol. 4, 294, and vol. 2, 109; hereafter cited in the text as Knox 1848, Knox 1854, and Knox 1864.

12. Jean-Paul Sartre, *Being and Nothingness: An Essay in Phenomenological Ontology,* trans. Hazel E. Barnes (London: Routledge, 1958), 73–102; hereafter cited in the text.

13. Echoing Calvin's theories that "there will never be plenitude or perfection" (Calvin, *Theological Treatises,* ed. and trans. J. K. S. Reid [Philadelphia: Westminster Press, 1954], 28), Knox's theories confirm God's "perpetual condemnation" (Knox 1854, 166) of man. According to them, "if we say we have no sin, (even after we are regenerated,) we deceive ourselves, and the verity of God is not into us" (Knox 1848, 107). For "no man on earth (Jesus Christ excepted) has given, gives or shall give in work that obedience to the Law which the Law requires" (Knox 1848, 108).

14. Similar instances of repressed emotional response can be found in several stories or novellas. In "Its Image on the Mirror," Jean Price hints at the local resistance to compassionate gestures. The agelong training to avoid personal involvement in any matter and to control—not to say repress—emotions clearly prevents the characters from losing face and faith: "It was for this conversation [the announcement of her brother's death] that I had learned to go *blank* in the presence of worry and pain" (*MHB,* 118; emphasis added). The achromatic quality of restraint that Jean reports in fact echoes the absence of movement implied by the phrase ("without a blink") that Linnet uses to describe just the same attitude.

15. In other stories, too, verbs of motion characterize emotions, as is to be expected (to move/to be moved), while verbs denoting immobility point to restraint, emotional isolation. In "Its Image on the Mirror," numerous passages highlight this formal characteristic. When envious Jean is at last invited to share her sister's sorrows over an unwanted pregnancy, spatial images convey her joy: "From that moment I *stopped* being the *stranger* on the *dark street* and I *moved into* the *bright rooms* of my sister's life. The *doors were opened* to me; everything had been *leading* to my *entrance,* my participation" (*MHB,* 149; emphasis added). The title character of "Bernadette" would also want to express her emotions—desperate, in her case—through action but is forced to control her impulse when her employer shows up: "A moment earlier, she had thought of *throwing herself down the stairs* and making it seem an accident. Robbie's sudden appearance had frightened her into *stillness*" (*MHB,* 20; emphasis added).

16. Thus in "The Accident" Shirley shows no despair or grief when her husband dies on their honeymoon. Later, in the follow-up *A Fairly Good Time,* she fails to communicate and show emotions, which causes her second marriage to dissolve. Her solution to her problem boils down to shutting herself up in a world of memories. No opening seems likely: her future remains bleak.

17. In "Its Image in the Mirror," when Mrs. Price sells the family house, her "gesture of total renunciation" is announced by a spatially laden image: "She *pushed* our past and our memories of Allenton as an Anglo-Scottish town *over a cliff*" (*MHB,* 60; emphasis added).

18. In "The Accident," while still enjoying her honeymoon, Shirley Higgins confirms this negative picture by commenting on real life, that is, adult life, in spatial terms. "So real life, the *grey* noon with *no limits,* had not yet begun. I distrusted real life, for I knew nothing about it. It was the middle-aged world without feeling, where no one was loved" (*EW,* 97; emphasis added).

19. This calls to mind a scene in "Its Image on the Mirror," where Jean Price witnesses similar patterns in her male colleagues' "finicky personal ceremony before the day's work" (*MHB,* 116).

20. In "Bernadette," Robbie Knight, it appears, allowed both his parents and wife to divert him from his literary inclinations: he has, for financial reasons and prestige, become a partner in his father's firm. Yet he wanted to put left-wing ideals into practice. In the narrative present, he cannot even oppose his wife when she erroneously presumes that he has had an affair with their French-Canadian maid, Bernadette. He is to support the financial burden of an institution where the latter can safely have the baby of another man, whose identity remains unknown to all, even to the victim.

21. My article "Squeezed 'Between Zero and One': Feminine Space in Mavis Gallant's *Home Truths,*" *Recherches anglaises et américaines* 22 (1989): 53–59, gives ampler information about the opportunities of women.

22. Jasper Ridley, *John Knox* (Oxford: Clarendon Press, 1968), 270. Knox claimed, Ridley adds, that since "no animal [is] prepared to be ruled by his female," why should man be? (270). So "to reign over man can never be the right to woman" (Eustace Percy, *John Knox* [Richmond, Va.: John Knox Press, s.d.], 218).

23. Thus Jean Price in "Its Image in the Mirror" visualizes how she "might have spent [her] life, creeping in her mother's shadow . . . if marriage, the only possible rescue, had not taken [her] away" (*MHB,* 66). Escaping the adults' world can only be secured through marriage, another form of confinement in Gallant's fiction not any more enviable than that of children.

24. Children's imprisonment is expressed both explicitly, through words of equivalent meaning, and implicitly, in the situations in which they find themselves. In "The Wedding Ring," when guests are expected, "the children—hostages released—are no longer required" (*EW,* 128) and are dispatched to relatives. Children thus know either imprisonment or exclusion. For

an overview of the limitations attendant on the lives of children in Gallant's fiction at large, see Kulyk Keefer's chapter "The Prison of Childhood" (1989, 89–118).

25.   Even when little outings are organized, as in "Thank You for the Lovely Tea" (*HT,* 2–16), no interaction comes out of them, as implied by the title's repeated rote thanks. Similarly, Jane, the first-person narrator of "The Wedding Ring," suffers from her mother's vixenish nature. The mother takes pleasure in making nasty comments that undermine her daughter's confidence.

26.   In the same vein, the "Old Presbyterians" (*MHB,* 65) in "Its Image on the Mirror" believe that everyone should be brought up like Jean Price and her mother: "[P]rudence, level-headedness and self-denial" (138) should take precedence over any personal expectation.

27.   Children need not be walled in; they can be walled off, as in "Bernadette," where the Knights send their daughters away to boarding school and, off term, to stay with friends. Ruled out of their parents' lives, the girls can never establish any contact with them.

28.   These make up the "descent into hell" (*HT,* 284) that Linnet experiences as she anxiously walks to meet her father and the "fall over the edge" (305) of the Earth that monolingual Montrealers fear should they try to establish contact with the other linguistic community.

29.   Charlotte Sturgess gives an interesting interpretation of the voices heard in the two quotations concerning parental attitudes toward children ("The Art of the Narrator in Mavis Gallant's Short Stories," *Etudes Canadiennes* 29 [1990]: 217–18).

30.   This makes Ruth Cook in "Thank You for the Lovely Tea" write "Life is Hell" (*HT,* 3) before the disastrous outing with her father's friend. Once out of the convent school's building, she also remarks that she is coming "out of jail" (8), a spatial image revealing her aversion.

31.   The spatial component of artistic creation will be discussed further in this chapter.

32.   Gallant's comments on her joys and fears as a writer echo the imagery of this passage and previous ones: "[W]hen [the actual writing] goes well . . . [o]ne seems to float. In between there come long periods of doubt, not floating, but sinking. Then there is the fantastic pleasure of solving a problem, when a door seems to open. . . . I am a slow writer, I move along like a glacier . . . an added source of worry and tension" (Michel Fabre, "An Interview with Mavis Gallant," *Commonwealth* 11, no. 2 [Spring 1989]: 99).

33.   Robert Martin Alter, *Partial Magic: The Novel as Self-Conscious Genre* (Berkeley and Los Angeles: University of California Press, 1975), x. Self-conscious plays are self-reflexive (Robert Scholes, "Metafiction," *Iowa Review* 1 [Fall 1970]: 100), thus trying to lay bare their potential. Like metafictional novels or stories, they "systematically [draw] attention to [their] status as an artefact in order to pose questions about the relationship between fiction and reality"

(Patricia Waugh, *Metafiction: The Theory and Practice of Self-Conscious Fiction* [London: Routledge, 1984], 2).

34. Other stories confirm this immutability. In "Its Image on the Mirror," Jean Price's parents, for instance, conceive of no interaction between the two communities: "French Canada *flows in* when English Canada *pulls away*" (*MHB,* 58; emphasis added). The in and out polarities clearly indicate the impossibility of even a brief encounter, let alone an unwanted overlapping. The sharp delimitations of territory explain the disarray of the Collier girls in "Orphans' Progress" (*HT,* 56–62), who are tossed about from one linguistic area to the other: each time they have to reject their previous command of language and thus gradually lose both affective response and identity.

35. In "Let it Pass" (*New Yorker,* 18 May 1987, 38–64), Steve remembers that his former wife "had the old Quebec-Irish inflection" (39) that made it easy for anyone to know where she came from. His noticing that her daughter "[talks] in the accents of modern Montreal—accents that render the speaker unplaceable except within vast regional boundaries" (39) marks his nostalgia for a past where spatial, and therefore social, labels could be stamped on anyone.

36. In "The Chosen Husband," Madame Carrette notices that Louis Driscoll, her youngest daughter's prospective husband, "[has] somewhere acquired a common Montreal accent." Her wondering "who his friends [are] and how Marie's children [will] sound" reveals the weight of one's background (Mavis Gallant, *Across the Bridge: New Stories* [Toronto: McClelland and Stewart, 1993], 45; hereafter cited in the text as *AB*).

37. Coral Ann Howells, "Mavis Gallant: *Home Truths,*" *Private and Fictional Words: Canadian Women Novelists of the 1970s and 1980s* (London: Methuen, 1987), 102; hereafter cited in the text. Linnet's lot easily compares with that of the immigrant Jean Price meets at her sister's in "Its Image on the Mirror": he is "a German refugee and his father was a professor of philosophy but he is nothing under a kind Canadian stare. He will never make it; if he marries, his children will never fit in" (*MHB,* 97).

38. The cause of the banishment—or rather "the romantic crime" (*HT,* 271)—is often "just the inability to sit for an examination, to stay at a university, to handle an allowance, to gain a toehold in a profession, or even to decide what he wanted to do—an ineptitude so maddening to live with that the Father preferred to *shell out* forever rather than watch his heir *fall apart* before his eyes" (*HT,* 271; emphasis added).

39. Mavis Gallant, "Good Morning and Goodbye," *Preview* 22 (December 1944): 2.

40. Mavis Gallant, "Three Brick Walls," *Preview* 22 (December 1944): 6.

41. My article "Mavis Gallant's Montreal: A Harbour for Immigrants?" *Etudes Canadiennes* 29 (1990): 195–201, offers further views on immigrants and the space allotted to them in Canadian culture.

42.   For a detailed discussion of the temporal and geographical structure of dissolution in the story, see chapter 4.

Chapter Seven

1.   Witness her essay on Marguerite Yourcenar, and her reviews of books by or about Giraudoux, Simone de Beauvoir, Colette, Simenon. Witness also her 1968 *Paris Notebooks:* from an external observer's standpoint, she describes the *évènements de Mai 68,* conveying the uproar caused by the students' revolt and the illusion that it would bring about drastic changes to French society. Also with full knowledge, she recounts the Gabrielle Russier case—the affair of a teacher with one of her pupils that ended up with preventive detention, a partial trial, unemployment, and suicide—highlighting the gendered, social, and racist bias of the French legal system.

2.   Neil Besner mentions Gallant's recurrent reference "to paintings, to pictures, and to characters watching them" ("A Broken Dialogue: History and Memory in Mavis Gallant's Short Fiction," *Essays in Canadian Writing* 33 [Fall 1986]: 95). Her appreciation also manifests itself through the careful pictures she creates as she describes places and people. For a discussion of the way Gallant exploits techniques from the visual arts, see the articles of Lesley D. Clement: 1991, 57–73; "Mavis Gallant's Apprenticeship Stories 1944–1950: Breaking the Frame," *English Studies in Canada* 18 (1992): 317–34; "Mavis Gallant's Stories of the 1950s: Learning to Look," *American Review of Canadian Studies* 24, no. 1 (Spring 1994): 57–73.

3.   Roland Barthes, *Image, Music, Text,* trans. Stephen Heath (New York: Noonday Press, 1977), 39; hereafter cited in the text as Barthes 1977.

4.   Roland Barthes, *Camera Lucida: Reflections on Photography,* trans. Richard Howard (New York: Noonday Press, 1981), 117; hereafter cited in the text as Barthes 1981.

5.   Ironically, the man who said these words echoed Goebbels, Hitler's minister for propaganda, who is credited with saying: "When I hear the word Culture, I take out my gun."

6.   The titles of the engravings are "Le Petit Palais—The Petit Palais; Place Vendôme—Place Vendôme; Rue de la Paix—Rue de la Paix" (*HT,* 299).

7.   Besides social topics, Gallant often chose to cover cultural and artistic subjects in her articles. Among those dealing with art, see "Above the Crowd in French Canada," *Harper's Bazaar,* July 1946, 58–59, 128–129; "Fresco Class," *The Standard,* Section Rotogravure, 9 November 1946, 12–13; "An Art Curator and His Critics," *Standard Magazine,* 12 June 1948, 3, 16, 22; "Art for the Family Pocket," *Standard Magazine,* 6 November 1948, 5, 22; "Success Story of a Canadian Artist," *Standard Magazine,* 29 April 1950, 18–19.

8.   Mary Condé, "The Chapel Paintings in Mavis Gallant's 'In the Tunnel,' " in *Image et récit: Littérature(s) et arts visuels du Canada,* ed. Jean-Michel

Lacroix, Simone Vauthier, and Héliane Venture (Paris: Presse de la Sorbonne Nouvelle, 1993), 98, 110.

9. Umberto Eco, *La Production des signes* (Paris: Librairie Générale Française, 1992), 72–79. See Condé's fine analysis for a further discussion of the various ways in which text and image intersect.

10. Mavis Gallant, *Overhead in a Balloon: Stories of Paris* (Toronto: Macmillan, 1985), 73; hereafter cited in the text as *OB*.

11. As Neil Besner rightly points out, the common concern with art is not the only aspect that links these two stories. Indeed, they both focus in different degrees on Sandor Speck, an art dealer, and his assistant, Walter: Gallant examines their place in French society and their political and ideological response to the situation they are confronted with (1988, 141).

12. I am indebted to Wolfgang Hochbruck for drawing my attention to the similarity in discourse. See Sándor Petöfi's poem "Magyars, Rise, Your Country Calls You!" in *Petöfi by Himself*, trans. Watson Kirkconnell (Budapest: Corvina Press, 1973), 29–32.

13. John Marlyn, *Under the Ribs of Death* (Toronto: McClelland and Stewart, 1957). Again, my thanks go to Wolfgang Hochbruck for reminding me of the name change in the earlier novel, allowing me to exploit the interpretation of the aptronym to the full.

14. Charlotte Sturgess makes such a point in an unpublished paper entitled "Pictorial Representation and Narrative in Mavis Gallant's 'Speck's Idea' " read in Strasbourg in May 1991.

15. Ronald Hatch rightly remarks that "Speck's Idea" "portrays the sense of disarray arising from a resurgence of right-wing politics in contemporary French society" ("Mavis Gallant and the Fascism of Everyday Life," *Essays in Canadian Writing* 42 [Winter 1990]: 37).

16. Charlotte Sturgess, "Narrative Strategies in 'Overhead in a Balloon,' " *Journal of the Short Story in English* 12 (Spring 1989): 47; hereafter cited in the text.

17. *Mise en abyme* refers to self-duplication within the finished work, such as a painting within the painting, representing the latter, or a story within the story, mirroring the latter. The work within the work need not be a certified copy; it may summarize, schematize, transpose, or even announce in different ways what it represents. See Lucien Dällenbach, *Le Récit spéculaire* (Paris: Seuils, 1977); Jean Ricardou, *Le Nouveau roman* (Paris: Seuils, 1978), 47–65; Linda Hutcheon, *Narcissistic Narrative: The Metafictional Paradox* (London: Routledge, 1980), 53–56.

18. John Ruskin, *The Two Paths: Being Lectures on Art and Its Application to Decoration and Manufacture* (London: George Allen, 1900), Lecture 2, 57.

19. Her views on writers are not any less critical. Witness her satirical descriptions of Prism and Grippes. In "A Flying Start," Prism attempts to write a novel about himself and his benefactress, rejects the idea, and instantly

becomes a literary critic. Grippes, on the other hand, does write, but he only produces mediocre novels about reactionary, provincial young men inspired by his tax collector, Poche, whose figure he changes slightly for the purpose of each new novel, following right-wing ideology dictating linear plots whose end can only be death (148). When Poche disappears, so does his inspiration, and Grippes starts clinging to an image from his past, the figure of a religious woman in gray whom he cannot summon to his imagination "because to depict life is to attract its ill-fortune" (146). Like Poche cornering him with his tax forms, Grippes would like to corner the woman to discover how to use her as a character. Both lifelikeness and pure creativity escape him altogether.

20. Linda Hutcheon, *Splitting Ironies: Contemporary Canadian Ironies* (Toronto: Oxford University Press, 1991), 113.

Chapter Eight

1. Witness the causticity and extremely measured tone of the following description delineating the mother-daughter relationship in "In Youth Is Pleasure": "[My mother] was impulsive, generous, in some ways better than most other people, but without any feeling for cause and effect; this made her at the least unpredictable and at the most a serious element of danger. I was fascinated by her, though she worried me; then all at once I lost interest. . . . As for my mother, whatever I thought, felt, said, wrote, and wore had always been a source of exasperation. From time to time she attempted to alter the form, the outward shape at least, of the creatures she thought she was modelling" (*HT,* 218–19). The picture is remarkable for the detachment that characterizes the daughter's analysis of her relationship to her mother, not just of the mother's to her.

2. These words appear in a review by Gallant in which she appraises Marguerite Yourcenar's careful use of her native language, so akin to Gallant's own experience.

3. Although William John Keith devotes a chapter to Gallant in his book on style in English-Canadian fiction, he does not develop any systematic stylistic argument, recurring to general statements about "Gallant's capacity to find the right word and the appropriate cadence [that] may well surpass that of any contemporary Canadian writer" (*A Sense of Style: Studies in the Art of Fiction in English-Speaking Canada* [Toronto: ECW Press, 1988], 115). Mainly interested in the relation between language and the art of living and the relation between language and creation, he focuses on thematic, rather than stylistic, characteristics. Janice Kulyk Keefer in part discusses Gallant's style, but her preoccupation with language is primarily connected with the narrative voice. Neil Besner touches on specific aspects of Gallant's style in several chapters but does not provide a rigorous investigation, for his, too, is an essentially thematic approach. Lois Ellen Grant identifies some specific linguistic features and gives some valuable hints on style but restricts her examination to the shifts from the original in the French translations of three stories ("Translating Mavis Gallant

into French: The Effect of Translation Shifts on Narrative Style" [M.A. thesis, Simon Fraser University, 1990]).

4.   This story exemplifies the stylistic contribution to message in Gallant's oeuvre at large. Although the story was originally intended as the beginning of *A Fairly Good Time,* Gallant "didn't want it and rewrote it as a story" (iHancock, 58).

5.   Throughout the chapter, bracketed numbers in the quotations from the story are added for the sake of clarity. I am indebted to Geoffrey N. Leech and Michael H. Short for their useful discussion of style and the various patterns they distinguish (*Style in Fiction: A Linguistic Introduction to English Fictional Prose* [Harlow, Essex: Longman, 1969]); hereafter cited as Leech and Short).

6.   Gallant favors this device; most of her fiction relies on the disturbing oscillation between omniscience and a figural point of view, forcing the consideration of different, and often clashing, views, one of the sources of her irony.

7.   Stasis recurrently typifies the lives of characters who cannot live fully, as for instance in *Home Truths,* where Linnet Muir expresses her compatriots' lifelessness with negated verbs of action.

8.   Another of Gallant's favored stylistic features, the pairing of contradictory words also contributes to the ironic effect of her prose.

9.   Gallant's allusion to the repeated use of "the silent cry" ridicules the tendency of Parisian journalists in the 1960s to reiterate certain striking phrases such as "the silent cry." Her appropriation of the phrase adds another layer of interpretation: a duplicate of duplicates, the phrase alerts the readers to the inevitable reproduction of certain patterns, to the nauseating repetition of trite phrases and clichés. Taken a step further, the argument would lead to Jorge Luis Borges's no less cynical conclusion in "The Library of Babel" that "the certainty that everything has been already written nullifies or makes phantoms of us all" (in *Fictions,* ed. and trans. Anthony Kerrigan [London: Calder and Boyars, 1965], 79). Or, to quote Linda Hutcheon, the presentation of anything "multiply reproduced . . . becomes the ironic repetition of the loss of individuality, of the unmaking of subjectivity, by mass reproductive technology" (1992b, 40).

10.   Edvard Munch, *The Scream,* 1893, National Gallery, Oslo. Munch himself recalls this scene in his diary: "I was out walking with two friends—the sun began to set—suddenly the sky turned blood-red—I paused, feeling exhausted, and leaned on a fence—there was blood and tongues of fire above the blue-black fjord and the city—my friends walked on, and there I stood, trembling with fear—I sensed an endless scream passing through nature" (as quoted in Ulrich Bischoff, *Edvard Munch: 1863–1944* [Cologne: Benedikt Taschen Verlag, 1990], 53; hereafter cited in the text).

11.   The title of the articles also calls to mind A. B. Yehoshua's title story "The Continuing Silence of a Poet," in *The Continuing Silence of a Poet: Collected Stories,* trans. Miriam Arad, et al. (New York: Penguin, 1991). Anguished by his own inability to voice his feelings, the old poet sinks into a mental world

of silence only disturbed by his feebleminded son's attempts at restoring some of his discarded lines to life.

12.   The analogy is definitely drawn in further passages with lexical echoes to this one.

13.   "She had / A heart—how shall I say?—too soon made glad, / Too easily impressed; she liked whatever / She looked on, and her looks went everywhere" (Robert Browning, "My Last Duchess," in *Poems* [London and New York: Oxford University Press, 1909], 21–25).

14.   Also a recurrent device in her fiction, repetitions of patterns allow Gallant to draw ironic parallels that poke fun at the characters.

15.   Edvard Munch, *The Dance of Life*, 1899/1900, National Gallery, Oslo.

16.   The following graph and its interpretation are based on Leech and Short's useful study in which they illustrate the architecture of parallelism and stress its implications (15–17, 59–60, 141–43).

17.   The parentheses or dashes including this information make it quite clear that Philippe did not dwell on these ideas, mentioning them in passing as an afterthought.

18.   *The Pegnitz Junction*, to give a striking example, offers a harrowing combination of both with its train deviated from its route and stranded in the middle of unwelcoming German regions.

19.   Edvard Munch, *The Three Stages of Woman*, 1894, Rasmus Meyer Collection, Bergen.

20.   Edvard Munch, *Despair*, 1892, Thielska Gallery, Stockholm; *Jealousy*, 1895, Rasmus Meyer Collection, Bergen; *Jealousy I*, 1896, Munch Museum, Oslo; *Jealousy II*, 1896, Munch Museum, Oslo; *Separation*, 1896, Munch Museum, Oslo; *Separation I*, 1896, Rasmus Meyer Collection, Bergen; *Separation II*, 1896, Munch Museum, Oslo.

21.   Edvard Munch, *The Lonely Ones*, 1906/1907, Folkwang Museum, Essen.

22.   Edvard Munch, *The Girls on the Bridge*, 1901, National Gallery, Oslo; *Melancholy*, 1892, Rasmus Meyer Collection, Bergen; *Three Girls on the Jetty*, 1903, National Gallery, Oslo.

23.   Robert Cluett, *Canadian Literary Prose: A Preliminary Stylistic Atlas* (Toronto: ECW Press, 1990), 162.

24.   M. A. K. Haliday, "Linguistic Function and Literary Style: An Inquiry into the Language of William Golding's *The Inheritors*," in *Literary Style: A Symposium*, ed. Seymour Chapman (London and New York: Oxford University Press, 1971), 347.

Chapter Nine

1.   Janice Kulyk Keefer, review of *Across the Bridge: New Stories*, by Mavis Gallant, *Quill and Quire* 59, no. 10 (October 1993): 26.

2. Norman Holland, *Poems in Persons: An Introduction to the Psychoanalysis of Literature* (New York: Norton, 1973), 77.

3. George Brassens, "Les Amoureux des bancs publics," *La Mauvaise réputation,* compact disc, Philips, n.d. (original long-playing recording by Phonogram, 1953). Throwing light on the elation attendant on the first stages of amorous relationships, Brassens claims that when looking back, the couples realize that they experienced the best phase of their love on one of those famous public benches. Oblivious of passersby, lovers monopolize public benches to kiss and dream of their future children, home, and life. "Across the Bridge" does not exemplify the bewitching enchantment usually presiding in such encounters on account of Arnaud's down-to-earth, indeed detached, approach to their future life.

4. Although the reasons for rejection differ, the result does not. Christian Rossi was banned for having been involved with his French teacher, Gabrielle Russier, an affair that made the front page of many a major French newspaper and drew the attention of Mavis Gallant, who then reported the case in the *New Yorker.*

5. Alice Munro, *Lives of Girls and Women* (Toronto: McGraw-Hill, 1971); Isabel Huggan, *The Elizabeth Stories* (Ottawa: Oberon, 1984); Margaret Laurence, *A Bird in the House* (Toronto: McClelland and Stewart, 1970).

6. Politically engaged people show no more perspicacity than 10-year-old Pascal Brouet, who sees "the candidates [for the elections] lined up like rugby teams" since rugby players are "the embodiment of action and its outcome, in an ideal form" (*AB,* 58–59). Television dominates the world's thinking, even for the worst.

7. Roland Barthes, *The Pleasure of the Text,* trans. Richard Miller (Oxford: Blackwell, 1990).

8. Wolfgang Iser, "The Current Situation of Literary Theory: Key Concepts and the Imaginary," *New Literary History* 11, no. 1 (1979): 15.

Selected Bibliography

PRIMARY SOURCES

Fiction

Across the Bridge: New Stories. Toronto: McClelland and Stewart, 1993. Reprint, New York: Random House, 1993.

The Collected Stories of Mavis Gallant. New York: Random House, 1996. Reprinted as *The Selected Stories of Mavis Gallant,* Toronto: McClelland and Stewart, 1996.

The End of the World and Other Stories. With an introduction by Robert Weaver. New Canadian Library 91. Toronto: McClelland and Stewart, 1974.

A Fairly Good Time: A Novel. New York: Random House, 1970. Reprint, Toronto: Macmillan (Laurentian Library 79), 1983.

From the Fifteenth District: A Novella and Eight Short Stories. New York: Random House, 1979. Reprint, Toronto: Macmillan, 1979.

Green Water, Green Sky: A Novel. Cambridge, Mass.: Houghton Mifflin, 1959. Reprint, Toronto: Macmillan (Laurentian Library 78), 1983.

Home Truths: Selected Canadian Stories. Toronto: Macmillan, 1981. Reprint, New York: Random House, 1981.

In Transit. Markham, Ont.: Viking-Penguin, 1988. Reprint, New York: Random House, 1988.

The Moslem Wife and Other Stories. With an afterword by Mordecai Richler. New Canadian Library. Toronto: McClelland and Stewart, 1993.

My Heart Is Broken: Eight Stories and a Short Novel. New York: Random House, 1964. Reprint, Toronto: General Publishing (New Press Canadian Classics), 1982.

The Other Paris: Stories. Boston: Houghton Mifflin, 1956. Reprint, Toronto: Macmillan, 1986.

Overhead in a Balloon: Stories of Paris. Toronto: Macmillan, 1985. Reprint, New York: Random House, 1985.

The Pegnitz Junction: A Novella and Five Short Stories. New York: Random House, 1973. Reprint, Toronto: Macmillan (Laurentian Library 69), 1982.

Play

What Is to Be Done? Dunvegan, Ont.: Quadrant, 1983.

Essays and Reviews

Paris Notebooks: Essays and Reviews. Toronto: Macmillan, 1988. Reprint, New York: Random House, 1988.

Interviews

Beattie, Earl. "Interview with Mavis Gallant." *Anthology.* CBC Radio, 24 May 1969.

Boyce, Pleuke. "Image and Memory: Interview with Mavis Gallant." *Books in Canada* 19, no. 1 (January–February 1990): 29–31.

Engel, Howard. "Interview with Mavis Gallant." *Anthology.* CBC Radio, 9 January 1982.

Fabre, Michel. "An Interview with Mavis Gallant." *Commonwealth* 11, no. 2 (Spring 1989): 95–103.

Gabriel, Barbara. "Fairly Good Times: An Interview with Mavis Gallant." *Forum* 66, no. 766 (February 1987): 23–27.

Gibson, Graeme. "Interview with Mavis Gallant." *Anthology.* CBC Radio, 31 August 1974.

Girard, Anne-Marie, and Claude Pamela Valette. "Entretien avec Mavis Gallant." *Journal of the Short Story in English* 2 (January 1984): 79–94.

Gzowski, Peter. "Interview with Mavis Gallant and Urjo Kareda." CBC *Morningside,* 11 November 1982.

Hancock, Geoff. "An Interview with Mavis Gallant." *Canadian Fiction Magazine* 28 (1978) [special Gallant issue]: 19–67; reprinted in Hancock's *Canadian Writers at Work* (Toronto: Oxford University Press, 1987).

Leith, Linda. "Remembering Montreal in the '40s: A Conversation with Mavis Gallant." *Border/Lines* 13 (Fall 1988): 4–5.

Leslie, Susan. "An Interview with Mavis Gallant." *Audience.* CBC FM, 6 February 1982.

McLean, Stuart. "Interview with Mavis Gallant." *Sunday Morning.* CBC Radio, 19 April 1981.

Markle, Fletcher. "Interview with Mavis Gallant." *Telescope.* Channel 6, Toronto, 22 and 29 January 1969.

Martens, Debra. "An Interview with Mavis Gallant." *Rubicon* (Winter 1984–1985): 151–82.

Rogers, Sheila. "Conversation with Mavis Gallant." *Morningside.* CBC Radio, 24 January 1997.

Twigg, Alan. "Mavis Gallant. *Strong Voices: Conversations with Fifty Canadian Authors.* Madeira Park, B.C.: Harbour Publishing, 1988: 102–7.

SECONDARY SOURCES

Bibliography

Grant, Judith Skelton, and Douglas Malcolm. "Mavis Gallant: An Annotated Bibliography." In *The Annotated Bibliography of Canada's Major Authors,* edited by Robert Lecker and Jack David, 179–230. Vol. 5. Downsview, Ont.: ECW Press, 1984. Lists Gallant's books, audiovisual material, manuscripts, and contributions to periodicals and books.

Books and Articles

Alexander, Flora. "Quebec Storytellers: Mavis Gallant's Narrators in Their Settings." *British Journal of Canadian Studies* 6, no. 2 (1991): 304–12. Compares the narrators in "Its Image on the Mirror" and the Linnet Muir sequence.

Besner, Neil K. "A Broken Dialogue: History and Memory in Mavis Gallant's Short Fiction." *Essays on Canadian Writing* 33 (Fall 1986): 89–99. Discusses the ambiguities of setting, functions of the characters, and treatment of time in several narratives.

————. "The Corruption of Memory: Mavis Gallant's 'An Autobiography.' " *Recherches anglaises et américaines* 20 (1987): 35–40. Addresses the impulse to suppress the memory of the past in the story.

————. *The Light of Imagination: Mavis Gallant's Fiction.* Vancouver: University of British Columbia Press, 1988. Explores the role of memory and invention in Gallant's fictional recreation of the cultural, social, and political history of the West in the last 80 years, examining narrative strategies.

Blodgett, E. D. "Heresy and the Other Arts: A Measure of Mavis Gallant's Fiction." *Essays in Canadian Writing* 42 (Winter 1990) [special Gallant issue]: 1–8. Introduces the special issue as a celebration of a writer too long neglected by parochial critics.

————. "The Letter and Its Gloss: A Reading of Mavis Gallant's *A Fairly Good Time.*" *Essays in Canadian Writing* 42 (Winter 1990) [special Gallant issue]: 173–190. Discusses the protagonist's unreproduced letter and its gloss in the opening of the novel, stressing the ironies of language.

Clement, Lesley D. "Artistry in Mavis Gallant's *Green Water, Green Sky:* The Composition of Structure, Pattern, and Gyre." *Canadian Literature* 129 (Summer 1991): 57–73. Discusses Gallant's exploitation of visual effects as structural designs.

————. "Mavis Gallant's Apprenticeship Stories 1944–1950: Breaking the Frame." *English Studies in Canada* 18 (1992): 317–34. Analyzes the dynamic medium provided by techniques from the visual arts in Gallant's early stories.

────. "Mavis Gallant's Stories of the 1950s: Learning to Look." *American Review of Canadian Studies* 24, no. 1 (Spring 1994): 57–73. Argues that Gallant's use of visual techniques contributes to multidimensional compositions.

Condé, Mary. "The Chapel Paintings in Mavis Gallant's 'In the Tunnel.'" In *Image et récit: Littérature(s) et arts visuels du Canada,* edited by Jean-Michel Lacroix, Simone Vauthier, and Héliane Ventura, 99–100. Paris: Presses de la Sorbonne Nouvelle, 1993. Discusses the interaction between the text and the paintings described in the story.

Dahlie, Hallvard. "From the Old World: A Canadian in Paris." In *Varieties of Exile: The Canadian Experience,* 115–43. Vancouver: University of British Columbia Press, 1986. Draws a parallel between the lives of Sarah Jeannette Duncan and Gallant and their prose artistry, distinguishing their approach to the theme of exile.

Darling, Michael. "'Voices Lost in Snow': Verbal Irony in Mavis Gallant's 'Bernadette.'" In *New Directions from Old,* edited by J. R. Struthers, 74–86. Canadian Storytellers 1. Guelph, Ont.: Red Kite Press, 1991. Identifies and decodes verbal irony in "Bernadette."

Davies, Robertson. "The Novels of Mavis Gallant." *Canadian Fiction Magazine* 28 (1978) [special Gallant issue]: 69–73. Argues that Gallant's novels enlarge the readers' understanding of life.

Fabre, Michel. "'Orphans' Progress,' Reader's Progress: Voice and Understatement in Mavis Gallant's Stories." In *Gaining Ground: European Critics on Canadian Literature,* translated by Eva Schacherl and Michel Fabre, edited by Robert Kroetsch and Reingard M. Nischik, 150–60. Western Canadian Literary Documents 6. Edmonton, Alberta: NeWest Press, 1988. Discusses the problematics of enunciation and perspective in "Orphans' Progress" and "Luc and His Father."

Gadpaille, Michelle. "Mavis Gallant." In *The Canadian Short Story,* 38–56. Perspectives on Canadian Culture. Toronto: Oxford University Press, 1988. Presents Gallant as one of the forerunners of present-day Canadian short-story writers.

Godard, Barbara. "Modalities of the Edge: Towards a Semiotics of Irony: The Case of Mavis Gallant." *Essays in Canadian Writing* 42 (Winter 1990) [special Gallant issue]: 72–101. Explores how irony as self-reflexive element dismantles conventional plots, focusing on several stories, novels, and the play.

Grant, Judith Skelton. "Mavis Gallant." In *Canadian Writers and Their Works,* edited by Robert Lecker, Jack David, and Ellen Quigley, 23–80. Vol 8. Toronto: ECW, 1989. Discusses Gallantian discontinuity, circling structures, characterization, and situations as puzzles.

Hatch, Ronald. "The Three Stages of Mavis Gallant's Short Fiction." *Canadian Fiction Magazine* 28 (1978) [special Gallant issue]: 92–114. Traces the development of Gallant's short fiction until the 1970s, focusing on characterization.

————. "Mavis Gallant: Returning Home." *Atlantis* 4 (Autumn 1978): 95–102. Discusses the switch from detached critiques of romantic individualism to a more personal approach of the fragmentation of society.

————. "Mavis Gallant and the Expatriate Character." *Zeitschrift der Gesellschaft für Kanada-Studien* 1 (January 1981): 133–43. Explores Gallant's fascination with the notions of exile and "foreignness," focusing on different stories.

————. "Mavis Gallant and the Creation of Consciousness." In *Present Tense: A Critical Anthology,* edited by John Moss. Vol. 4 of *The Canadian Novel.* Toronto: NC Press, 1985: 46–71. Explores how the past inhabits the present in *Green Water, Green Sky, A Fairly Good Time,* and *The Pegnitz Junction.*

————. "Mavis Gallant and the Fascism of Everyday Life." *Essays in Canadian Writing* 42 (Winter 1990) [special Gallant issue]: 9–40. Addresses the issue of fascist tendencies in Gallant's characters.

Howells, Coral Ann. "Mavis Gallant: *Home Truths.*" In *Private and Fictional Words: Canadian Women Novelists of the 1970s and 1980s,* 89–105. London and New York: Methuen, 1987. Discusses the sense of displacement, language manipulation, and shifts in point of view in *Home Truths.*

Irvine, Lorna. "Maternal Vitality in Gallant's Fiction." In *Sub/Version,* 131–47. Toronto: ECW, 1986. Contends that the female protagonists in "The Pegnitz Junction" and the Linnet Muir sequence choose creation over destruction.

————. "Starting from the Beginning Every Time." In *A Mazing Space: Writing Canadian Women Writing,* edited by Shirley Neuman and Smaro Kamboureli, 246–55. Edmonton: Longspoon/NeWest, 1986. Discusses Gallant's fictional daughters in *Green Water, Green Sky, A Fairly Good Time, The Pegnitz Junction, My Heart Is Broken,* and *Home Truths.*

Jarrett, Mary. "The Presentation of Montreal in Mavis Gallant's 'Between Zero and One' and of Toronto in Margaret Atwood's *Cat's Eye.*" *Etudes Canadiennes* (Talence) 29 (1990): 173–81. Discusses the similarities and dissimilarities in the portrayal of both metropolises.

Jewison, Donald. "Speaking of Mirrors: Imagery and Narration in Two Novellas by Mavis Gallant." *Studies in Canadian Literature* 10, nos. 1–2 (1985): 94–109. Explores the vision of dislocation in *Green Water, Green Sky* and "Its Image on the Mirror" as well as the modernist subtlety of their narrative voice and imagery.

————. "Children of the Wars: A Discussion of *From the Fifteenth District* by Mavis Gallant." *Commonwealth* 9, no. 1 (Autumn 1986): 112–20. Analyzes the sense of defeat in "The Latehomecomer" and "Baum, Gabriel, 1935–( )" and compares it to its milder appearances in the other stories of the collection.

Keith, William John. "Mavis Gallant." In *A Sense of Style: Studies in the Art of Fiction in English-Speaking Canada*, 96–115. Toronto: ECW Press, 1988. Examines the relation between language and the art of living and between language and creation in some fictional narratives.

Kulyk Keefer, Janice. "Mavis Gallant: A Profile." In *The Macmillan Anthology 1*, edited by John Metcalf and Leon Rooke, 192–215. Toronto: Macmillan, 1988. Reviews the striking features of Gallant's life and writing, emphasizing among others her baffling irony, acerbic vision, detachment, fractured narratives.

———. *Reading Mavis Gallant*. Oxford: Oxford University Press, 1989. Explores the narrative voice and structure of Gallant's fiction as well as the disconcerting vision of her fiction, drama, and journalism, focusing on Gallant's oppressive world of children and women and her social and historical narratives.

———. "Bridges and Chasms: Multiculturalism and Mavis Gallant's 'Virus X.'" *World Literature Written in English* 31, no. 2 (Autumn 1993): 100–111. Emphasizes the multicultural components in "Virus X."

Leith, Linda. "The Scream: Mavis Gallant's *A Fairly Good Time*." *American Review of Canadian Studies* 18, no. 2 (Summer 1988): 213–21. Discusses the combination of personal and political considerations in *A Fairly Good Time*, focusing on "the silent cry," a metaphor intertwining hilarity and anguish.

Mathews, Laurence. "Ghosts and Saints: Notes on Mavis Gallant's *From the Fifteenth District*." *Essays in Canadian Writing* 42 (Winter 1990) [special Gallant issue]: 154–72. Stresses the ironic use of the character within the passage of time.

Merler, Grazia. *Mavis Gallant: Narrative Patterns and Devices*. Ottawa: Tecumseh Press, 1978. Structuralist and formalist analysis of the short stories leading to the discovery of a single creative framework.

Murray, Heather. "'Its Image on the Mirror': Canada, Canonicity, the Uncanny." *Essays in Canadian Writing* 42 (Winter 1990) [special Gallant issue]: 102–30. Discusses Gallant's reception in Canada, focusing on Freud's notion of the uncanny.

O'Rourke, David. "Exiles in Time: Gallant's 'My Heart Is Broken.'" *Canadian Literature* 93 (Summer 1982): 98–107. Explores the theme of exile in the stories collected in *My Heart Is Broken*.

Richler, Mordecai. Afterword to *The Moslem Wife and Other Stories*, by Mavis Gallant, 247–52. New Canadian Library. Toronto: McClelland and Stewart, 1993. Justifies his selection of stories by stressing Gallant's convincing delineation of characters and social background.

Rooke, Constance. "Fear of the Open Heart." In *A Mazing Space: Writing Canadian Women Writing*, edited by Shirley Neuman and Smaro Kamboureli, 256–69. Edmonton: Longspoon/NeWest, 1986. Reprinted in *Fear of the Open Heart: Essays on Contemporary Canadian Writing*, 9–26. Toronto:

Coach House Press, 1989. Explores the significance of the phrase "the fear of the open heart" in "Its Image on the Mirror."

———. "Waiting for a Final Explanation: Mavis Gallant's 'Irina.' " In *Fear of the Open Heart: Essays on Contemporary Canadian Writing,* 27–40. Toronto: Coach House Press, 1989. Discusses the title character's ascendency and acceptance of the mystery of life.

Schaub, Danielle. "Canadian Culture and Fragmentation: Mavis Gallant's Canadians in Search of Their Identity." In *At the Edge: Canadian Literature and Culture at Century's End,* edited by Richard Sherwin, Seymour Mayne, and Ruth Amossi, 100–113. Jerusalem: Magnes Press, 1995. Argues that the characters' unsuccessful quest for identity is caused by their fragmented perception of life, focusing on the Canadian stories in *My Heart Is Broken, Home Truths, Across the Bridge,* and three uncollected stories.

Schrank, Bernice. "Popular Culture and Political Consciousness in Mavis Gallant's *My Heart Is Broken.*" *Essays in Canadian Writing* 42 (Winter 1990) [special Gallant issue]: 57–71. Explores the significance of the reference to films and books in *My Heart Is Broken.*

Siemerling, Winfried. "Perception, Memory, Irony: Mavis Gallant Greets Proust and Flaubert." *Essays in Canadian Writing* 42 (Winter 1990) [special Gallant issue]: 131–53. Discusses the importance of memory and the use of irony in Gallant's fiction.

Simmons, Diane. "Remittance Men: Exile and Identity in the Short Stories of Mavis Gallant." In *Canadian Women Writing Fiction,* edited by Mickey Pearlman. Jackson: University Press of Mississippi, 1993. Argues that the remittance man serves as a model for Gallant's exiles, their sense of loss and nonexistent identity.

Smythe, Karen. "*Green Water, Green Sky:* Gallant's Discourse of Dislocation." *Studies in Canadian Literature* 14, no. 1 (1989): 73–84. Feminist analysis of the voice of the decentralized speaker.

———. "The Silent Cry: Empathy and Elegy in Mavis Gallant's Novels." *Studies in Canadian Literature* 15, no. 2 (1990): 116–35. Argues that *Green Water, Green Sky, Its Image on the Mirror,* and *A Fairly Good Time* are elegiac texts that call for the readers' empathetic participation.

———."To Be (and Not to Be) Continued: Closure and Consolation in Gallant's 'Linnet Muir Sequence.' " *Canadian Literature* 129 (Summer 1991): 74–86. Discusses resistance to closure and consolation resulting from the reinvention of the past in the Linnet Muir sequence.

———. "The 'Home Truth' about *Home Truths:* Gallant's Ironic Introduction." In *Double-Talking: Essays on Verbal and Visual Ironies in Contemporary Canadian Art and Literature,* edited by Linda Hutcheon, 106–14. Toronto: ECW Press, 1992. Analyzes Gallant's introduction to *Home Truths* and its ironic subversion of conventions.

———. *Gallant, Munro, and the Poetics of Elegy.* Montreal and Kingston, McGill-Queen's University Press, 1992. Discusses Gallant's sad stories calling for the readers' empathy and the ethics of reading in Gallant's fiction.

Stevens, Peter. "Perils of Compassion." *Canadian Literature* 56 (Spring 1973): 61–70. The earliest article on Gallant, discusses the double-edged theme of closeness and domination in *Green Water, Green Sky, Its Image on the Mirror*, and *A Fairly Good Time*.

Sturgess, Charlotte. "The Art of the Narrator in Mavis Gallant's Short Stories." *Etudes Canadiennes* (Talence) 29 (1990): 213–22. Discusses the paradoxical omnipresence and absence of control of the narrative voice.

————. "Mavis Gallant's *In Transit:* Stories from the Border." *British Journal of Canadian Studies* 6, no. 2 (1991): 313–18. Discusses authorial voice and narrativity in "April Fish."

————. "Voices of Time in 'The Pegnitz Junction' by Mavis Gallant." *Visions Critiques* 6 (1991): 61–69. Explores the novella's multiple strands and voices of time.

Vauthier, Simone. "Listening In to Mavis Gallant's 'Voices Lost in Snow.' " In *Reverberations: Explorations in the Canadian Short Story*, 177–208. Concord: Anansi, 1993. Explores the narratorial and linguistic structures that govern the narrative.

Weaver, Robert. Introduction to *The End of the World and Other Stories*, by Mavis Gallant, 7–13. New Canadian Library 91. Toronto: McClelland and Stewart, 1974. Reviews Gallant's fictional and nonfictional production and its emphasis on expatriation.

Woodcock, George. "Memory, Imagination, Artifice: The Late Short Fiction of Mavis Gallant." *Canadian Fiction Magazine* 28 (1978) [special Gallant issue]: 74–91. Discusses Gallant's short fiction of the 1960s and 1970s, focusing on common thematic and stylistic aspects.

Woolford, Daniel. "Mavis Gallant's *Overhead in a Balloon:* Politics and Religion, Language and Art." *Studies in Canadian Literature* 14, no. 2 (1989): 27–47. Explores the interactions of politics, religion, and art, as well as the pitfalls of language in various stories collected in *Overhead in a Balloon*.

Index

INDEX

227

multiple perspectives, 11, 47, 51, 168, 177; of author, 24, 90; clashing, 58; combination of, 25; uncountable, 28. *See also* multiple lenses; multiple viewpoints

multiple viewpoints, 9. *See also* multiple lenses; multiple perspectives

multiple voices, 26–54, 145, 168, 179, 180, 181. *See also* polyphony

Munch, Edvard, 143, 148, 154, 155, 159, 160, 161, 207n. 10, 208nn. 15, 19, 20, 21, 22; *Dance of Life, The,* 154, 159, 160, 161; *Girls on a Bridge, The,* 161; *Jealousy,* 160, 161; *Lonely Ones, The,* 160; *Melancholy,* 161; *Scream, The,* 148, 154, 160, 161; *Separation,* 160; *Three Girls on the Jetty,* 161; *Three Stages of Woman, The,* 160, 161

Munro, Alice, 4, 168, 209n. 5

Nabokov, Vladimir, 186n. 15

name: chain-link, 133; impression evoked by, 76; ironic, 107; play on, 129; symbolism, 129, 131. *See also* aptronym

narration: multivoiced, 9; split levels of, 89. *See also* multiple voices; polyphony

narrative: chronological, 63; double, 89; enforcing reflection, 89; fractured, 14, 18, 28; ironic, 88, 90; third-person, 140

narrative perspective: discontinuous, 22; double, 144. *See also* multiple lenses; multiple perspectives; multiple viewpoints; standpoint

narrative present, 144, 150

narrative strategies, 8, 63, 182; contradictory, 162

narrative techniques: experiment with, 28, 29, 33; subversive exploitation of, 183

narrative voice, 86; disembodied, 114; not neutral, 150

narrator: first-person, 47, 48, 59; indulgent smile of, 169; involved and detached, 177; omniscient, 28, 29, 30, 32, 33, 34, 44

nationalism, lack of interest in, 5

omniscience, 12, 144; editorial, 13; limited, 144

Ondaatje, Michael, 187n. 23

opening, 8, 64; allusive, 140, 141, 143; assertive, 142; chapter, 58; compelling statement of, 142; ironic, 142; paragraph, 60, 64, 88, 152; parallelism of, 144; reductive, 141; revelatory, 141; sentence, 59, 60, 67, 140, 141; sentence, detached, 143; sharp and incisive, 144; unforgettable, 142

opposition, 162; spatial, 107; stylistic, 181

oxymoron, 130, 143, 147, 161

Palmer, Frank R., 193n. 52

paradox, 135, 138, 162; of character's appreciation, 81; of characters' facets, 58

parallel, 144, 153, 156; comic, 156; of construction, 152; between couples, 158; and equation, 147; ironic, 154; between love and revolution, 106

parallelism, 156

parallel structures, 158, 161, 162, 181; clarifying outlook, 158; enhancing pattern, 156; imperative, 114; in opening sentence, 144; reflecting mood, 159; revealing pattern in life, 158

parody, 131

Pascal, Roy, 191n. 23

pathos, 165

perception: of atmosphere, 102; clarity of, 94; detached, 90; fluid, 96; fractured, 53; illusory, 94; ironic, 13, 37; of irony, 78; naive, 86; spatial, 96, 105, 115, 116; subjective, 90, 92

perspective: changed, 35; changing, 9; clashing, 58; conflicting, 10, 182; contradictory, 9, 21; detached, 9, 11, 21; different, 53; disappointing, 117; indeterminate, 12; ironic, 10, 13, 77, 91; lack of, 79; nonexistent, 103; omniscient, 14, 144; reduplicated, 78;

The Author

Danielle Schaub was born in Kuala Belait, Sultanate of Brunei, and raised all over the world. She received her Ph.D. from the Université Libre de Bruxelles. She taught at the University of Cambridge, England, and then at the Université Libre de Bruxelles, before joining the English Department of Oranim, University of Haifa, Israel, where she teaches, among other subjects, Canadian fiction, a first in the country. She has published numerous articles on Canadian literature, most particularly on women writers, in such journals as *Canadian Literature, Studies in Canadian Literature,* the *International Journal of Canadian Studies, Critique, Etudes Canadiennes,* and the *British Journal of Canadian Studies.* She has coedited a collection of literary essays entitled *Precarious Present/Promising Future? Ethnicity and Identities in Canadian Literature* (1996).

The Editor

Robert Lecker is professor of English at McGill University in Montreal. He received his Ph.D. from York University. Professor Lecker is the author of numerous critical studies, including *On the Line* (1982), *Robert Kroetch* (1986), *An Other I* (1988), and *Making It Real: The Canonization of English-Canadian Literature* (1995). He is the editor of the critical journal *Essays on Canadian Writing* and of many collections of critical essays, most recent of which is *Canadian Canons: Essays in Literary Value* (1991). He is the founding and current general editor of Twayne's Masterwork Studies, and the editor of the Twayne World Authors Series on Canadian writers. He is also the general editor of G. K. Hall's Critical Essays on World Literature series.